M000034964

For the Good of the Children

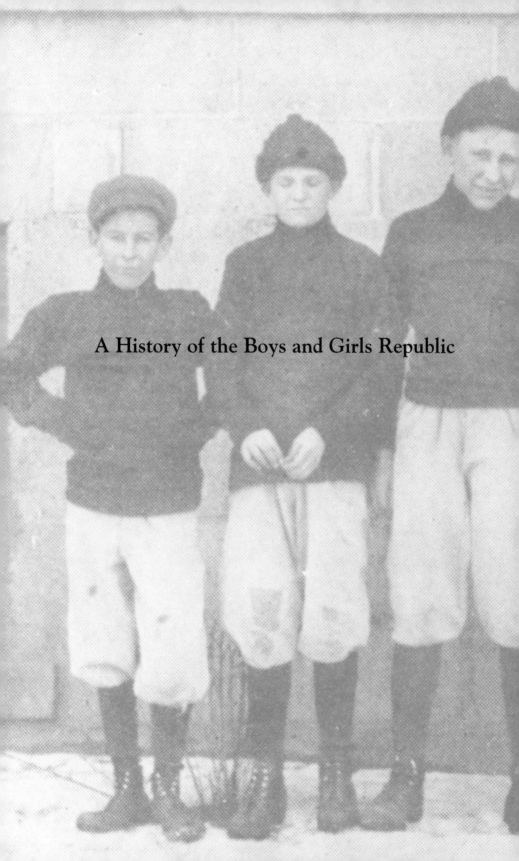

A History of the Boys and Girls Republic

For the Good of the
CHILDREN

Gay Pitman Zieger

Wayne State
University Press
DETROIT

GREAT LAKES BOOKS

A complete listing of the books in this series can be found at the back of this volume.

PHILIP P. MASON, EDITOR
Department of History, Wayne State University

DR. CHARLES K. HYDE, ASSOCIATE EDITOR
Department of History, Wayne State University

Copyright © 2003 by Wayne State University Press,
Detroit, Michigan 48201. All rights are reserved.
No part of this book may be reproduced without formal permission.
Manufactured in the United States of America.
07 06 05 04 03   5 4 3 2 1

Library of Congress Cataloging-in-Publication Data

Zieger, Gay.
For the good of the children : a history of the boys and girls Republic /
Gay Zieger.
    p.   cm.—(Great Lakes books)
Includes bibliographical reference and index.
ISBN 0-8143-3086-X
    1. Boys and Girls Republic (Juvenile home)—History   2. Children—
Institutional care—Michigan History.   3. Youth—Institutional care—
Michigan—History.   4. Problem children—Institutional care—Michigan—
History.   5. Problem youth—Institutional care—Michigan—History.
I. Title.   II. Series.
    HV864.M5 Z54   2003
    362.73'2'0977438—dc21   2002014910

♾ The paper used in this publication meets the minimum requirements of
the American National Standard for Information Sciences—Permanence
of Paper for Printed Library Materials, ANSI Z39.48–1984.

Contents

Preface

The story of the republic came to me from the happy circumstance of being in the right place at the right time. Former director and chief proponent of the need to bring public awareness to this remarkable turn-of-the-century institution, Clyde L. Reed, was looking for a researcher and writer. I was teaching part-time in the English Department at Wayne State University in Detroit and working as a feature writer for the *Detroit Metro Times* and a drama critic for *The Birmingham Eccentric*, having previously been a newspaper film, book, and theater critic in various states. Reed advertised for an author and my work was flexible enough for me to apply. Therein began a close association with Clyde and Elaine Reed, with the republic staff, and eventually with the collected republic papers housed in the Archives of Union and Labor History, the Walter P. Reuther Archives.

Personal interest was almost immediate, in part because of the poignancy of the boys' tales and the love and dedication of those who worked with them. Each superintendent brought a vision, a determination to strengthen what was and to augment change where needed. Each was seminal in bringing the institution to its current status. The boys—and later girls—added the justification to the enterprise. They deserved—and most often earned—a chance to become successful and productive citizens.

In respect for their right to anonymity, the citizens will not, with a few exceptions, be identified but rather will be rendered as composites of particular types. This is their story as much as it is that of the people who made it possible. Clyde L. Reed died in 1987 and it is to him that this history is dedicated. Elaine Reed, who died in 1991, carried on where he left off, and she shares in my gratitude.

7

Many others provided inspiration, practical advice, and access to material. Many thanks to LeRoy Ashby, Jane Hoehner, Annie Martin, Jennifer Backer, Tom Featherstone, Margaret Raucher, Phil Mason, Werner Pflug, Brigette Weeks, Kathy Mac Farlane, Arthur Evans, Alice Nigoghosian, and Elizabeth Clemens.

My husband, Bob, has set the ideal with his own body of work and has been a constant source of inspiration and support in all my endeavors. Both he and son Robert have always encouraged and inspired me just by being there and being who they are.

Introduction

In the world of our dreams, every child has a nurturing mother, a proud father, doting grandparents, shelter, clothing, food, a time for seriousness, a time for laughter. Too often reality is not the stuff dreams are made of, however, and many children are deprived of the ingredients that promise at least a degree of personal fulfillment. Historical records note an awareness of the problem of dependent, homeless, and/or neglected children in America as early as the 1700s, but it was not until the age of industrialism that the situation became serious enough to warrant organized courses of action.

Back in the days when small towns and villages predominated and learning, work, and pleasure centered on the home, most children had a degree of security and certainty. As John Dewey noted later, "There was always something which really needed to be done, and a real necessity that each member of the household . . . do his own part faithfully and in cooperation with others." And, he added, "Personalities which became effective in action were bred and tested in the medium of action."[1]

These small communities tended to foster a sense of otherness, a feeling that each member was as important as the self. Hence, when disaster befell one family, another most often would come to the rescue. A youngster suddenly orphaned or in need of adult supervision would be taken in by neighbors, friends, or relatives.

As farmers and townspeople drifted to the cities in search of better lives, however, family unity was threatened. Mothers became the primary teachers of values and, as such, were widely heralded. But when they, too, were lured to the city, the traditional family was further disrupted and fears grew that the old virtues of hard work, cooperation, and loyalty would be lost forever.

9

Youngsters who had little or no familial support were the focus of such concerns. The early nineteenth-century solution of providing homeless or neglected children with the bare essentials in almshouses would no longer do. Of necessity, with numbers anywhere from fifty to two thousand, these institutions emphasized discipline and routine. They could not, therefore, provide the kind of instruction and guidance that would turn out ethical and moral young people. In response to the problem, an anti-institutional movement began to grow.

In 1854 the Children's Aid Society of New York proposed "draining the city of destitute children" by following a plan conceived by Charles Loring Brace, founder of the organization and clergyman and social reformer. Trainloads of children were sent out into the Midwestern countryside where clean air, healthful living, and wide-open spaces would "re-create" them. Unfortunately, not all farmers who came to the train stations looking for likely candidates to help with the chores were people of conscience. Most chose the older, stronger-looking children, leaving the younger, more frail ones behind to either return to the city streets or find a way of surviving on country lanes.

For awhile, child savers advocated "placing out," or putting youngsters in homes that might eventually turn into adoptive ones. Later followed a boarding-out system where families received a nominal payment for keeping a child. But with the lack of controls and adequate follow-up supervision, these plans sometimes proved disastrous.[2]

Still, it was apparent that a family setting was preferable for molding character and by the end of the nineteenth century the anti-institutional trend was well established. An 1899 statement issued by the National Conference of Charities and Corrections Committee called for preserving the home, but if this was not possible, for placing or boarding children only after "careful investigation and [with] constant supervision." According to historian Walter Trattner, "The 19th century, which began with attempts to get needy children into institutions, ended with attempts to get them out of those institutions."[3]

The demographic features of the United States at the turn of the century posed unique problems and compounded already existing ones. It was a time of increased urbanization, industrialization, and immigration, all of which had a profound impact on family life and particularly on children. Country people flocked to the city, bright with its promise of work—in the factories, in communications, in law enforcement, and in transportation. Farms and rural schools fell to disrepair and disuse.

Thousands of immigrants flooded U.S. shores seeking freedom and opportunities, thus adding to the problem. Without the financial resources to buy farms or farm equipment, they had to abandon the lives they knew best to become the cities' unskilled labor force and as such often were the first fired. Generally they had many mouths to feed: newly arrived Poles led the numbers, having an average of six children per family; French Canadians followed with five. City streets swarmed with multitudes in search of homes and jobs. Urban classrooms bulged, often having to accommodate more than sixty students each.

During this period, Michigan reflected the general shifts in population. Once predominantly a state of farmers, lumberjacks, and miners, it was rapidly becoming industrialized. By 1910 the shift was complete, with city population figures exceeding rural ones. But even as early as the 1890s, one out of ten Michiganders lived in Detroit.

Detroit was a city with potential. Its waterways were ideal for industrial expansion, and its burgeoning industries cried out for workers. People came in hordes from rural countrysides and foreign lands, all in search of a good life. Poles, Germans, Italians, French Canadians, and Americans poured into the city to vie for jobs. Between 1880 and 1890, Detroit's population increased from 116,000 to 286,000. In the first decade of the new century, it rose to 466,000.[4]

Rural people and foreigners alike discovered soon enough that the city's streets were dusty, not gold covered. A smallpox epidemic in the 1890s spread terror and death. A massive depression beginning in 1893 cast a deadly pall over the city. One observer commented on the "pathetic sights of the unemployed, especially the foreign-born, as they roamed the streets hoping to find a job."[5]

Tensions grew as immigrants and natives competed for precious jobs. To make ends meet, many women were forced to go to work. Sometimes they found employment only because their labor came cheaper. There were no controls over the workplace and accidents killed and maimed scores of people. Epidemic diseases added to the death toll and increasing numbers of children were bereft of parents or adequate adult guidance.

Women who put in twelve-hour days in factories and shops could not afford governesses or babysitters. In desperation, some tied their children to bedposts. Many mothers turned to highly touted and widely advertised elixirs and patent medicines to quell the cries of their children and thus make marginal supervision possible. These innocuous-sounding remedies—Dr. Fowler's Strawberry and Peppermint Mixture, Dr. Moffett's Teething Powders, Dr. James' Soothing Syrup, and Dr. Miller's Anodyne for Babies, for example—were anything but. They worked, but unwitting mothers, swayed by the promises, failed to understand that they contained morphine, opium, chloroform, heroin, or knockout drops.[6]

When children became too old for calming sedatives, they often were consigned to the streets, where they formed gangs and engaged in organized thievery, sometimes out of need but mostly out of boredom. The streets of the city were alive with these waifs, many of whom did not have a home to return to. They hung around saloons for warmth or protection from heat and the elements. They slept in doorways or under makeshift huts. Half-hearted attempts were made to round them up and send them to school, but truancy was widespread and more often than not street urchins got into trouble. These were the conditions that led to an upswing in the child-saving movement in the late 1800s and early 1900s.

Many reformers looked on the past nostalgically. They harked back on the old values, fearing them forever irretrievable. They envisioned whole generations of youngsters growing up without an appreciation of the principles, the moral fiber, the dedication to hard work, and the pleasure in long hours that were essential for maintaining the greatness of America. They lamented the passing of a time when family life itself was the teacher, when the rewards of industry, cooperation, shared responsibility, and clean living were clearly evident, built right into the structure of the family unit.

Reformers across the country began searching for ways to instill American virtues and ideals in children who had no strong models or examples of productive living. Some established fresh-air camps and country outing programs designed specifically to replace decadent environs with bucolic ones conducive to the teaching of old-fashioned values.

This belief in the healing properties of the countryside was not new, having been invoked as early as the mid-nineteenth century when the first reform schools were developed, generally far from the teeming cities. Surprisingly, reformatories were considered a necessary evil by many reformers and not antithetical to family-setting treatment since they too were based on the premise that individualization and parental-type guidance would yield the best results. Many people concurred with Nelson Mc Lain, superintendent of the Illinois State Home for Delinquent Boys, who in 1901 said that delinquent (dependent) children needed to be "taken away from evil associations and temptations, away from the moral and physical filth and contagion, out of the gaslight and sewer gas; away out into the sunlight and starlight and the pure sweet air of the meadows."[7]

One reformer, William George, opened a home for potentially wayward youngsters in the mid-1890s in upstate New York. Called the Freeville Republic, later sometimes the George, Jr. Republic or Daddy George's Republic, it became a prototype for many similar projects. Another reformer, Edward Bradley, succumbed to the pleas of six youngsters not to return to the orphanage after their camping trip—and right there in Illinois in 1895 was born the Allendale Farm. And Marian Ogden, appalled that the courts routinely handed down adult punishments to children, began the Wisconsin Home and Farm School in the late 1890s.[8] A similar concern about the primitivism of the judicial and prison systems led Agnes D'Arcambal in 1890 to establish the parolee care facility that later evolved into the Boys Republic.

Chapter 1

Mother Agnes D'Arcambal and the
Home of Industry: 1890–1906

AGNES D'ARCAMBAL HAD ALWAYS BEEN sensitive to the needs of the downtrodden. Even as a young girl in the late 1830s in Kalamazoo, Michigan, she had visited local jails and Jackson Prison, bringing comfort, fruit, and flowers to the inmates. Early on she recognized that people were hauled in and tossed out with little interest in how they would adjust upon release to the very society that had imprisoned them.

On May 7, 1890, in firm resolution to aid discharged prisoners, she and nine other Detroit humanitarians—C. A. Newcomb, H. F. Hatch, Robert Y. Ogg, Caroline E. Osmun, Levi L. Barbour, Stephen Baldwin, M. W. O'Brien, George H. Smith, and George C. Wetherbee—filed the Articles of Association of the Home of Industry. In league with a coterie of volunteers, they embarked on a campaign to ease the transition from prison to civilian life. They provided parolees with shelter, clothing, job placement, and, most important, human caring.[1]

The way was not always easy, according to Mrs. D'Arcambal. She told of a dark, wintry night when she was in such great despair that she could neither pray nor cry. She feared the home would have to close due to lack of food and fuel. Still, she placed her bedroom lamp in the window to welcome any homeless wayfarer. As she lay in bed, her attention was drawn to the curtains that had parted ever so gently. She saw a haze, the color of "mountain mist on a spring morning." From the haze there emerged a visage "so exquisitely beautiful, full of divine love and tenderest pathos, touched with the silver light of suffering, and marked with the golden lines of sorrow" that she knew she was in the presence of her "Saviour." She reached for the picture of her daughter she always kept under her pillow and, finding she was not dreaming, gazed deeply into the "wondrous eyes" of her Lord. Her despair lifted, replaced by hope. Her daughter, a Catholic nun, believed that the Lord had come to her to give her the courage to carry on with her mission. Thereafter, when frightened or discouraged, she would think back on that night and find strength. [2]

From April 1, 1895, to April 1, 1896, the home, located in Detroit, served over twenty-nine thousand meals to those who had "stumbled on the rough road" but for whom "the mother's arm of love [had] ever been ready to encircle and uphold them, until they [were] able to step out firmly once more." By then Mother D'Arcambal was in failing health. [3]

In 1898 she was placed in a Battle Creek sanitarium but returned to the home on her birthday to "be with my boys." A *Detroit Journal* article from March 4, 1898, described the touching scene: "35 inmates, 'criminals' they are called by outsiders, marched past her couch to welcome her back to the home, their broken words and tearful eyes testifying eloquently to the love in which she is enshrined." On the trip back to Battle Creek, Mother stopped in Jackson and was "wheeled in her reclining chair into the chapel of the prison, 'not to preach to them,' she said, but just to let them know that Mother was on her way home to wait for them." [4]

Agnes D'Arcambal died in 1899, leaving behind devotees determined to carry on her good work. She was, said one friend and associate, "an example of exalted womanhood, worthy of emulation by all." The association minutes contain more glowing tributes. Mrs. S. Baldwin remembered a sadly dissipated man who came to her home for fresh clothing, rather than have Mother bear witness to his "shame" and "deplorable condition." She told of the great love and "respect for her at all times and in all places [that] her boys" felt. Mrs. D'Arcambal's dying wishes were contained in a letter read to the association on April 12, 1899: "Should there be any word as to a memorial of any kind for me . . . all the monument or memorial I want is to carry on and extend the work of this 'Home,' gather in all the help possible; if should such a thing occur that there is at any time a surplus, reach out to others but make this an enduring monument to the 'Mother' if you think her worthy and her faithful helpers."[5]

True to the spirit of the founder and in compliance with these last wishes, the members continued to reach out. In April 1902 they visited sixty-eight offenders; supervised six boys under court appointment; found food and shelter for three and clothing for an additional three; loaned cash to two; secured employment for three; visited three state prisons, the Asylum for Insane Criminals, and the Ionia Jail; and wrote nearly two hundred letters to or on behalf of offenders.[6]

In the early 1900s reformers and journalists drew national attention to the problems inherent in prisons and a number of reform laws were enacted. Later legislation created an effective parole system. With many of the needs of parolees and prisoners being met by the state, the D'Arcambal Home Association no longer needed to support a probation officer and decided to broaden its concept and include preventive work among potentially wayward youngsters. With an eye toward saving children, members began searching the streets for likely candidates. They were easy to find—in the bars, on the docks, sleeping in hallways—many purporting to be busily engaged in the business of selling newspapers.

Some people admired the independent spirit of these "newsies," as they were called. The forcefulness and enterprise learned on the streets would serve them well later on, they believed. But studies showed that more often than not these children fell under evil influences and learned about drinking, smoking, gambling, and thievery. The "school of hard knocks" taught them negative survival skills rather than positive ones.

Many a night found home members out well after dark, rounding up children. A 1905 Home of Industry Report proudly proclaims that they had "spent the last two hours before midnight on the streets for the past 4 months and [had] taken to their homes 36 different boys . . . and through appeals or threats to their parents, the aid of the police, or the boys' good sense . . . put a stop to much of this practice."[7]

These yearly home reports were issued to advise supporters of the status of the organization and to appeal to the community conscience. "It is more economical, practical, and humane to save the boy than to wait until prison life and associations have made the task more difficult. Are you willing to invest in the saving of some boy?" they asked. "A Fence at the Top of a Precipice Is Better than an Ambulance at the Bottom. Put a Rail in the Fence," they urged. They heralded the home as the first to shelter boys apart from adults. As of 1905, it had housed 206 youngsters. Of 38 former truants, only four had repeated the offense while still at the home. All had "advanced in their grades by the close of the term." The bulletin for that year conveys the dramatic story of one John Genter through a series of news releases:

News, December 15, 1904
John Genter, absent from home, found asleep in basement on Lafayette Avenue this morning. Such a boy I never saw, sobbed his mother.

Journal, April 7, 1905
What to do with Johnnie Genter is a puzzle that Lieut. Breault of Truant Squad is trying to solve. He would rather sell papers until all hours of the night than go to school. Of fear he knows nothing, being just as free from fright when rummaging through dark alleys in search of an empty dry goods box as bed as in daylight. Nor have the police or dungeon cells any terror for him. I have picked Johnnie up more than 20 times in the last years, and he is getting worse.

News, June 24, 1905
Johnnie Genter played "yogi" on Woodward Avenue. 8 year

old youngster feigned blindness and begged pennies from passers-by at 11 P.M.

Free Press, July 1, 1905
Johnnie Genter—Again. Hardened young criminal has bobbed up once more.

News, July 5, 1905, "Mention of Bath Scarded [*sic*] 'Yogi'"
Curled up under a desk, with a pile of papers, "Yogi" John Genter, 9 year old gamin, whose exploits have attracted so much attention, was discovered early this morning asleep in the "*News* Office." Later arrested for stealing stamps.

News, July 6, 1905
Nine year old Johnnie Genter arrested for stealing watches. The detectives say he is the toughest youth of his age they have ever had to deal with.

News, July 10, 1905
Johnnie caught cooking chicken in back yard of Lafayette Place.

News, July 26, 1905
Johnnie tried for stealing segars [*sic*]—and placed on probation.

His story had a happy ending: "Since John was received in the Home on probation, September 1st, he has regularly attended the public school; received his class prize in October for best record. No longer associates with his old companions. Never on the street after 5:30 P.M. And the indications are that the improvement will continue."[8]

Hard statistics were also on the home's side. Figures for the period January 1, 1902–March 1, 1906 showed that 143 "News-boys, Juvenile peddlers and beggars [were] sent from streets and saloons from 9:30 P.M. to 2 A.M." and 43 "School boys found on streets, docks, and Exhibits in school hours [were] reported to Schools or Police." In a shorter period, March 1, 1906–February 28, 1907, nearly as many—105—were rounded up at night and just as many—43—were handled during the day.

In May 1906 the organization officially became the Boys' Home and D'Arcambal Association, with a superintendent, J. Morris Fisher, and a housemaster and matron, Mr. and Mrs. C. S. Carney. It moved from Jefferson Avenue in Detroit to 192 Lafayette Avenue. It asked the public to contribute apples, potatoes, turnips, cabbages, beets, squash, onions, carrots, and other vegetables; boys' clothing or bedding; and old rubber—for fund-raising sales in the spring. It boasted, "Boys who have habitually frequented the cheap theatres, or been accustomed to late hours on the streets, or spending days and nights away from their homes, have been discharged after a term of probation, and give no further trouble this way."[9]

By this time the organization counted many prominent Detroit-area personages among its supporters. Their names appear frequently in the records: Fred Butzel, Dr. Rollin H. Stevens, Dexter M. Ferry, Joseph L. Hudson, E. L. Ford, Clarence Lightner, Leonard Laurense, Hon. Alfred J. Murphy, Rabbi L. M. Franklin, James Inglis, Rev. L. J. McCollester, Rev. William B. Forbush, Rev. A. H. Barr, Sherman D. Callender, George M. Lane, Hon. Lucius C. Storrs, Rev. Spencer B. Meeser, Prof. Frederick L. Bliss, P. F. Gaines, Ormand F. Hunt, and Herman Krolik. None was more responsible for helping set the foundation of the emerging Boys Republic than Butzel.

Fred M. Butzel, lawyer, social worker, and humanitarian, once said that the trouble with being a leader was that you never could be sure if "people were following you or chasing you." In his case, there is no evidence of the latter. Throughout his life Butzel earned respect, love, and high praise. For his fiftieth birthday celebration in 1927, a friend wrote that Butzel was a rich man—"rich in the service of mankind, rich in the esteem of a great community, rich in the thoughts of a whole people— the powerful and the weak, the Jew and the non-Jew." Another said, "His leadership arises from the extraordinarily keen qualities of his mind and the broad and deep sympathies of his heart."[10]

Butzel spent more hours helping people than practicing law. Newcomers to the city learned quickly enough that if they needed help, maybe just a little boost during a hard time, Fred Butzel's law office door was always open. Another friend observed, "If you are down and out, desperately in need of money or advice, if you are torn in mind and soul and you know not which way to turn, he is the one man in all Detroit who will never fail you and who for half a century has never failed others who have been in trouble."[11] Not all who turned to him had such dramatic problems, but the most remarkable thing was that Butzel offered his services without fanfare, hoopla, or self-aggrandizement. He just helped—and no one knows how many lives he touched.

He cared about people and was responsible for such things as bringing the Boy Scouts to Detroit and helping organize the Community Chest. He held offices in the United Jewish Charities, the Jewish Welfare Federation, and the Detroit Urban League, and he was on the Board of Associated Charities. He taught English and civics to boys at the Jewish Institute and opened the first night school for refugees. Through his efforts, truancy eventually came under the province of a truant officer instead of the police department, allowing truants to be handled, according to friend and associate Monsignor Edward Hickey, by an "educator rather than a cop." Butzel was also instrumental in establishing the juvenile court in Wayne County.[12]

When one of his most cherished projects, the Boys' Home and D'Arcambal Association, was faced with a potentially escalating discipline problem, Butzel sought a solution. The boys were staging a minor rebellion by refusing to wash their hands regularly. The housemaster, a dedicated, caring man, was exasperated, but no amount of cajoling would spur the boys to action. Butzel discussed the situation with his friend Homer Lane, who, as director of the public playground, had shown he could command rather than demand respect from young people.

Though a relative newcomer to the city, Lane already had a reputation as an innovator. He annoyed traditionalists with his theories about boys and radical ways, but he also seemed to be getting results. He had a way of understanding the workings of youthful minds. Hence, when Butzel presented the problem to him, he came up with a plan within a few minutes. "Give me $1.00 and I'll get them to wash," he said, adding, "Meet me at the home tonight."

This was the sort of challenge Lane loved. He believed that unless the "why" of a thing was clear to youngsters, any rule would seem merely an arbitrary dictum made by those with power on those without. They needed to *want* to wash their hands and to understand why doing so was important.

That night Lane arrived at the home with a brown parcel tucked under his arm. Asking Butzel to keep the boys occupied, he headed for the kitchen. Butzel played games with them for quite some time, but they were growing restless. And when wondrous aromas came wafting in from the kitchen, he could contain them no longer. They dashed in and found Lane, wearing a spotless white apron, sleeves rolled up, stirring something in a large pot on the stove. He was making molasses taffy. When the time came for pulling, Lane asked Butzel and the cook to join in on the fun. Naturally the boys clamored for a turn, but Lane would not hear of it. "You'd poison the candy with those hands," he said. They rushed off to wash but could not rid themselves of the accumulated filth and grime. One enterprising boy asked Lane if he could come back with more candy makings the next week and see if their hands were clean enough by then. Lane agreed, adding that it would take at least three washings a day to take effect. Lane had given them a reason to achieve the desired goal of cleanliness.

Butzel knew at that moment that the Boys' Home would flourish under Homer Lane's direction. Without a second thought, he offered him the superintendency—and Lane accepted. Thus it was that the simple challenge of a prominent Detroit humanitarian to a rough-hewn innovative educator resulted in establishing the framework of an institution that would change through the years but would never lose sight of the inherent worth of all living creatures, even wayward youths.[13]

Chapter 2

Homer Lane and the Republic Ideal: 1906–1912

HOMER TERRIL LANE WAS THIRTY-ONE years old when he assumed the superintendency of the Boys' Home and D'Arcambal Association. The appointment seemed a natural culmination of his years of study and interest in education, manual training, and work with disadvantaged youth. By the time of his death eighteen years later, he had an international reputation, the respect and admiration of scholars, politicians, heads of schools and state, British officials, and ordinary folks, and had been called everything from a visionary genius to a scoundrel. He had also helped spawn a movement that would take hold on two continents and would forever change the way children and their education were viewed.

A. S. Neill, creator of the famed experiment in progressive education, Summerhill, noted on reading of Lane's death in the papers: "I found myself smiling. At first this seemed like hard-heartedness, but later I got the true explanation: I was free at last. Up to then, I had relied entirely on him—what would Homer say? Now I had to stand on my own feet."[1] And in 1930, W. H. Auden wrote in Poem No. XXII:

> Lawrence was brought down by Smut-hounds, Blake
> went dotty as he sang,
> Homer Lane was killed in action by the
> Twickenham Baptist gang.

HOMER LANE'S REPUBLIC

Lane was delighted with the Boys' Home appointment. His mind was already brimming with theories regarding the causes and prevention of delinquent behavior and now he had a chance to put those theories to practical application. He approached the job with characteristic enthusiasm and excitement.

Lane was never one to do anything half-heartedly or to take life for granted. Born in Hudson, New Hampshire, on September 22, 1875, he seemed very much the product of seven generations of solid Puritan stock. With his strong good looks, warm voice, luminous smile, and energy, he inspired confidence and a belief that good things were just ahead. His wife would note years later that sometimes when her life seemed too much to bear, "Daddy would come in with his grin and a cheery word and everything would seem worthwhile again."[2]

Though his father's railroad work necessitated frequent uprooting of the family, Homer showed great adaptability, taking each move in stride. The family finally settled in Framingham, Massachusetts, in 1881 where they spent the next twelve years.

Homer had a regular job by the time he was fourteen, rising every morning at four o'clock to collect and distribute milk from neighboring farms. Fearful that he might succumb to the temptation to cover his head with a pillow when he knew he should get up in the morning, he devised a powerful alarm system that was sure to get him on his feet. At fifteen he was a grocery boy, collecting shopping lists from housewives in the morning and delivering provisions in the afternoon. He held a number of jobs in the ensuing years until at eighteen, after a two-year stint as a railway clerk, he moved to nearby Southborough and once again worked as a delivery boy, this time for McMasters Stores. Besides ordinary responsibilities, he had to care for his own horse and wagon and on most afternoons help out in the store, soda-jerking at the newly installed ice cream fountain.

Southborough proved to be a good place for Homer. He liked

the independence that came from living on his own, away from the watchful eyes of his parents. He also made two new friends, both of whom would have a profound effect on his life. Cora Barney, one of four daughters of the local police chief, was charming and after a proper courtship they were married. Their first child, Raymond, was born in 1899 and a second, Cora, in 1901.

The other pivotal person in Southborough was Claude Jones, a prominent, well-to-do physician who liked to invest in the future by helping young people. Jones saw in Lane a man of promise, one who could achieve great things given half a chance. He could not bear to see Lane waste his talents, forever shackled by uninspiring jobs. Thus when Lane expressed an interest in working with his hands, Jones saw an ideal opportunity to realize a longtime dream of his while at the same time securing a brighter tomorrow for the young man. He would send Lane to the Sloyd Training School in Boston. Sloyd, with its name derived from the Finnish word for "skill," was in its experimental stage in the United States and was a precursor of industrial arts programs. Jones would help the family financially until Lane could return and offer his own course in Southborough.

Lane flourished in Boston. He understood perfectly the underlying principles of Sloyd: learning and understanding could come from physical work with the hands as well as from textbooks and passive study. Shortly after graduation, he established a very successful manual training class at Southborough's high school.

Lane delighted in showing youngsters immediate results, in helping them understand that hard, careful work could produce something tangible, something they could see and feel. His satisfaction was short-lived however. As a new program, his was the first to go during a school funding crisis, and his great plans suffered a setback.

A far more devastating blow had befallen him by this time. His young wife had contracted pneumonia and had died. It was 1901 and she had just borne his second child. Homer had been deliriously happy about having a little girl and had managed to coax Cora into a night of celebration at the theater. Not fully recovered from childbirth, she caught a chill during the horse-drawn sleigh ride to town and within a few days was gone.

Lane was no stranger to death nor to feeling responsible for it. As a young boy, he had been asked to keep an eye on his two-and-a-half-year-old sister. But he and his brother Judson were anxious to try out a canoe they had constructed of cheese boxes and canvas, so they sent Bessie back to the house while they headed for the pond. She returned dutifully to her mother but did not find women's chores nearly as fascinating as boys' play and soon was out in the yard. Finding the boys gone, she went in search of them and wandered over to the railroad track. A brakeman on a passing freight saw the train bearing down on her and lunged over the side of his car, snatching her out of its path, but not before she had received a fatal blow.

Homer was ravaged with despair and guilt. His mother, always a fair, rational woman, consoled him, saying that he was not to blame. Nevertheless, Lane may have never forgiven himself for bringing death upon someone who meant so much to him. So, 1901 found him once more, this time at age twenty-six, grieving the loss of a loved one, believing he could have prevented it. Some theorists contend that these two incidents imprinted themselves upon Lane in such a way that success would always be followed by failure, that an achievement was sure to bring disaster, and that he would always need to punish himself disproportionately for what he deemed a character defect. Psychoanalytic conjecture is inconclusive at best, and what mysterious forces drew Lane into a maelstrom of achievements and failures will never be clear. But he was certainly bound for a kind of glory that would bring him personal fulfillment and, ultimately, personal shame.

His glory ride started in Detroit. The city, alive with excitement and growth potential, had advertised for two manual training instructors and Lane was hired to fill one of the posts in 1902. Within three years, he had riled his principal with his radicalism to such a degree that he was appointed superintendent of playgrounds, partially to rid the school administration of a thorn and partially to give him a good outlet for his creativity and innovative ways.

Lane found the playground post ideal for working through his theory that boys need unstructured playtime. He believed that delinquent behavior was merely misdirected good behavior, that the same impulses that led boys to acts of destruction were those that made them vital, creative human beings. When city streets served as play areas, children were certain to antagonize adults trying to go about their business or travel down the streets unhampered. And boys, once cognizant of their power to annoy, were bound to look for new ways to do so. Adults and children thus became adversaries. Overly supervised playgrounds were no better, Lane contended. He cited as proof a study of two urban playgrounds, one controlled by adults, the other giving children free rein. The park that allowed children to make their own games and govern their own playtime had fewer incidences of delinquency.

While playground superintendent, Lane received funding to take youngsters on six-week summer camping trips, and he began work with a settlement project for recent immigrants. It was during this period, in 1904, that he met Fred Butzel, another person who would figure prominently in his life and provide him with his greatest challenge.[3]

Butzel, like Jones, marked Lane as a man of destiny. He saw in him a genius for knowing something instinctively without long hours of study, for being able to size up a situation and take direct action, for getting to the heart of youngsters and gaining their trust. (Forty years later, Butzel said that it was his association with Lane more than any other person or event that "formed his attitude to social problems . . . his whole philosophy of life.") So when Lane earned the $1 by giving the boys an incentive for personal hygiene, Butzel knew that the home needed him. And Lane happily obliged, becoming superintendent in 1907.[4]

Strongly believing it essential for the boys to be removed from the environment that had bred them, Lane promoted the home's board of trustees' purchase of a seventy-acre farm near Clarenceville. The site was ideal: wooded countryside, a creek, gentle hills, and room to grow. The large old farmhouse was over-run with chickens—indeed the owner had even had to shoo a rooster from a chair so that she and a board member could close the deal—but it was structurally sound. The land proved too boggy for crops, but a landfill project later resolved that problem.

The board proposed a massive cleanup campaign to ready the place for the new inhabitants, but Lane asked that it be left as is. The boys would be far more appreciative of their home if they were involved in making it livable. He recalled some years later the pride with which the boys showed newcomers "the barn we shin-gled, the henhouse and icehouse and blacksmith shop we built."[5]

In 1907 Lane and second wife, Mabel (Cora's sister), their two children and his one (his eldest daughter was still with her grand-parents), and thirty boys headed for Clarenceville. The first weeks found them busily engaged in reconstruction, cleaning up, and clearing out. Within a short time they were joined by Mr. and Mrs. Mel Barney (Mabel's brother and sister-in-law), who would help in daily operations; a schoolteacher named Anna Bingham; two youngsters the Lanes had been caring for; and a young woman to tend to the Lanes' children. They all, thirty boys included, lived in the farmhouse. It was soon clear that they needed new accommo-dations, so Lane and the boys began constructing another build-ing. He drew up the plans and they all dug the foundation, mixed and poured the concrete, and began raising the walls.

They were proceeding quite nicely when disaster struck. A fire started in the boys' sleeping quarters. Nineteen of the youngsters were marshaled through the door, but four remained trapped in the attic. Lane managed to reach them but, with flames blocking an escape, had to drop them out the window to a makeshift safety net. He jumped, at last, but proved too heavy for the hand-held blanket and crashed to the ground. He professed to be uninjured, but after arranging shelter for the boys in nearby homes and barns, learned he had broken his wrist.

His main concern was for the boys. Still wearing his charred and smoky clothing, a dramatic but effective gesture, he visited Mrs. E. L. Ford, an earlier benefactor, and told her of his desperate situation. Thanks to the generosity of Mrs. Ford and her two daughters, Mrs. H. N. Torrey and Mrs. Stella Schlotman, the association was able to finish the building. In honor of the family that had made it possible, the organization was renamed Ford Republic.

Right from the beginning Lane had an eye toward complete self-government, but the floating population in the early years made that virtually impossible. In the first year alone, 145 boys were admitted to the home, with no more than 60 residing at a given time.

The boys had varied backgrounds. Of the first 386 admitted, 320 were sent by court order (most for truancy or larceny, and some for both). There were also nine felons and one vagrant. Thirty-eight were committed by their parents as a result of poverty, domestic trouble, or discipline problems. Others were runaways, homeless, or neglected. One hundred and sixty-six of these boys were under age thirteen, with one as young as seven. The oldest in residence was eighteen. Only 55 of them stayed for one or more years, with 258 leaving after six or fewer months, and 100 of those after less than one month.[6]

Letters poured in from private sources asking for placement of needy boys. The records are filled with sad, poignant, sometimes sadly funny letters about youngsters who were not "bad" but who had "undesirable companions" or were "under the influence of tobacco." One writer was thoroughly exasperated, saying he had told the boy to "get a pipe and cut out the cigarettes" but to no avail. He asked that the boy be kept until he came "to his reasoning power," adding that he would not "stand to have him lay around and do nothing but smoke and other bad things that go along with it."[7]

One letter writer advised Lane to "give it to [his] boy good and hard if he don't behave himself." Another assured him that "under a man's control" the boy would come out all right—"for his mother is so nice." One particularly heart-wrenching letter from Mary McNabb Johnston, excerpted here, reached the home in September 1909:

I want to . . . send . . . a boy [who] is not naughty at all but
his father is dead and his mother can get a place to work
and bring her tiny daughter. Few employers would care to
have two children, however, so the boy will have to be given
away. . . . The child is a sturdy little chap, nearly nine. He
says he can milk cows to pay for his board, but I told him I
thought that sort of work was generally given to boys a little
older, but he could do something else. Your big heart will find
a place to stow him away, I'm sure, and some employment for
his willing little fingers.

Some letters asked for boys. One man wanted a fifteen-year-old
for office work and specified that he need not know everything
but should be able to "write legible." He added: "The less he
knows about the details of office work the better." Another man
requested a "Protestant child of good size, hair preferred to be
dark curly, and good looking." He said that although he would
not adopt the child, he would "do right by him," provided he
was not "untidy . . . or in any way deranged." The poor youngster
who came close to fitting the bill was returned two months later
because "he [had] a breaking out rash [they couldn't] seem to cure."
Generally, there were more applicants than there were facilities
to provide for them, and most came from the courts.[8]

The boys sent to the home usually were those adjudged delinquent by the Wayne County Juvenile Court. They were boys who
did not fit in the Detroit school system, who were chronic truants,
who disrupted classes and disturbed teachers when they did attend
class, and hence were labeled "incorrigible." Lane felt that most of
these boys had no "bad instincts" but through poor associations or
background, city conditions, and a "lack of opportunity to work off
[their] surplus spirits through a healthful and interesting channel"
had "drifted . . . into a disregard for law, order, and decency." And
then, with the scoldings from those in power, with dirty clothes
and face and sloppiness eliciting more chiding, they had lost self-
respect, the "mental condition that precedes the commission of a
crime."[9]

He believed that their "natural impulses [were] virtuous" and that it was the "perversion by demoralizing street conditions that [made for] wrong doing and law breaking." He argued that all boys passed through a "savage" stage in which the dream of a hero slaying his foes and conquering his enemies was foremost in their minds. Witness only the popular reading material among Detroit-area thirteen-year-olds, the "Indian and 'Deadwood Dick' stories." We had only to see the boys through the stage, to temper criticism with praise. Since all boys wanted to assert themselves, to claim their rights as individuals, that first bad act might have just been an experiment, a step toward independence. Children with loving parents could tolerate being disciplined because they also received acceptance. But with street kids, scoldings predominated. Lane said: "Correction of the unfortunate boy cannot be forced into him from the outside; it must be the growth of an internal experience that well-doing and honesty is more satisfactory and more fun than dishonesty and deceit."[10]

Lane believed that the first thing he needed to do was help the boys regain their self-respect. He theorized that this particular quality was "the cornerstone of manhood, good citizenship, and healthy morals." Self-respect could come in a multitude of ways, sometimes by a boy's being able to run the fastest, jump the highest, "stand on his head longer, walk on his hands further." His goal with each child was to find the triumphs, to look for the good in every boy. Once self-respect was firmly entrenched, the child could go on to self-reliance and finally to his greatest need—self-restraint.[11]

Lane had strong convictions regarding methods for instilling these virtues in young people. He had worked in a Pennsylvania reformatory for a while and knew that, if anything, wayward youths consigned there just learned new ways to behave badly. "It is not self restraint that keeps these boys from lawlessness, but external restraint," he observed. He likened outside restraints to splinting up a perfectly well leg for a few weeks. "It will be useless when [the splints] are removed. It [will be] weak and [unable to] perform its natural functions from disuse." He concluded:

"Surround a boy with restrictions and routine which prevent him from using his self-restraint and judgment for a year or two, and these virtues, which are absolutely necessary in a community of human units, are not present when an occasion for their use arises." Sometimes Lane launched a boy on the road to self-respect before even being formally introduced to him.[12]

Representatives from the home attended weekly juvenile court sessions to spot likely candidates for admission. The judge, in cahoots with Lane, would express doubt about a particular lad's ability to make a go of it at the farm. Lane would rise to his feet in protest, saying, "If that boy isn't first-rate material, Your Honor, I'll eat my shirt." The seed of pride, of self-respect, was planted and the boy would soon learn by example what sorts of behavior earned praise.[13]

Once a boy arrived at the home he was undoubtedly shocked. He was prepared to resist authority, to break through restraints. But there were no fences and no bars. Escaping would be a cinch. Staying would be a matter of choice—his decision. Ergo, the first lesson in self-determination and self-restraint.

Lane did not believe that bars and ironclad rules could show youngsters how to restrain themselves. Neither could lectures about proper behavior and attitudes. Children needed to first have freedom of choice so that they could then see that good behavior brought more rewards than bad behavior. He was convinced that children were inherently good and that bad behavior was simply misdirected energy. Give children an understanding of why some behavior is acceptable and some is not, and they will do the right thing; they will not fail you.

Lane had toyed with the idea of self-government for a long time, seeing it as the optimal way of encouraging youngsters to become self-directed. He was familiar with the republic concept of the Freeville Republic in New York, although he claimed that the plan he devised owed little to William George's program. While the two men's visions were similar in most respects, they differed radically in one. George utilized a jail system; Lane would have no part of that. He was offended by the idea of a replication of a crime-and-punishment procedure that had proved ineffective as a deterrent in the first place. A republic could not hope to teach self-restraint by using restraint. Lane was convinced that the principle of self-government would work well, especially since the home, unlike the George Jr. Republic, accepted younger as well as older boys.[14]

By 1909, with the population stabilizing somewhat, Lane was ready to set the gears of self-government in motion. He sat down with the boys and drew up a constitution—probably with himself as the most vocal contributor. The boys would make the laws and establish a means of dealing with those who broke them. Lane had already led his charges into decisions that affected them all directly. Now they would have rules and written procedures.

The constitution established four main governing bodies: managing, executive, legislative, and judicial. The trustees of the Ford Republic were recognized as the owners of the property and had as their representative the superintendent. It fell under his jurisdiction to deal with any instances that in any way hurt the successful operation of the Republic, also known as the "State," or resulted in the loss of board property. As protector of the board's interests, he was chief justice of the supreme court and administered punishment for neglect of duty, stealing, lying, insolence, running away, or property destruction. The penalties could range from expulsion to corporal punishment. The chief justice had the power to veto any legislative decision, though his veto could be overridden by a two-thirds majority vote of the total citizenry.

The executive was made up of a president and vice president, both elected officials with prescribed functions and specific responsibilities. The legislative was made up of all citizens over ten years old. The boys ran the republic themselves with no rules or laws established that had not first been voted on and accepted by the citizenry. Every citizen, including the superintendent, the matron, and other adults, had just one vote.[15]

Because Lane insisted that the boys keep accurate minutes of their weekly legislative assemblies, some priceless, charming, funny, and *very* serious edicts are part of today's historical record.

A typical state meeting would begin with the president calling (sometimes shouting) the assemblage to order. Rambunctious citizens were, on occasion, dismissed and sent to bed. Generally the group behaved because the proceedings affected them directly and hence were of great interest. When quiet prevailed, the secretary would read the minutes of the last meeting, and then the work of the evening would commence:

> Moved by Mr. Savitski, seconded by Mr. Novak, that taking eggs from the Barn or Hen House and sucking them shall be against the law.

> Moved by Walter Brake and seconded by William Schalkowski that grabbing for food, putting elbows on table, saying "O Beans!" etc. is a misdemeanor.

> Moved by Mr. Klatt that no boy shall come to the table unless face, neck, ears are clean and hair combed. Seconded.

> Moved by Mr. William Schalkowski that the teacher of the State is not allowed to put a dirty cloth around a citizen's mouth. Carried.

> Matron ordered by President to put all who wet the beds on a separate table.

> Moved by Mr. Rose that dish boys be made to stay in the kitchen and not go to the toilet. Carried.

> Moved by Mr. Klatt that Mr. Priest show his hands to the citizens. Carried. (Hands shown and declared very dirty.)

> Moved by Mr. Rose that a committee be appointed to buy Priest a pair of gloves. Carried.

March 27, 1909, seemed especially ripe for rule-making gems:

Moved by Mr. Lane that when a citizen is too ill to do his work, that he shall not be allowed to go fishing. Carried.

Moved by Mr. Rose and seconded by Mr. Schwab that no boy be allowed to kick the pigs. Carried.

Moved by Henry Nichols that no boy be allowed to jump on beds that are not occupied. Carried.

Moved by Mr. Klatt that no citizen shall dump coffee grounds in drinking fountains. Carried.

Moved by Mr. Rose that the big boys who work outside ought to have coffee for dinner. Opposed.

Moved by Mr. Schalkowski that the working boys have coffee for dinner. Ruled out of order by the President.

Moved by Henry Nichols that we ought to get better meals for outdoor boys. Carried.

Moved by Henry Nichols that we get it pretty soon. Carried.

At the April 3 meeting, tired of the constant begging, Lane moved that they have apple pie and ice cream three times a day. A very happy Mr. Cohen seconded the motion. The cook was sorely distressed but was asked to abide by the rules of the republic. The boys were delighted. For three days they basked in the pleasures of ice cream and pie. Then the week's budget was spent. The cook reported that there was little else in the larder than beans—and beans would have to do. The boys were quite moderate in their demands after that.

Subsequent state meetings yielded equally impressive codes:

Moved by Mr. Lane that Rose be sent out of the room and to bed. Seconded by Mr. Schalkowski.

> Moved by August Schwab that the boys don't call me
> "Crabby" any more. Seconded by Marshall Davidson and
> opposed.

> Moved by Tom Navrot that the boys stop calling me "Green
> Horn." Seconded by Mr. Parmantye. Ruled out of order.

> Moved by Mr. Van Dyke that Mr. Lane be called "Crabby."
> Ruled out of order by the chairman.

> Moved by Henry Nichols that I can have a meeting whenever
> I want one and Mr. Lane don't have to tell me when to hold
> one. Ruled out of order by the chairman.

And then:

> Moved by Mr. Klatt that no boy is allowed to trip the
> little pigs and make believe to kill them. Seconded by Mr.
> Bojanczyk and carried.

It is no wonder that Mr. Lane was once banished from the courtroom for laughing out loud at a decision handed down by the young judge.

Court sessions *were* sometimes funny because of the very seriousness of the pronouncements. But to boys who seldom had any say in their lives, these proceedings were of the utmost importance. And rightfully so.[16]

The judicial arm of the government was made up of a judge and a sheriff to help ensure that sentences were carried out. Since the boys made the laws and understood why they were necessary, they endorsed punishment for breaking them. The judge was someone they elected. There were no policemen, no lawyers. The citizens themselves were responsible for reporting violations, and not to do so was in itself a crime. Anyone with a grievance against another, Mr. Lane included, needed to fill out an official complaint form. It had to be given to the judge in advance, who saw that justice was administered during a court session. A citizen with a complaint against him had to be notified ahead of time so that he could prepare a defense.

The crimes were as varied as the punishments. A boy could be reported for violating a rule; for using tobacco or bad language; for being a nuisance, lazy, disorderly, or tardy; for being out of bed after bells, or in the kitchen, dining room, engine house, boiler room, blacksmith shop or barn without permission; for talking or running at inappropriate times; and for bullying, quarreling, or calling names.

He could be put on probation, especially if he was a new boy, or he could be ostracized, put on extra work detail, or forced to stand in the dining room during meals. A special favorite punishment was the merry-go-round, an oval garden bordered by a path, that a boy would have to walk for an hour or so. The actual walking did not hurt as much as the jeers that others were encouraged to hurl. A lesser punishment entailed being called "Crabby" for a length of time determined by the court. Sometimes, if nothing else seemed to work, the boy would be paddled by hand on bare flesh by the state officers.

For a while the boys experimented gleefully with stocks, but this practice was put to a well-deserved death. One odd provision of the constitution called for a truant to be punished by "being placed under arrest for two weeks, being held to close bounds for a month, and being forced to wear a dress." Only a supreme court judge pardon could save him from this humiliation, which, though seldom used, was apparently endorsed by Lane.

Said Lane, "Every boy hears every law discussed for and against. The whys and wherefore of its enaction are understood by every citizen. . . . The motive behind the opinions expressed is as pure and wholesome and sweet as is that of any legislature ever enacted. Every penalty imposed by the Court is a just penalty, and every experience which the individual has in wrong-doing is participated in by the community."[17]

One citizen was found guilty of cheating because he pulled the top blanket of his bed up to cover rucked up sheets underneath and was sentenced to one hour on the merry-go-round. Two others were sent to bed for contempt of court because they had failed to comb their hair. One boy who broke a window had his case turned over to the supreme court because it involved the destruction of state-owned property. Another received a suspended sentence for having tobacco, since his mother had given it to him, but he was referred to the chief justice for a lecture on the "evils of smoking," in itself amusing, considering Lane's own habit. A paper-wad thrower had to spend three days after school throwing wads at a chair. Officers were not exempt. The president himself had to split a half cord of wood for wasting corn when feeding the pigs. And the matron was once reprimanded but put on probation for failing to provide clean nightshirts one week. Records show some odd punishments, like the pouring of cold cups of water down sleeves and dunkings in the creek. Lane said that "probably no lecture or advice couched in the best of English and delivered in a much more impressive manner, [could] ever [have as much of an] effect upon the new citizen [as a] homely, ungrammatical and somewhat stern statement on the part of [a] boy judge."[18]

Lane was not averse to using physical persuasion when necessary. Butzel told of a couple of instances when Lane had given a boy a "thorough licking." But generally Lane believed that forced, or enforced, goodness was as bad as forced education. Of the latter he said: "We may awaken interest by the stick, but not in the subject."[19]

The most frequently used punishment was the assessing of a fine, anywhere from fifty cents to several dollars. An important aspect of republic operations was a monetary system under which the boys were paid for labor and almost every bit of effort exerted on behalf of the citizenry, including going to school. In turn they paid for room and board, laundry, taxes, and extras. They kept careful records of the hours devoted to each activity and then received republic scrip, which was roughly equivalent to U.S. currency and good for paying for their keep and purchases at the Ford store. Though no one was forced to work, laziness was frowned upon. A debtor would be carried by the state, though not cheerfully, until he was able to make his own way. Such a boy might be put on state labor, having to work for the sheriff without pay for a prescribed time. He would not be able to walk in the woods, go swimming, or play ball but would be assigned to tough jobs like sawing wood or scrubbing floors. When not working he would have to sit on the steps and watch the others at play. A boy leaving the republic could exchange his funds for real money, usually at a percentage rate, mostly dependent on the state of the treasury.[20]

This experience with finances, keeping a time card, and figuring income and expenses was invaluable for the boys. Understandably, accuracy was of the utmost importance and the boys had a vested interest in the outcome. Lane pointed with pride to a time card made out in 1909 by a boy who "three months earlier had been unable to read or write."[21]

Lane knew that if the boys were ever to gain respect for themselves, others, and the property of others, they had to understand a system based on pay for work. They had to see that if they did not work, they would not earn the money to buy necessities, much less luxuries. One boy adapted particularly well to the republic concept and by the time he died at age thirteen was something of an area celebrity.

Fred Bloman was only nine when the police found him soliciting coins from some "hobos" down on the docks. Homeless, without memory of his parents, he was a foul-mouthed, tobacco-chewing, street-savvy ragamuffin of little promise. Though one tramp tried to claim him as his own, Fred was turned over to the Boys' Home for want of any other place to send him.[22]

After nearly a year, the boy began to blossom. He lost some of his old ways and habits and began to show signs of leadership. The other boys liked him for his good head and maturity and also for his occasional naughtiness. So great was his popularity that he was elected judge of the citizen's court, served two half-year terms, and was reelected while dying in the hospital.

Fred was an ideal judge, so good in fact that the court was often visited by outsiders—citizens, judges, lawyers—all anxious to catch the boy judge in action. He had an uncanny ability to get to the heart of the matter, to assess the problem, weigh the evidence, and impose fair penalties. He had a keen mind, good perceptions, and a way of inspiring trust. The boys had elected him and respected his judgments. How could they help but admire a person so honest as to first turn himself in for a violation—smoking—before adjudicating against the others involved.

Some of his "legal" observations, while lacking in sophistication and knowledge, rang with a certain truth: "A crook is a fellow who is willing to be called a crook" and "A fellow who has to hire a lawyer to defend him must be a crook." He also showed a certain astuteness in dealing with boy fights. He determined that when all other avenues of recourse had been explored, the two parties could go out behind the barn and fight under two conditions: there could be no witnesses (thereby fighting would not be as much fun) and the loser would first have to declare himself as such and then would have to be the one to report the outcome of the fight to the president.

When Fred died of heart failure, brought on by years of untreated illnesses, he left behind him a legacy and an impressive array of mourners. His friends at the republic were devastated and carried on their own memorial service for him while the official one was going on. Each boy stood and recounted some way that Fred had touched his life. The public ceremony was attended by three state supreme court justices. Both the Wayne County Juvenile Court and the state supreme court suspended operations for the day and Judge Henry Butzel was a pallbearer. Secretary of the republic, Clarence Lightner, quoted Booker T. Washington: "It is not the height a man attains that denotes his character, but rather the distance that he rose in getting there." The thirteen-year-old had reached the stature of a man.

Fred Bloman was buried at the Grand Lawn Cemetery in Redford Township on Grand Avenue. Lightner visited his gravesite regularly and a memorial fountain was constructed at the republic. In a few short years this youngster had become a symbol, the very epitome, of the republic concept.[23]

The boy's story attracted much attention in the community and Homer Lane used the opportunity to become the republic's chief advocate and publicist and to champion his and the republic's cause. In a series of informational reports on the status of the institution and in five articles published in *Detroit Saturday Night* from March to May 1909, he familiarized the public with his work, his ideals, and his boy successes.

In a 1907 publication titled *The Boy Farm,* Lane presented a vivid picture of the modus operandi of the republic: "The institution is devoted to the purpose of correcting the wrong impression which hundreds of city boys get, that the world is against them and so they must be against the world." (It is interesting to note here that the only fault the boys had was that they were getting a "wrong impression" and it was the impression that needed correcting, not the boys, further proof that he was always on the side of the boy.) The article then discussed the significance of a farm setting: "The farm, with its crops, its stock, etc., furnishes the boy with a progressive interest in his work. He is taught to plow, sow, cultivate, weed and harvest. . . . By the time the onion bed needs weeding the second time, the onions have grown so much that it does not seem like a repetition of the work." Each boy also had the thrill of growing whatever flowers and vegetables he wanted in his own garden from a supply of thirty varieties. Lane added that the "constant demand for repairs and construction to buildings furnishes . . . many opportunities for [developing] mechanical skill and [learning] arithmetic from interesting and practical experience."[24]

He made it clear that play was every bit as important as "plowing the potato patch." The boys had time for baseball, swimming, walking in the woods, and nutting. Of relationships on the farm, he noted:

> There is no separate residence for the Superintendent or . . .
> adults . . . ; all live together, occupy the same dining room at
> the same time and eat the same food; there is the same close
> contact and intimate relationship . . . [in] this large family

as . . . [in] a small family. Every boy is encouraged to tell his
private woes and trials to the father. . . . The Matron is never
too busy . . . to take out a sliver or bandage up a bruise, or
administer the common remedies . . . for minor illness. Boys
are treated as reasoning and independent beings . . . are made
to feel that the accomplishment of their tasks is . . . the result
of their own efforts and not the result of force exerted by
adults.[25]

Homer Lane's plans for re-creating the boy seemed to be working. But not all the republic officials immediately embraced him
and his policies. Board Secretary Rollin Stevens viewed him with
reservation, and thinking of his appointment as temporary asked
sociologist Charles Cooley from the University of Michigan to observe Lane and his methods and draw some conclusions. Cooley's
response was most enthusiastic and must have reassured Stevens
somewhat: "Of Lane's remarkable natural aptitude for boys' work
there can be no question. His sympathy with them and faith in
them, and freedom from all insincerity or formalism are such that
he needs only to be among them to ensure their devotion. I have
never seen a better man in this regard."[26]

Cooley got to the core of Lane's philosophy when he said: "His
main principle is that the way to bring out the best in them is to
inculcate an ideal or group tradition by personal influence and let
it work itself out without interference [even if the process] seems
slow and disorderly." To this end, Lane often pretended to forget a
rule so that the boys would have to remind him of it, or he would
feign ignorance so that they could teach him. Noted Cooley, "His
ideas are in harmony with the best psychology and pedagogy."[27]

By 1911 Lane had gained a widespread reputation. In Detroit
and throughout Michigan he was now considered a leading authority on the treatment of juvenile delinquency. He was also
gaining some international renown. An emissary from England
visited the republic to observe operations and talk to Lane about a
similar project being established in his country.[28] Lane enjoyed the
recognition and envisioned extensive application of his methods.

Although at times he may have overstated his case and claimed some questionable victories, he nevertheless was having an effect and was being watched, read, and listened to.

In that year's report to the board, Lane cited the lack of a serious illness in four hundred boys in four years as testament to the virtues of "out-of-door activities . . . fresh air . . . and a diet which is plain but wholesome and abundant." In perhaps his strongest statement justifying self-government, Lane said:

> If arbitrary discipline, the unreasonable rule of the rod, the blind following of monarchial edict without reason of self-interest, is the kind of discipline essential in character building, the Ford Republic is weak—but if the kind of discipline that builds character and makes for citizens who appreciate the rights of their neighbors, who do not require policemen to keep them respectful toward the law, who have the interest of their neighborhood, city and state at heart, then the Ford Republic is developing a quality of discipline which will produce citizens upon which the State may depend for intelligent and unselfish service.[29]

Homer Lane was, indisputably, a charismatic, keenly intelligent, shrewd observer of people and their environment. He inspired awe, evoked love, commanded attention, and alternately riled and beguiled his associates. His methods were unorthodox, and he had little patience with routine, with regulations, with accepted and time-honored procedures. He was impetuous and careless, often obscuring the lines between personal and business expenses. He easily could have driven the republic's treasurer crazy. He cashed checks before they were good, incurred new debts before old ones were paid off, and generally refused to care much about the whole thing. A letter written by Treasurer Frank Thiesen on June 11, 1909, is telling: "Last year we had three cows and nine hogs. This year we have two cows and two hogs. What happened to one cow and seven hogs? The books show that one hog sold for $20."[30]

And, on the subject of livestock, Lane managed to ruffle a few feathers when he declined board member Rabbi Leo Franklin's offer of a cow. He simply did not want the animal at that time but obviously got some flack from the board and an apology, of sorts, was in order:

My dear Doctor,

I have a letter from Mr. Gaines taking me to task because I told you we were not ready for the cow. It seems that he and Mr. Clark and Mr. Barney have talked the matter over concerning cows, and have decided to increase their dairy. I was not aware of that, and in talking to you expressed the last opinion that I heard from the Farm Committee on the subject. I am requested by Mr. Gaines to withdraw my objection to your donation of a cow, and hereby do so. Therefore we are very much in need of a cow, must have one, and any action on your part which will relieve our distress will be greatly appreciated. I would suggest however privately, that you do not allow our cow distress to interfere in any way with your vacation.

Very respectfully, Homer T. Lane[31]

Lane was irresponsible, sometimes thoughtless, always genuine, and always inspired. Once, when spending way beyond his means on Christmas presents for every friend he had, he blithely told Fred Butzel that God would provide. Many years later Butzel made it clear that in fact it was he, himself, upon whom Lane called to do the Lord's work. But generally people accepted Lane's unacceptable behavior as something to be endured since it was coupled with his genius for handling boys.[32]

When Lane was making motions toward taking a position in Pittsburgh in 1910, Clarence Lightner wrote to the board, saying: "We think that there is a growing sense of appreciation for Mr.

Lane's services in this community and we hope that the Trustees . . . will not be the last in Detroit to understand that Mr. Lane, personally, as well as the Association, is an important factor in the children's welfare work in Detroit."[33]

Lane himself submitted a rather astonishing document: "In naming my successor I have in mind the qualifications necessary—[and] am aware of the difficulty of finding a man who can play baseball and lead a band—who can repair a pump and treat the mumps—who can teach manual training and weed onions—who is big enough to direct the moral training of boys and not too big to do so as Judge of the Supreme Court of the Ford Republic."[34]

Self-congratulatory, yes, but accurate and indicative of Lane's hold on people and his way of manipulating them. He was no ordinary man and, like men of his ilk, was subjected to close scrutiny. Scandal followed him through the last twenty years of his life.

He was not deceitful but was known on occasion to embellish the truth, to fabricate, to make up a fact if it would further illustrate his point or clarify his position. Thus, when in 1906, in defense of abortion, he declared that he himself had borne the expense of an abortion rather than bring an unwanted child into the world, he may or may not have meant that he got some girl in trouble. Biographer David Wills suggests that Lane may have been talking about what he would do if the situation should arise. At any rate, a newspaper reporter had threatened to expose Lane to the City Fathers, and in response he had resigned as supervisor of playgrounds. This was the first in a cycle of accusations, all unproven, that led him to withdraw rather than counter the charges.[35]

Just as easily as he gave force to scandal, he appeared unable to explain or defend himself. In 1911 when a board member of the Ford Republic saw him exiting a rooming house with his secretary and confronted him, Lane elected to neither confess nor clear his name, resigning instead. There is no mention in the association minutes of Lane's departure. He just left.

LANE: THE SUCCEEDING YEARS

After a year of working as a laborer, Lane was called to England to help get a newly established youth correction facility called the Little Commonwealth off the ground. So brilliant was his concept and so skillful its implementation that the school became a prototype for similar operations. But as surely as day must yield to night, Lane became embroiled in yet another scandal. Two young delinquent girls, hoping to gain their freedom, accused him of sexual improprieties. Lane, first wishing to spare the girls from the consequences of their lying, later responding to the self-righteousness and pomposity of the Home Office–appointed investigator, dug himself into a hole so deep that the board, rather than bowing to pressure to fire him, closed the school altogether.

Lane's subsequent foray into a private psychotherapy practice broadened his coterie of admirers, which now included, in addition to doctors, teachers, and students, such luminaries as Lord Lytton—later viceroy of India—and Dr. David, the rugby headmaster who became bishop of Liverpool. It also drew a charge of adultery from a female patient. The authorities, still leery of the man from the Commonwealth but lacking any hard evidence of criminal misconduct, charged him with failure as an alien to report an address change. Rather than contest the charge Lane submitted to deportation.

He contracted pneumonia, complicated by typhoid fever, and died in France on September 5, 1925, with Mabel at his bedside. He was cremated two days later. A friend said that though Lane had not committed suicide, he certainly had given up, believing that people brought on themselves the illnesses that they in some way needed. He had once more chosen not to defend himself.

A former colleague at the Commonwealth and later biographer, E. T. Bazeley, said of him: "Homer Lane was one who expanded humanity for all who knew him . . . though however much you thought you did know him you always [realized] that there were worlds more of him you had not yet had time or capacity to know." She added: "[He was] strong at every point except that one of self conservation. There danger found him and we and children and sick folk are daily the poorer for his loss."[36]

Homer Lane's death did not mark the end of his teaching, his wisdom, and the far-reaching effects of his love. Though little remains of his writing—he was, at best, clumsy in expressing himself on paper and some of his correspondence was, sadly enough, discarded, possibly because of grammatical infractions—his students collected his lectures in a volume titled *Talks to Parents*. And Bazeley's loving tribute to the man is recorded in *Homer Lane: A Biography*.[37] The republic proudly acknowledges the man whose wisdom, strength of character, beauty, and "way with boys" set the foundation for a noble enterprise that has helped thousands of young people regain their footing—and self-respect.

Chapter 3

Charles McIndoo (1912–1922) and
Claude P. Jones (1922–1933): Ushering in a New Era

OVER THE NEXT TWENTY-ONE YEARS the Ford Republic underwent subtle but nevertheless dramatic changes. From a self-governing commonwealth it evolved into an institution in which only marginally autonomous boys were directed by a strong administrative hand. The years saw a gradual drifting away from Homer Lane's vision and the first tentative steps toward becoming the residential care treatment center it is today.

A number of factors brought change. Increasingly sophisticated methods for foster care placement reduced the republic's potential clientele to more emotionally disturbed youngsters who were less successful in handling the responsibilities inherent in self-government. These boys were a breed apart from the ones who helped Lane launch his republic. At its inception the home cared for boys who were less often wayward than simply homeless or neglected. Lane's remarkable achievements stood undiminished, but the new population needed new approaches.

In addition, staffing needed to reflect the great strides that had been made in the areas of mental health and social welfare. Says historian/sociologist Susan Tiffin, "By 1920 . . . in both placing agencies and institutions, the quality of diagnosis and treatment services had risen substantially . . . child welfare was becoming professionalized . . . social workers were formally trained in case-work techniques [and], aided by new investigative methods, they were better able to offer an individualized solution to a child's problems."[1] Social welfare and psychiatric professionals had to be hired, as did clerical people to handle the paperwork created by greater state controls, yet another change that had to be contended with.

From 1912 to 1933 three superintendents oversaw the staffing, philosophic, and population changes: a school administrator, a doctor from Lane's Southborough days, and a republic teacher/bookkeeper.

THE BEGINNING OF A NEW ERA

Homer Lane's abrupt departure in 1912 threw the organization into a state of chaos. His practically nonexistent record keeping gave rise to many questions regarding actual operating costs. His haphazard bill paying and lack of compunction about buying on credit had created some ill will among area grocers and suppliers. His "God will provide" mentality left the republic with a rather tenuous hold on the future. Fortunately the board of trustees chose his successor well.

John McIndoo was a young, enthusiastic educator with considerable administrative and organizational skills. He was just finishing his Ph.D. at Clark University in Massachusetts under noted psychologist, philosopher, and academician G. Stanley Hall when Lane's position became vacant. The possibilities in such a place as the republic intrigued him. He was a firm believer in the healing properties of country living, possibly because of his own rearing in rural Illinois. He was convinced that active involvement in farming and nature could turn city ruffians into upstanding citizens. And as an experienced teacher of high school English, he was confident that he could instruct boys on how to lead productive lives.

But first he had to work his way through the web of unpaid bills and accounts in arrears he had inherited from his predecessor. His earlier experience as superintendent of schools in Broken

Bow, Nebraska, proved invaluable. He assessed the situation and systematically set about to balance the accounts. He was just what the republic needed.

In approaches to the problem of delinquency and dependency, McIndoo and Lane had differing philosophies. Lane believed that growth had to come from within the boy, and he was willing to wait for it to emerge, naturally, when the boy was ready. McIndoo, though far from being an advocate of rigid rules and procedures, was less patient, feeling that a boy had to be "trained" to "habits of obedience . . . of respect and reverence."[2]

In regard to the self-governing capabilities of youngsters, McIndoo was somewhat skeptical. He thought the concept noble but impractical. In an October 21, 1913, letter to his Clark mentor, he expressed his reservations and concerns: "There are many problems here as yet unsolved. One . . . is that of self-government for the juvenile—just how much self-government there should be and how much of the parental." Part of the problem, he explained, was that boys from ten to sixteen are in the "gang stage." While he understood the psychology of this stage, he felt that "nationality" also had to be taken into consideration. It was his experience that, for some unexplained reason, Irish, French, and Jewish boys were "more efficient" in governing themselves and that there was a "smaller percent of leaders among . . . Polish boys." Since a large percentage of the citizenry was Polish, he concluded that a "pure republic among boys of the gang age [was], in the nature of this, an impossibility." He added, "Such an organization resolves itself naturally into an oligarchy ruled by the few gang leaders." He questioned the efficacy of pursuing the republic concept when they naturally resisted it.[3] Hall, having heard of opposition to McIndoo's viewpoint, suggested that "republic" would be a misnomer in anything but a self-governing institution. But republic records show no evidence of serious conflict and apparently McIndoo, unchallenged, forged ahead with his plans.

From the outset he showed greater concern with the physical environment, with improving living conditions, than with helping the yet untapped inner energies of the boys to emerge. He began with a massive dental and physical hygiene campaign. Each boy was given his own towel, washcloth, and toothbrush, and his own designated spot in a cupboard for storing them. He began a program of health inspections conducted by an elected health officer.

The boys, who now lined up for meals, were expected to have their hands, faces, and necks well scrubbed. Not to was to suffer a reprimand or a fine. As noted by longtime republic teacher, supervisor, and later interim superintendent Ruth Jones Colebank, "Five minutes before the last bell [would ring, the boys would fall] into line standing erect, looking neither to right or left, under the supervision of their president." The health officer would stand at the top of the basement stairs and scrutinize them "with an eagle eye." Saturdays saw special ablutions with the health commissioner before court sessions combing "wet hair into sleek, shining divisions."[4]

Historian LeRoy Ashby calls this an early sign of the changing nature of the institution. He notes that "Lane had left the decision of clean hands with each boy, who was supposed to gauge his conduct in terms of self-interest: Shedding dirt paid off in terms of producing desirable consequences. But with the health officer system, individual conduct came more in response to external rules and regulations than from internalization of values."[5]

One young citizen declared in a report before the board: "I am very good. I am doing my duty. I have to see that the boys' hands and faces are clean. If there is any nuisance I must get someone and clean it. I must see that the boys are not sloppy. If they have a coat button torn off, they must go to [the] matron of the home. The boys must have their coats off at the meals."[6]

McIndoo also began improvements of the property. He arranged for an electricity hook up; completely refurbished Ford Hall; and, in conjunction with the boys, built a gymnasium and a barn. He installed a tile drainage system for the land and, as chronicled by Colebank, imported "car loads of manure from the Chicago stock yards" to build up the soil. With the acquisition of additional acreage, he was able to begin a crop rotation process.

He turned the republic into a working, productive farm community. He set aside a fourteen-by-sixteen-foot plot of land for each boy where he could grow whatever fruits and vegetables he wanted. The republic would buy his produce, but his greatest thrill, undoubtedly, would be in sending visitors home with things he had produced through his own labors.[7]

McIndoo used these small garden plots for instilling the pride of ownership and respect for property in his charges. He spoke of the "school of practical agriculture." Colebank made note of a herd of thoroughbred Holstein cattle and a flock of thoroughbred Rhode Island Red chickens that he built up. She said of those days: "There was an abundance of milk and cream and we began to churn out our own butter. There were eggs for cooking only, the rest were sold to help make the farm pay for itself."[8]

McIndoo put great faith in the therapeutic powers of nature. The republic's rural setting was ideal, with "wild flowers . . . in rank profusion . . . a wooded glen where songbirds . . . build their nests and rear their young . . . [a glen which] chipmunk, rabbit, and squirrel call . . . home . . . and [where] big green bull-frogs and sleek, shiny muskrats hold forth." He claimed that a visitor could ask any boy "where to find the frogs in the early fall" and be taken to "where the grass grows tall in swampy land." He boasted that the boys also knew the location of every nut-bearing tree and that "every rabbit hole and bird nest is as carefully marked as a prospector's claim." McIndoo believed in using this setting, permitting learning to involve everyday problems and situations that need resolution. Through outdoor work and classes, the boys could gain practical experience in dealing with the environment and could gain valuable information about nature. How much better it was, he thought, to actually see "a hornet's nest or perchance a mushroom growth" than to learn of it through textbook abstractions. And boys actively involved in growing crops and maintaining buildings could see the contributions they made to the community.[9]

In the superintendent's report to the board of February 28, 1917, McIndoo wrote of an "Indian camp" on the grounds "where the boys rehearse in a harmless way, in play, some of their primitive instincts." Primitivism is a major theme throughout his written discourse. He felt that boys had to have outlets for their untamed urges so that what was civilized in them could come to the fore. One "primitive occupation" he encouraged was cave digging. But he also encouraged the boys to become observers of nature. To this end, he had them construct and set out birdhouses and then watch the occupants. He claimed that his boys, curiosity piqued, learned of bird variety in species, songs, colors, eggs, nesting habits, and rearing of young. A dammed-up rock and gravel bed stream provided an excellent swimming hole for the boys and the beautiful adjacent glen was perfect for picnics and play.[10]

McIndoo was very much aware of the importance of boy play, particularly in organized sports. He saw competitive physical activities as a way to channel energies. The "play spirit" would evolve into "team spirit" with its inherent unselfishness, helpfulness, and courage. The boys would gain a sense of belonging, of achieving, through cooperation, a desired end. He gave the boys latitude in what sorts of sports they wanted to engage in but made certain that someone was always there to help them improve.

He took great pride in "a ball field that is not bounded by expensive window panes; football grounds where it is not necessary to dodge the year's increment of tin cans, glass, and junk." He rejoiced in a field that was a field and not a city street filled with city trash. In 1914 the two senior soccer teams were known as the "Fords" and the "D'Arcambs." The boys also played basketball and marbles, went skating and coasting, and made kites.

In 1913 McIndoo ran a vastly ambitious fly extermination campaign, the slogan of which was "a flyless Ford Republic." The boys, armed with swatters and buckets, slapped their way around the buildings and grounds, spurred on by a payment of fifteen cents per hundred. Ruth Colebank recalled later what a messy business it had been and how eventually the boys were reimbursed based on the weight of the dead flies they had accumulated, not on how many. She remarked in the 1950s, "[E]ven today I prefer a live fly to a dead one."[11] McIndoo believed that more was at stake than

extermination of the verminous fly. He observed that besides being a constant source of income for a boy, the campaign taught him
"lessons of cleanliness and an aversion to filth as well as teaching
him other lessons in civic biology."[12]

McIndoo showed his sense of humor and his flair for word play
in the 1914 bulletin discussion of paying boys in candy: "Stick
candy was found to be a better fly exterminator than sticky fly
paper. It may be truthfully said that the most striking thing about
the Ford Republic is the fly swatting campaign. It was a hit every
time." He also showed his appreciation of fanciful language and
imagery: "We are sure . . . that very few flies were left . . . to crawl
away into crevices for the winter . . . and that when those . . . escaping emerge from their winter quarters next spring, their coming forth will be looked forward to by the boys and their chances
for survival very slim." The bulletin further noted that unlike
those institutions seeking reform through "external forces," the
republic did not try to "stamp out . . . primitive gang instincts,"
but rather "channel" them along right lines through wise direction from "adults in charge."[13]

This is a significant modification of the one citizen–one vote
concept fostered by Lane. The adults were "in charge," not mere
citizens. While Lane wanted as little a direct say in their lives as
possible and was willing to wait out the emergence of the "good
in all boys," McIndoo felt the need for a stronger say, except in
the school, which he felt operated exceedingly well with a kind
of self-governance that put disciplinary measures for tardiness or
absenteeism directly in the hands of the boys.

Fred Butzel himself had second thoughts about the validity of
a self-governing operation. In a 1916 article in *Detroit Saturday
Night*, he half apologized for the radicalism of the fathers of the
republic in thinking that all boys were good and were capable
of handling their own affairs. This slightly misguided notion, he
suggested, had had the good effect, however, of forcing the "reac-
tionaries" toward a more viable center.[14]

McIndoo maintained the court system, feeling it served to satisfy a boy need for retribution and to give smaller boys a chance for

power. He said that the court showed "self-government methods
exemplified in their highest forms." Noted Colebank, "The court
was used as a simple way of handling discipline. . . . The president
had certain functions which were expedient to the smooth running of the boy-life. But elections were held by acclamation and
there were no state meetings."[15]

Boy rules, regulations, and punishments did not change much
from those in effect during Lane's tenure. Boys were chided and
penalized for not "cleaning milk cans . . . not playing fair . . .
buttin' in . . . smoking, stealing, lying . . . swearing and destroying property." The guilty party might be "dismissed, fined, arrested,
spanked" or, as noted in the 1914 bulletin, forced to sit "all day
in de apple tree fer swipin' dem green apples."[16]

Some laws showed a newfound regimentation:

> Boys should not roll up their sleeves in dining room or school
> room.

> Boys must remember that they are not to whisper or talk
> while in line . . . this means—in line for meals, in line for
> bed, and in line in school room.

Some rules suggested greater routinization, more order, and greater
attention to smaller details:

> Boys must get out of bed before starting to dress.

> When undressing, boys should take off one thing at a time.

> Boys must not put their feet on the bed while lacing their
> shoes.

> Boys must not curl up and pull nightgown over their feet
> while waiting for prayers.

It was also ruled that they should not:

Wash hands in the horse trough.

Keep potato bugs in the cubehole [sic].

Make any noise with there [sic] stools.[17]

And in 1921:

Mrs McIndoo said the boys should write more to their parents.

Susie Balliet McIndoo played an active role in republic affairs. When it became apparent that some boys were gambling with their wages and others were stealing, she helped devise a ledger system with credits on one side and charges on the other. Each week individual accounts would be settled, but the boys would only be given actual funds for purchases or paying court fines. The money was kept in a box in the store.[18]

McIndoo took great pains to organize the school department so that it would correspond with the public school system, in which most boys would have to operate. School was very flexible, providing much individual instruction to bring the boys up to grade level. Some boys were prepared for getting working papers and some were helped in securing jobs. In August 1921 McIndoo hired Bertha Flowers, a special education teacher with an appreciation of wildlife, gardening, and handicrafts and some background in intelligence testing. He also hired Frank Stone, a physical education instructor who became director of recreation, a post he held for fourteen years.

The boys, perhaps, were the best spokesmen for the school system. In a presentation before the board, one youngster observed: "Sometimes the 4th and 5th grades go to the woods. [We] look for birds and tracks of muskrats and skunks and for different kinds of trees. We chase squirrels but we never catch them and we saw a crow's nest. Once D. Daley fell in the creek." And: "Mr. Colebank teaches us Arithmetic and writing. He is a pretty good writer and makes lots of curves when he writes." And: "Miss Jones' room sings every morning and noon. She makes so much noise that the 4th and 5th grades can just about do their work. They were dragging a song the other morning."[19]

McIndoo had high hopes for a strong industrial arts program. He wanted to gear it around interests and practicality. If the kitchen needed a new table, the kitchen workers would make it. An ironing board could be constructed by the laundry boys. He wanted to provide instruction in toy, wagon, sled, and kite making and in shoe repair. He wanted to install a knitting machine for making stockings and a printing press. The boys already had a school weekly. He hoped, too, to "give boys the fundamental principles of handling tools . . . [and] . . . ease and dexterity."[20]

He saw this as a "plastic age" where boys could be molded for good or ill. Apparently most were molded for good because a discharge report prepared by researcher Roy Olson showed that between January 1, 1912, and November 24, 1924, 186 of the 284 boys located from a list of 800 were leading reasonably productive lives. Ninety-one others required additional institutionalizing, but 24 of those later became "good citizens." Juvenile court and recorder's court records showed that 84 were "not doing useful work" and 46 were in correctional facilities.[21]

By 1922 John McIndoo had experienced considerable success with the boys, had seen the republic through to solvency, and, most remarkably, had incurred no new debts. But in that year he was recruited into a new enterprise and in the early months submitted his resignation. His successor was waiting in the wings.

THE JONES YEARS

Dr. Claude P. Jones, Lane's old friend and benefactor, had maintained a lively interest in the problem of delinquency and dependence. And in the back of his mind was the idea that when his financial state permitted, he would become involved with his protégé's boys' home. When the superintendent position became vacant, he was ready to fill it. He was aware of his limitations—medical doctors are not necessarily skilled in dealing with problem youths. But he was committed to Lane and his philosophy and felt it would be a great honor to be able to continue the man's noble work.

His ties with the republic had been particularly close during most of McIndoo's tenure. His daughter, Ruth, after a chance encounter with Lane at the Vineland (New Jersey) Training Center, had come to Detroit and later been hired by the republic as a teacher/bookkeeper. Thus, in 1922, when the superintendency became a possibility, he was well-versed in day-to-day operations.[22]

Claude Jones decided to let his daughter judge the wisdom of his candidacy and sent her his application along with a note to send it on to Fred Butzel if she deemed it appropriate. Ruth did indeed think her father suitable for the position. He had intelligence, an abiding interest in young people, and an eternal youthfulness in his favor. The board agreed and Jones was appointed. Because he could not settle his affairs until July 1, his daughter was appointed interim superintendent.

Ruth Jones Colebank had been called on many times—and would be in the next thirty-two years—to use her judgment, to lead. Her life was the republic and many felt that had she been a man she would most certainly have headed the organization. She was a strong woman, strong enough to laugh at her foibles and admit to mistakes. She was highly intelligent, keenly insightful, meticulously organized, and warm and loving. She was closer to the heart of the republic longer than anyone had been or would be.

While not given to embracing Lane's philosophy about the goodness in all boys, she held fast to his belief that youngsters learned best through example and by self-determination. The tendency of administrators to step in when the boys appeared to be heading in an undesirable direction distressed her. Such controls did not allow for growth, she believed, and boys living under imposed rules would not get practical experience in self-restraint. The boys needed to make mistakes in order to see what worked and what did not. Thus, when serving in the interim she, with the help of Bertha Flowers and Frank Stone, set about trying to revive the republic concept.

First they dusted off the constitution, rewriting and discarding segments. Then they began the process of electing officers: a president, vice president, judge, sheriff, yard commissioner, and health officer. Candidates were nominated freely, without a limit on the number, at a general assembly. A primary narrowed the number to two for each office. The boys quickly got into the spirit of the event. They made speeches, promising everything under the sun. Campaign posters, some very artistic, sprang up everywhere. By election day feelings ran high. Balloting was secret and controlled, with boys counting in the presence of other boys.

The republic once again had state meetings and a feeling of community grew. In a splendid 1950s forty-seven-page manuscript chronicling her days at the republic, Ruth Colebank recalled that that spring the boys enjoyed freedom from the constraints imposed by the McIndoo superintendency. The glen was used more widely, and, although there were rules, they were mutually agreed upon. Mrs. Colebank noted that as the complexion of the residents changed, the old rules had to be reinstated, but those early months were special ones.[23]

In the succeeding years, she was to enjoy similar closeness with the boys, though in a different capacity. One colleague remembered that when a boy had a complaint against Henry Colebank (who had been hired in 1913 as a teacher and bookkeeper and whom Ruth married in 1925), perhaps for expecting too much or for showing impatience, he would go to her. This was typical of her relationship with the boys. Some of them were big and tough, but she seemed bigger and tougher—and ever gentle—and they respected her. She was praised widely for her work with the republic. One colleague called her "the brain behind the gun," adding, "If Fred Butzel was the dominant spirit on our Board, it was Ruth Colebank that ran the show." Said another: "Ruth had a stability and understanding of social work far beyond any college experience she ever had."[24]

She had strong administrative skills, a deep commitment to her work, and an ability to handle on-the-spot problems with dignity and grace. Above all, she was blessed with a spirited sense of humor. Her manuscript abounds with insightful introspection and a keen appreciation of life's absurdities. Throughout, she allows the reader to feel the pulse of the republic, to see it as it was, in the language and with the color of the days.

Of the boys' clothing she recalled, "When I arrived the boys were wearing blue chambray shirts and khaki knickers with long black ribbed stockings." Because these were inexpensive and easily washed, they continued to be republic garb long after style dictated otherwise. Wanting to avoid the appearance of uniforms, the republic staff tried "grey covert cloth pants, but we learned that they were more deadly than the khaki ever could be. It was not until the blue jeans and T shirts became the universal [attire] of the male American adolescent that we achieved our desire—to have our boys look like all the other boys. There had been a time when the Michigan State Police could spot one of our run-aways in other parts of the state by the clothes he was wearing."[25]

Of daily menus in the early days she said:

> The food was fairly good but monotonous. It was the day
> of one kind of meal for the boys and another for the staff,
> [all] planned by the cook. Mrs. Jones made good apple pie
> but she made it six days a week. On the seventh we had ice
> cream. One man cook used to make baking powder biscuits
> for breakfast seven mornings a week. You can get awfully tired
> of biscuits. This same man gave us stew every noon and on
> Saturday we could still detect the remains of Monday's stew.

In a revealing August 14, 1956, letter to then Superintendent Milton Huber regarding the content of her manuscript, Ruth Colebank said that she had "made no mention of the trials and troubles [they] went through periodically with truancy, low population, interfering busybodies, and that most devastating of all troubles, staff bickering and disloyalty . . . because in retrospect these were overshadowed by the good elements of each adminis-tration."[26]

Mrs. Colebank was certainly a positive force in the repub-lic. In 1953 Superintendent Charles Henry characterized her as "kind, considerate, patient . . . invaluable." He most admired her "spirit . . . love of youth . . . flexibility and willingness to accept and use new and promising ideas."[27] It is no wonder that when Claude P. Jones assumed the superintendency in July 1922 he found the republic operating in high gear under the competent guidance of his daughter.

Jones was thrilled at the prospect of helping to ensure the fur-therance of his friend and protégé's dream. In a letter to Fred Butzel, he wrote, "The one lasting thing I have done in life so far was the education of Homer Lane."[28]

However, like McIndoo before him, he found a different sort of boy awaiting him. The truants, ragamuffins, and newsies of Lane's day had been joined by confused delinquents with a multitude of emotional scars. Although in harmony with Lane's best thinking, Jones began to conclude that while self-government might be viable for some, others were not capable of functioning with that degree of leeway. Over the next eleven years Jones worked toward segregating those who would sabotage the system from those who could benefit from it. His tenure also brought improvements in the physical plant, greater involvement in the community, and the augmentation of a program of psychological approaches to the problems of youths.

Jones had been at the republic just a few short weeks when tragedy struck: a typhoid epidemic swept through the place, send-ing thirteen boys to the hospital, one of whom died. Two boys were desperately ill and many others suffered severe intestinal disrup-tion. He had planned to institute a typhoid vaccination program, but the disease had struck first. After some painful and distressing weeks, a degree of order was reestablished and Jones was able to get down to the business of running the republic.[29]

Through the years he had kept abreast of changing concepts in youth work. He had helped organize a scout troop in the New

Jersey town where he practiced medicine (Jones was an 1893 Harvard Medical School graduate), and his interest in children had led him to a study of the new field of psychological testing. One thing was certain: he was willing to experiment and adapt if doing so helped increase the chance that young people would become productive adults.

Thus, when money became available through a bequest designated for non-operational expenses, Jones recommended hiring a dentist, a psychiatrist, and a social worker—and building a separate facility for those too young intellectually or chronologically to govern their own affairs successfully. This was one more step toward the home's becoming a complete residential care institution.

Jones may not have been far afield in his view of the new types of boys being admitted to the republic. A statistical study in 1930 conducted by Wayne State University doctoral student Courtland Van Vechten seemed to bear out his theory that some boys had suffered too many emotional upheavals to settle easily into controlling their own lives in a free setting. Though statistical analyses were relatively unsophisticated back in the 1930s and some of Van Vechten's categories are abstruse and in need of further definition, his data merit note.

Van Vechten studied one thousand consecutive admissions to the home, numbers 601 to 1600 inclusive, from April 20, 1922, to September 5, 1929. His sources were republic and juvenile court records and police reports. Admitting that the records were often inconclusive and at best spotty, he nevertheless was able to trace patterns and to illuminate trends.

Without providing the kind of substantive evidence needed for the reader to concur or accept, he concluded that the republic philosophy was only viable with youngsters of at least ordinary intelligence, stability, and health who were steeped in the principles of democracy. Of the 1,000 boys, 108 were born in foreign countries, 41 in the democratic countries of Canada and the British Isles. Of significance is Van Vechten's observation that only one-third of the total had "more than their own experience in democracy" and "four hundred and twenty-eight [hadn't gone] to American Public Schools." The remaining two-thirds probably had little contact with "American democratic theory."

Van Vechten determined that "[The Republic] is receiving a much larger percentage of boys who are deadweight as far as the active participation in affairs of state are [sic] concerned—boys who must be carried by the more socially-minded ones." The greatest number of boys came from Polish backgrounds (343), followed by what he classified "American" and then Italian. Of interest also, though not directly pertaining to his self-governing thesis, is that 514 were Roman Catholic, 259 Protestant, 29 Greek Orthodox, and 27 Jewish.

Of direct significance was that only 46 percent came from intact families (those free from divorce and separation). The majority of the children had suffered some sort of upset in the family: death of a parent (sometimes both parents); parental desertion; divorce or separation; or the introduction of a step-parent into the family. Some children came from other child welfare agencies; only two were homeless. Many children came from families where there were roomers and/or relatives living with them.

Many boys suffered the effects of family members' criminal behavior, the offenses ranging from bootlegging, drunkenness, and disorderliness to physical abuse, sexual offenses, and prostitution. There were also many parents suffering from physical or emotional problems. Several were afflicted with syphilis or gonorrhea, and the emotional afflictions ranged from feeble-mindedness to imbecility to psychopathic tendencies. A small number came from families where a parent had committed suicide. The majority of boys, however, had parents without criminal records or emotional problems. The boys mostly came from working-class families. Few were desperately poor, though most lived in undesirable neighborhoods. Many were gang members, a few of them actual leaders.

Nine hundred and twenty-six of the boys were Wayne County Court appointees; forty-three were paying residents placed by parents in lieu of having them sent to the Boys' Vocational School.

Nine hundred and forty-four boys were white; fifty-six were of another race or mixed race.[30]

Reasons for commitment varied. Most boys were remanded for breaking and entering (343), larceny (594), and home and school truancy (879). Some boys had been charged with robberies, sexual offenses, incorrigibility, assaults, and auto misuse; one was charged with murder. The average age of a boy beginning a delinquent lifestyle was eleven years old. Observed Monsignor Edward Hickey:

> They came from the homes of recent immigrants . . . who had more recently come to our city and were the first ones to be out of jobs. Sometimes they'd send their youngsters out to push coal off freight trains, and gather it up, to break and enter and bring home food or clothing. Then, they would break and enter themselves . . . Or wait for the bars to close and go over the pockets of some persons only half sober . . . take their watch and their money . . . take automobiles, strip them, and sell their parts.[31]

Notable is the fact that of the one thousand boys admitted in those years, only twenty-five were classified as neglected or dependent.

Of 137 boys given comprehensive psychological testing, a large percentage showed signs of instability. The categories are intriguing and the terminology marks a vast change in the ways boys were observed:

NEUROTIC	8
SCHIZOID	4
PARANOID	2
CONSTITUTIONALLY PSYCHOPATHIC	20
TENDING TOWARD DEMENTIA PRAECOX	1
UNSTABLE, IMPULSIVE	27
HYPER-SUGGESTIVE	7
INFANTILE	28
HAVING PSYCHOPATHIC FANTASY LIFE	6

SELF-PITYING	3
BLUNTED EMOTIONALLY	2
SENSITIVE	5
UNINHIBITED	2
PRIMITIVE	2
IDEALISTIC	2
CAREFREE	1

Van Vechten found that of fifty boys given psychological testing prior to admittance, thirty-eight showed signs characteristic of troubled youths. If these fifty were representative, over "three-fourths of the [population had] some fairly well marked mental or emotional abnormality," he wrote.[32]

Some boys had physical problems, but eventually a new screening system weeded out those with serious problems, and minor ones such as hernias and astigmatism were corrected prior to admission. Still, one-third of the boys were handicapped from undernourishment and lesser concerns. A few were retarded, but gradually the screening system saw that such boys were placed elsewhere. In addition, some were intellectually deficient. The average IQ was only 80.6, with 22.1 percent of the boys falling below 71.[33] The boys were clearly different from the ones who had set up the self-governing community with Lane. Jones's request for a separate facility to house boys with greater needs reflected his awareness of the change.

The new Baldwin Building was officially dedicated in 1925. Designed for seventy-two youngsters who needed more supervision, it had its own house mother, house father, teachers, cooks, baker, and service employees. The Baldwin boys were able to air their grievances during roundtable meetings with a supervisor, but they did not have state sessions or make or enforce laws. They were divided into groups of not more than twenty-five, each under the guidance of a staff member. In the next five years, they had less and less contact with the self-governing Ford Hall boys. In the 1930 annual report Jones noted "the most complete separation of the Baldwin and Ford groups that we have made."[34]

These were years of growth. Henry Colebank and the boys constructed the Lane cottage, which eventually housed four couples.
Ruth Colebank, staff, and citizens dug a north-south road and
Henry built a bridge to span it. They all set out five thousand
spruce trees. Colebank attributed the sense of unity back then to
the difficulties in reaching and leaving the farm. When something
needed to be done, they all did it. When it was time for play, they
all played. She noted, "Just as the dam for the swimming area was
built by the whole community, so was that road built by us all."
Improved methods of transportation resulted in a loss of some of
that closeness.[35]

Soon the republic had a hospital, a new heating plant, a milk
house, a settling basin, and an addition to the gym. There Frank
Stone painted a shuffleboard court, set aside space for a form of
bowling, put out boxing equipment, and eventually brought in
table games and dartboards. Later the republic had four tennis
courts and four softball diamonds, and intramural basketball and
softball leagues.

The school program improved greatly. Because of better transportation, teachers could take evening classes at area colleges and
receive more training. A visiting teacher, Gertrude Brock, was
hired to teach math and to spend one day a week in the boys' family residences. She served as an important liaison and was received
so well that sometimes she was called on as a friend to help with
a sewing project or to make arrangements for emergency medical
treatment. Because of the effectiveness of the program, most of the
other teachers became involved. Once a week one person would
stay at the republic school and oversee quiet desk work assigned to
the students while the others visited three to four family homes
each, usually in the same neighborhood. Sometimes they compared notes at lunch. Because their schedules were flexible, they
were able to establish good relationships with the parents, giving
each family the time needed during a particular session. They always discussed the visits with the boys, thus keeping them in touch
with their families and showing them that everyone was involved
in helping them overcome their difficulties. In 1927 and 1928,

teachers visited 431 homes, conducted 828 interviews, and made 322 administrative calls to schools and child welfare agencies.[36]

The visiting teacher program paved the way for one providing follow-up counseling. In 1927, with the approval of the juvenile court, Roy Sharp and Earl Baxtresser were hired to work closely with newly released boys instead of returning them to their probation officers. In 1928 alone they handled 341 cases, conducted 2,106 interviews, and paid 2,510 visits to homes and schools. Each year decreasing numbers of boys were sent to the vocational school in Lansing and more and more needed farm placement or help in finding other employment. Through the efforts of these men, boys often returned to homes that had been appreciably repaired and to families that had a better understanding of how to live peaceably and effectively.[37]

Perhaps more than any other document of the period, the 1924 constitution with seven pages of laws best reflects the general change in attitude toward the republic concept. The boys still made and enforced the regulations, but the chief justice of the supreme court—the superintendent—had absolute veto power, as the constitution noted three times. Gone was the two-thirds majority overriding vote of the citizenry. Though Jones used this power only three times, in each case to make a ruling less harsh, the trend toward greater administrative control was set. Rules covered leaning, sitting, touching, tardiness, "insolence to officers or employees (like saying 'Tough luck')," dressing, wetting the bed, loud talking, hanging up towels, putting away toothbrushes, wearing neckties, parent visitation, removing hats in buildings, cutting across lawns, getting up before rising bell, closing doors, using the Baldwin toilet, and reading papers during school hours.[38]

A *Redford Record* reporter visiting the republic in 1927 saw a "simon pure democracy." She was especially impressed with the orderliness of the luncheon crowd and with the absence of noise— just low talk. No one sat until the president "bid them be seated." One boy who forgot his manners and put his hand on the white tablecloth was required, by the table head, to spend the time standing up, face to the wall. When the reporter showed surprise at an open locker policy, Jones explained that he wanted to "build up the will to resist." There were no locks anywhere because "when they leave here and return to the world, we want them strong enough to keep their hands off the property of others." Pointing to some particularly well-dressed lads in the dining room who were buying second desserts, Jones said that the "loafer" learns that "extras—new clothing, desserts, candy—come from work."[39]

The reporter was equally impressed with the reenactment of Lane's "ice-cream-at-every-meal" ploy. She was convinced that when boys make an untenable demand, get their wish, and then see it as untenable, they learn an invaluable lesson. She noted:

> The boys, instead of being forced to obey adult-made rules without understanding the necessity of their existence, and without the almost inevitable result that they will continue in their habit of breaking any law that irks them, learn through experience that laws, and an observance of them, are vitally necessary if the world is to go along smoothly and everyone receive his fair share of comfort and enjoyment.[40]

Jones contended that he did not want to "crush [the gang] instinct but to direct it along worthwhile lines." He said that the whole election procedure exemplified how energy could be used creatively. The boys campaigned, made posters, held rallies, gave speeches, and canvassed voters. He said: "We capitalize on this spirit of leadership and this willingness to follow a leader."

Other republic activities enabled the boys to rid themselves of excess energy. They all looked forward to the annual ice harvest. The pond usually yielded one hundred and fifty tons of ice blocks, which were stored after the boys sawed and loaded them onto wagons. One boy said that the "chain gang" had the best deal of all because after hauling twenty blocks, they could rest around the fire and have hot cocoa and cakes while a replacement team worked. The boys also produced and performed in plays and held pageants. They learned techniques of lighting and constructing scenery. The reporter observed that once inside the republic "all signs of adult rule disappear."[41]

To a large extent this was true. In 1927 the boys still made some laws and determined penalties. When Jones ruled against the use of corporal punishment, the boys protested so vigorously that he decided that maybe they did know best how to handle each other. For a serious infraction, a boy was brought to an executive session at which seventy older boys each gave him a slap on his bare bottom. The offender also lost his free time for a specified period and was forced to wear a girl's dress in the school classroom, dining room, and on campus.

One former resident remembered those days well. In a 1981 republic-conducted historical survey of board members, teachers, staff, and former residents, he recalled, "This punishment was cruel. When seventy-two boys were through slapping your butt, it was bleading [sic]. If they didn't slap you hard, they would get two slaps themselves. You could not sit down for a week without pain." Still, he felt indebted to the republic. He had been antagonistic and had run away a few times, but then was elected to various judicial posts and finally "made Judge." He noted: "I felt like a big shot, but I treated the boys fairly when they did something wrong." He learned how to drive a team of horses, grow crops, work with machinery, and was never in trouble again, having learned how to be a "better person." He recalled that some boys were so reluctant to leave when they were supposed to at seventeen that they stayed on and "worked for room and board."[42]

The 1930 Van Vechten study included a follow-up report with an attempt at gauging degrees of successful adaptation. Again the definitions are amorphous. How does one measure success? But of the 1,000 boys studied, 613 were adjudged to have attained a "satisfactory" mode of living. Of 237 who were later sent to other institutions for delinquents, 92 had never been "recommended for release by the Ford Republic." One hundred and ninety-five boys had run off and had not been returned to the republic. Ten boys had died.[43]

An undated though much later board of trustees bulletin noted that the Van Vechten study, along with spot checks and a "survey by Wayne State University," attributed a success rate of 75 percent to the republic, adding, "Yet this outstanding degree of reclamation has been done with the Republic consistently accepting and successfully working with youngsters that other private schools may have rejected because of race, creed, or nationality; in some cases below normal intelligence or with difficult problems involved."[44]

The republic continued to grow and expand. It became associated with the Community Fund and the Council of Social Agencies, thereby having greater access to financial resources and more substantial accreditation. In 1931 it sent two Detroit police officers who had been assigned to the juvenile court to the University of Chicago for three months to study under a leading authority on youthful criminality. Jones also arranged for the first regular religious services for Catholic and Protestant boys, and Jewish boys were allowed to return to their homes for special observances.

To provide an added incentive toward achievement, Jones began awarding high grades with money. A student whose average in all subjects was below 80 received $2 a week for his labor. Those making marks over 85 got $3. The star student had 95+ and got $6.

In spite of all sorts of figures showing a relatively high rate of success, Jones was not content. In a rather angry-sounding report to the board in 1931 he said:

> It does not satisfy me that our very fine activities of self-government, school athletics, and visiting teachers' splendid follow-up are greatly lessening our failures. It is not enough to keep these boys within the law. It is important to understand methods for developing their talents for success. . . . I want to live to make an annual report . . . which will show the striking success of many of the seventy percent whom we now can only classify as not having been failures.

In a bid for an increased psychiatric staff, he said:

> In 1928 you added to our better understanding of the cause
> of our boys being in trouble by having a thorough study of
> the boy made by the Clinic for Child Study at the Detention
> Home. It added to our enthusiasm to know that Johnny was
> here because of an inferiority complex and to understand
> that this was due to his mother having another baby when
> Johnny was four years old, and neglecting Johnny for the new
> baby. Also we got a thrill from knowing that Willie was a
> homosexual and was becoming delinquent from that cause. In
> fact, this knowledge, new to us, was so interesting that it was
> a year or more before some of us awoke to the fact that our
> knowing it did not help Johnny or Willie because we did not
> know a thing to do about it.

He went on to say that fifteen employees handled one hundred and fifty boys. Each employee had to read about forty case pages per boy in his spare time, when not working at his full-time job. He wrote, "I don't know how soon the staff found out they were in over their heads, but I know I was the first one to holler for help." He concluded, "It is not enough to keep these boys within the law. It is important to understand methods for developing their talents for success. . . . We need the mental hygiene direction of a practical psychiatrist."[45]

Despite ongoing program changes, attempts at finding new ways of dealing with old problems, and a relatively high level of operation, the republic was going through a troublesome period. Waves of discontent led to an increase in truancies and attempted runaways. The juvenile court was beginning to question the efficacy, in some cases, of returning the boys they had picked up. By late 1933 it was apparent that the republic needed some new direction. Clyde L. Reed was anxious to provide it.

Chapter 4

The Clyde L. Reed Years: 1933–1948

IN THE 1930S AND 1940S, young people continued to be the unwitting victims of economic and political change. During the depression, some children were sent from their homes to fend for themselves; others ran away. World War II also gave rise to new problems. Historian Alan Clive notes the phenomenon of mothers seeking outside employment, flocking into war plants and civilian industries, an estimated sixty thousand in Wayne County alone, "leaving forty-five thousand children in need of [day] care." This period witnessed the first latchkey child, though many youngsters, "unable to enter homes locked for the day by their war-worker parents . . . roamed the streets of industrial communities."

According to Clive, "children were in a constant state of excitation, a condition that often produced deeply disturbing side effects." They feared not only for the fathers and brothers in the service but also for themselves. They had to deal with the conflicting emotions of "pride, fear, guilt, hatred and love—all directed at the absent [person]."[1]

Disruption in the family led to anxiety, loneliness, and sometimes divorce. Michigan divorces climbed from 12,054 in 1940 to 29,158 in 1946. The lack of supervision in the home extended to the schools, many of which were meeting the wartime government's urging that they operate at 200 percent capacity. The problem was compounded by the exodus of military-age faculty. Notes Clive, "The man-power shortage also deprived communities of needed police and social workers. Juvenile authorities [had] predicted that involvement in the war would incite a rise in deviant behavior, and juvenile delinquency statistics bore them out." In Detroit, truancy rates soared and the number of runaways more than doubled. There was also a notable rise in crime among children under ten.

A late 1930s study of Michigan delinquency patterns concluded that the Detroit area was the "storm center of disturbance, accounting for fifty percent of the total cases." Still, according to Clive, it was not until a "youth gang war erupted in the city" that Detroit authorities were brought "face to face with the magnitude of the war-time delinquency problem."[2]

Ninety percent of the republic boys in the 1930s and 1940s came from Michigan juvenile courts, half from Wayne County. Ten percent came from Ohio and Illinois. Most were of average intelligence, or slightly below, and had problems that seemed to stem from gang affiliations. According to Rev. John J. Wittsock, the republic Catholic chaplain from 1936 to 1966, "In the forties and fifties many more lads came from homes where a mother was working and the lads got no supervision."[3]

The breaches of good conduct remained the same as earlier: breaking and entering, robbery, truancy, incorrigibility. But a few boys had committed serious crimes: murder, arson, statutory sex offenses. Thus was the climate when Clyde L. Reed began his association with the republic.

REED AND THE REPUBLIC

Clyde L. Reed was well suited for work with delinquent and disadvantaged boys. He was born on June 15, 1909, in Battle Creek, Michigan, where he became an active member of the Boy Scouts of America. After high school graduation, he enrolled at the University of Michigan, working primarily in business administration at the gentle urging of his aunt and uncle who were helping him with college expenses. But the world of "stocks, bonds, mortgages, and balance sheets," he noted, did not fully engage him, as his grades so well reflected. After two years of pre-business courses and a first semester junior year with a heavy load of required ones, he sought out the services of the guidance and placement center. Extensive testing showed that, indeed, he needed to work with people rather than figures. A definite avocational pattern emerged: He should consider ministerial, YMCA, or social work. Without a word to anyone, he switched to a program that combined sociology and psychology. His grade-point average soared—and the foundation for his life's work was laid.

Upon graduation he was faced with a depressed economy, few jobs, and lots of job seekers. This was an ideal time to begin graduate studies. His own financial state was shaky, however, and he needed a place to stay. He found one at the Detroit House of Correction. He worked with the "Kindergarten," eighteen-year-old and younger committed felons, in return for a salary and sleeping quarters, taking classes and earning his degree in 1932. The experience at the correctional facility led him to the realization that his main interest was in the younger criminal, or delinquent, the boy who was still developing and could yet be molded or influenced.

Armed with twenty-four letters of recommendation, he recalled later, he "barnstormed [his] way through the East . . . and Midwest," looking for work in an institution. He received the same response everywhere: well-qualified, yes; available job, no; call back in six months. He decided to seek out that champion of the young, the great Detroit humanitarian Fred Butzel. Said Reed: "I came to [his] office with a master's degree in one hand and an empty pocketbook in the other." Something about the young man impressed Butzel and he asked him to stop by at the republic the next Saturday. He hired him on the spot and, without having had any "discussion of salary, remuneration, or what the job would be," Reed began work on the following Monday.

His first assignment was to oversee three boys in trash hauling—collecting rubbish in the republic dump truck. Reed knew that

"every individual working with children is a kind of model." He
believed that even as a dump truck driver, he needed to "counsel them about work, about attitudes toward work . . . toward
staff . . . toward the rules and regulations of the institution." He
observed, "There's an interpersonal relationship that immediately
develops between each child and some staff member." Later, as
superintendent, he advised his staff: "Remember that no matter
what your position—fireman, gardener, farmer—some boy at this
school is looking up to you," thinking of you as "his model, his
little tin god."[4]

Reed observed, "Every boy had a 'locked in' problem. Fortunate was the staff member who had the right key: An understanding housemother who could successfully play the role of mother
substitute; the psychiatrist who could diagnose the problem; the
recreation worker who had a way with a particular boy." Noted
Sam Rabinovitz, republic follow-up counselor from 1935 to 1943,
"Each person on the staff felt and knew he or she was part of this
total process."[5]

Within a short time Reed was assigned to the Recreation
Department where he helped boys "express themselves through
craft work [and] through play." He later taught for awhile, and
then became the assistant to the assistant superintendent, Ruth
Colebank.

Since he had already proven his competency at working with
boys, the twenty-four-year-old Reed was a natural choice for the
superintendency when Jones stepped down. He had no doubt,
however, that Colebank could have succeeded her father if society had been "ready for a female to be head of a school for delinquent boys."

Reed felt prepared for the job, given his background in aca-
demics, preparation in sociology, and his practical experience,
though his responsibilities were plentiful. He had to hire and fire
personnel, maintain the institution, handle finances, arrange for
fund-raising, and answer to the board of directors, in addition to
seeing after day-to-day operations and making policy decisions.
But he loved the challenge and met it head-on.

Reed had some strong feelings regarding the basic framework of the institution. He was skeptical of the leaning in similar facilities in the 1930s toward marching bands, parades, semi-military-type uniforms, and training. Not enough attention was paid to the individual, to how he was progressing, to what he was achieving.[6]

Reed did not want to lose sight of the individual and always attempted to make a clear distinction between the group emphasis of more military correctional facilities and the individual emphasis of his democratic organization. In 1935 he dismissed the notion that "Republic" was a euphemism for "Reformatory." His was not a place for "confin[ing] transgressors of the law," for "mak[ing] bad boys good" through the use of "high walls and spanking machines." Rather, the republic was a school for "delinquent, underprivileged and problem boys," from ten to seventeen, who, though not handicapped by substandard intelligence, had "poor parental discipline, a history of misconduct, or more than a year-long delinquency record."[7]

"The average Ford Republic youngster," noted writer William Norton in 1940, "is far from the tight-lipped youth typical of so many institutions. There is a noticeable spirit of normal happiness and boyish exuberance" as evidenced when the boys, upon court adjournment, "popped up from their seats and swarmed out comfortably, normally, instead of marching out in neatly regimented lines." He further observed: "A buzz of chatter filled the room, as everybody sauntered easily for the door. They wandered outside to the greenhouse to receive their regular afternoon apples."[8]

To Reed, the goal of the republic was and had always been to help a boy achieve a level of adjustment that would enable him to return to society as a productive member. The first step in the adjustment process, he felt, was to help the boy understand the difference between right and wrong.

Reed firmly believed that the most effective way to teach boys what is acceptable and what is not was by allowing them to make and enforce laws and then determine penalties for those who broke them. Through self-government the boys could learn to work together, begin to understand why rules are essential to the functioning of a group, and grow to understand the principles of democracy and the judicial system. They could learn not only from their own transgressions, not just from the personal experience of being caught and reprimanded, but also from witnessing group responses and reactions to the law-breaking of others. They also had the advantage of close daily contact with staff members who pointed out right and wrong approaches to problems or projects. A severe labor shortage during the war stretched the operation precariously thin at times and caused undue pressure on existing staff. However, a greater awareness of psychological approaches to boy problems led to the establishment of a clinic staffed by a social worker, a psychologist, and a visiting psychiatrist. A merit system was instituted in the 1930s whereby boys could earn their release.

Reed felt that there was nothing more conducive to good behavior than the disdain of peers for bad behavior. He believed that the certainty of being caught was much more of a deterrent than the nature or intensity of punishment. He agreed with some who viewed the merry-go-round punishment as meaningless in bearing a relationship to individual misdeeds, but felt that at least it was a form of punishment, a sure punishment. People who broke laws needed to suffer some unpleasant consequence.

The republic's crime-and-punishment system functioned much as it had previously, with boys being fined or assigned to work detail without pay or being made to walk or stand for specified periods of time. A bully might be told to go into a ring with someone slightly larger for three one-minute rounds under the close supervision of an adult. A boy who picked raisins out of his bread and threw them around the dining hall was sentenced to "toss a shot-put back and forth forty-five times." A boy who fed one of the republic's five dogs in the dormitory was fined fifty cents. Instead of being assigned to the merry-go-round, a boy might be expected to walk back and forth between two trees fifty feet apart.

Sometimes the boys needed help, nondictatorial help, in determining an appropriate punishment. In one case a boy was charged with stealing a hunting knife during a republic trip to a sportsman's show. One youngster suggested forgiving the boy because he was new. Another said that that was no excuse—he should have known better. Reed, appearing to be vocalizing some personal musings, said it was a real shame when the actions of a few affected the whole group. He related a story of some boys a few years earlier whose misbehavior at a local movie house had resulted in that establishment's becoming off-limits to the entire republic. It was not until some republic emissaries apologized to the manager that their good standing was reinstated. The judge listened carefully and, just as those boys had lost some privileges, so did the knife thief. Reed did not tell the boys how to handle the situation. He led them to see what the implications of the offense might be and what penalty would be fitting. According to Reed, "When a boy is charged by adults with committing an offense and the investigation as well as the discipline are in the hands of an adult, resentment is frequently felt. The boy is being handled by a person who is intellectually and physically his superior."

There was some corporal punishment—by hand or paddle—but no incidences of abuse or injury. When, on rare occasions, a worker caught up in the throes of the moment elected to mete out his own system of justice, it had to be reported and fully documented in the files.

In 1937 the boys, having "read about stocks in American history class," wanted to try out this novel form of punishment. Some staff members were horrified, but the boys were given permission to go ahead with the construction of the implement. Far from being deterred by the punishment, the boys determined that it was fun—a chance to sit in the shade and talk to buddies. The stock soon lost its fascination, however.

There were some imaginative penalties. A boy accused of spitting was sentenced to carrying mouthfuls of fountain water to a bucket ten or fifteen yards away until he accumulated two or three inches of spit. A boy who chose to whistle at an inopportune time was sentenced to a half hour of whistling behind the barn. The rather bizarre and potentially traumatic punishment of putting miscreants in dresses was eliminated. Noted Reed: "It is love, affection, and fitting in with the mores of the group . . . that help a child fit into what the society in which he lives demands of him."

Reed brought self-government back into full swing at the republic, though he later explained that the boys made laws governing their own conduct, not institutional operations. He called the program one of "student participation" in the hope of "put[ting] into operation the principles of democratic living." He valued a system that taught responsibility for oneself through a pay-for-work arrangement and toward others through the government. Such a framework taught self-reliance, community involvement, and cooperation, all the while allowing room for individual treatment for emotional and physical problems. The boys learned that industriousness paid, that labor brought satisfaction as well as financial rewards, and that money accumulated legally could bring greater material awards.

As in previous years, the question of ice cream rights came to the fore, this time in the form of a proposal that it be served twice a day. The proposition won unanimous approval. After a week Reed called the boys together to explain the food budget, saying that some part of the meals needed to be cut to allow the ice cream expense. The boys voted out vegetables. Meat went next. When they were down to bread, milk, and ice cream (in addition to a normal, healthy breakfast), they revoked the law.

One time the boys passed a ruling that made them responsible for all the cooking. After three or four of them prepared those foods that they were accustomed to at home, much to the dismay of others whose tastes differed, they decided to defer to the adult cook. Observed Reed: "Every staff member knew very well how this experiment would work out, but not one said, 'No, you cannot . . . try it.' The boys had to discover the real situation for themselves and learn through experience." He added: "Through making their own rules and observing . . . why some are good . . . and some . . . bad, boys are better equipped to understand the mechanism of real democracy. They actually learn to do by doing. They learn how to obey the rules of any society and [see] the advantages of [doing so]."

Reed noted, "The sky's the limit" as to how far they could go with self-government so long as they "don't hurt their health or injure institutional property. The level of citizenship fluctuates as the group changes. At periods, we have a fine upstanding sort of government. At other times we are beset by all the evils of 'rotten politics.'" Indeed, the citizens once impeached an officer for accepting bribes of jack-knives, fountain pens, and candy.

To help the boys develop an understanding of economics, the republic continued to use a fiat system that differed from earlier ones only in that the currency was stamped with the individual boy's number so that it could not be bartered, bet with, or stolen. The money system, according to Harry August, republic psychiatrist from 1929 to 1932, put the institution "far ahead" of others because "it promoted the development, maturation, and the esteem of these boys." They learned that hard work—industry—enabled them to enjoy such niceties as good clothing and second desserts. They learned the rewards of working and saving. They learned that being on "welfare," not paying their debt to the republic, meant no desserts, no field trips, and a good deal of scorn.

Reed recalls an instance of seeing a citizen reading outside a movie theater. Knowing how much the boy loved films, he asked why he was not inside. The boy answered that his parents were visiting the next Sunday and he really wanted to buy a new shirt for the occasion. The boy had taken one giant step toward maturity.

Some people voiced objections to boys being paid to attend school, saying that such a system set up unrealistic expectations and rewarded a physical presence rather than intellectual development, but to those boys, school was work, and getting them there represented a real achievement. And the financial rewards were based on ability and were always coupled with counseling. Said Reed: "There is no wish to create a highly protective environment. The boy . . . is from the first thrown into the hurly burly of vigorous, virile living. He has to grapple with all the day to day problems which occur in work, school, recreation, and group living situations." He added that "self-government offers to the problem boy a place in a society where he can be accepted; where his status is equal to that of his neighbor; where he learns by being a part of the government to respect the rights and properties of others."[9]

Esther Meredith, staff social worker from 1934 to 1945, hailed the system for conveying lessons that lectures could not have: "When a boy suddenly came up against another boy's taking something from him . . . something he had earned . . . worked for, gotten the money and purchased, [he experienced] his first awareness of what is meant by ownership, personal property. It was a very different concept to him than his blithely going out in the community and taking whatever was loose or he could grab."[10]

The boys also needed help in developing constructive ways to use leisure time. A widely read book by the warden of Sing Sing Prison had pointed out that 97 percent of prisoners were never associated with clubs where they could have learned about wholesome recreation. According to Reed, many of the boys had "spent their leisure time playing cards and dice, junking, robbing, or jack-rolling." They needed to be taught how to "play organized games and, even more important, how to occupy their time constructively when there [was] no supervision or organization."

The republic had a fully developed sports program under the Reed administration, though his thinking differed somewhat from that of his predecessor and the general approaches of the day. Competitiveness was fostered because it taught good sportsmanship, but the emphasis was on having widespread participation rather than on developing star athletes. The boys had varsity teams but they were encouraged to play intramural sports. Most of the games were strenuous ones (baseball, football, and handball) to help them work off excess energy.

A well-stocked library of 1,955 volumes (685 fiction and 1,270 nonfiction in 1941) gave the boys ample opportunities to spend free time constructively. Posters advised them of new acquisitions, as did their counselors. An added incentive was that they earned merit points for library use. Approximately 50 percent of the boys read an average of three books during their stay, which at that time was anywhere between six to sixteen months, usually eleven months. They read more nonfiction, though 75 percent of the boys read easy fiction. The 1941 Child Welfare League of America Report noted the republic's attempts to divert the boys from "trash literature—comic books"—a dilemma being faced nationwide.[11]

There were also craft clubs and special interest groups to help the boys discover hidden talents or work toward establishing a satisfying hobby. They could take up such activities as boxing; tap dancing; stamp collecting; leather, plastic, metal, or wood working; dramatics; or model airplane building. A bench and tools were available for boys inclined to make something. Said Reed: "If we can be of some assistance in helping the boy learn how to spend his time in other places than on the corner with his gang shooting dice or in other activities that are not constructive, we have helped in a measure to assist in his rehabilitation."[12]

The vocational projects were often tied in with community needs. For example, in June 1947, the cement class responded to an urgent need for repairs on a flood-burst dam. A *Battle Creek Enquirer and News* article noted, "At stake is their 'swimming hole' in a Rouge River tributary which flows through their land."[13] On another occasion, the boys worked on reseating the Fred Bloman memorial fountain.

Auto mechanics classes acquainted the boys with simple filling station services, such as tire changes, battery maintenance, radiator and brake repairs and installation, and car waxing. A diploma offered upon completion of the course helped many get jobs after release. An agricultural course consisting of a study of soil enrichment, crop rotation, animal husbandry, horticulture, and farm mechanics prepared a number of boys for farm work. Vegetable and flower planting sometimes led to later employment, or at least to a productive hobby.

In addition, the boys helped repair their own shoes and mend their own clothes, and were taught to knit afghans for the Red Cross. The main objectives of the vocational work were to train the boys in good work habits, give them manual dexterity, teach them to cooperate with others, and perhaps expose them to trades that might be useful in later life. They were always given theoretical and practical training.

A highlight in practical experience had to be the day in 1946 when Superintendent Reed arranged for the five boys in highest academic standing after final exams to do something highly unusual. Each would take a turn at the controls of an airplane. Pilot Graham Prince took them up, one by one, and let them fly over the republic. There was plenty of excitement in the air that day.

Admission procedures during the Reed years called for first determining a boy's emotional maturity, as well as noting his age and size, and then assigning him to either Ford or Baldwin Hall, the latter for those needing closer supervision. All boys were advised that they were responsible for their own actions, though a Big Brother was a close companion during the first week and clarified what was permissible and what was not. The Big Brother was a citizen of at least three months' standing who was not in debt and who seemed to be making a good adjustment. He helped a new boy (a "freshie") buy his first set of clothes; showed him his bed; sat with him in the cafeteria; acquainted him with the staff and the citizens; showed him places that were out-of-bounds; and generally filled him in on operations. A freshie spent about two hours a day with his counselor, who familiarized him with all aspects of the republic. They also discussed why the boy had come to the republic and what could be done to change his life course.

The boy was given a job, one that the staff placement committee felt best suited his interests, abilities, and needs. He was encouraged to ask for a transfer, however, if he found some other work he would rather do. Such jobs included building or grounds maintenance, laundry work, dishwashing, planting and harvesting, and building construction. A boy could volunteer for one of the more unpopular jobs if he needed money to make a special purchase at the store. Pay was based on effort, thus rewarding the limited boy who did as well as he could and penalizing the loafer.

A typical day in the 1930s and 1940s began at 7:00 A.M. with the wake-up bell. The boys would have thirty minutes for washing and dressing before breakfast at 7:30. The meal might consist of milk, fresh fruits, cooked cereal, and toast. It could be more elaborate or less so, depending on the food plan a boy had chosen. There were three options: economy at $4.20 a week, regular at $5.25 a week, or luxury at $5.70 a week.

There were problems, on occasion, with this system. Some boys cared more about money than nutrition and would be happy to save the few cents and always eat cheaply. While all the meals were balanced, only those boys who paid got the extras. Hence, noted the 1941 child welfare report, a youngster suffering from malnutrition who opted for economy might not get ample food to make up for his deficiency. Still, an earlier 1940 study had shown that seven out of ten boys gained weight within the first few weeks.

After breakfast the boys got their work assignments for the day. Some went to school, others to the fields, to counselors, to the doctor, or the dentist. At 11:30 they had to be back in their dorms where they could relax, play checkers, or listen to the radio until the noon meal. This was always the big meal of the day, so they were allotted forty minutes. The meal might consist of the following: salmon and peas, mashed potatoes, cabbage salad, bread, and milk; or spareribs, creamed potatoes, green beans, bread, milk, and mustard; or roast pork, mashed potatoes, gravy, buttered peas and carrots, bread, milk, and Jello.

After lunch the boys had free time until 1:30, when they were due back at work or school. At 4:45 they returned to their dorms for the roll call. Supper was at 6:00. Sometimes the meals were repetitious. The dinner menu for the week of June 20–26, 1941, was typical:

Friday, June 20
Economy: Creamed eggs on toast, bread, milk, graham crackers
Regular: Butter, sauce, cookies
Luxury: Deviled eggs

Saturday, June 21
Economy: Potato salad, kidney beans, bread, milk, rice
pudding
Regular: Butter, canned figs
Luxury: Liver and side pork

Sunday, June 22
Economy: Creamed eggs on toast, crackers, cheese, milk,
bread, ice cream, and cookies
Regular: Butter
Luxury: Fried potatoes

Monday, June 23
Economy: Italian spaghetti, spinach, bread, milk, stewed
prunes
Regular: Butter, dessert
Luxury: Cold meat

Tuesday, June 24
Economy: Side pork, boiled rice (unsweetened), brown sugar,
lettuce, bread, milk, and peanut butter
Regular: Butter
Luxury: Fried potatoes, two doughnuts

Wednesday, June 25
Economy: Baked beans, ketchup, stewed tomatoes, chocolate
pudding, bread, milk, fresh rolls, jam
Regular: Butter
Luxury: Cold meat

Thursday, June 26
Economy: Creamed dried beef on toast, lima beans au gratin,
bread, milk, peanut butter
Regular: Butter, sauce
Luxury: Vegetable

As these menus show, paying a bit more usually entitled a boy to butter and dessert. Luxury ensured him of an alternate main or side dish. On Tuesday, June 24, for example, the more the boy paid, the more likely he was to clog his arteries, at least according to modern medical studies. And surely Thursday's child felt shortchanged at the luxury of a vegetable choice.

The dichotomy between modern concepts of good nutrition and those of the 1930s and 1940s is dramatically apparent in Thursday's lunch and dinner menus:

Dinner (Lunch)
Economy: Frankfurters (1 1/2), browned potatoes, Harvard beets, bread, milk
Regular: Butter, dessert
Luxury: Pork chops, vegetables

Supper
Economy: Creamed dried beef on toast, lima beans au gratin, bread, milk, peanut butter
Regular: Butter, sauce
Luxury: Vegetable

The staff was always served the luxury meal.

Wednesday evenings were reserved for court sessions, and Fridays for movies and other recreational events. In the summer the boys had to take daily showers, which were reduced to two a week in winter. Bedtime was 9:30.[14] They did some "fancy things," observed Reed, at holiday times, such as staging Christmas plays and pageants. At Thanksgiving the staff served the boys, who loved having a chance to give orders.

Reed felt it imperative that the boys understand the advantages of being placed at the republic. He highlighted the differences between the republic and vocational and reform schools: The latter had "strict, rigid, stern, militaristic discipline; close supervision; severe discipline; no talking, and no talking over difficulties with those in charge." In fact, he added, there was "no talking at all."

The republic, on the other hand, did not have "strict, rigid, or stern discipline" but allowed for "personal attention to individual problems." In addition, "citizens were never required to snap into line, stand at attention for hours, or drill for hours; nor was a boy punished when he committed an infraction of the rules, without consideration of the circumstances." Hence, one boy, when charged with being absent for roll call, pled: "Guilty with defense, your Honor. I was dressing for the opera." (The Detroit Civic Light Opera Association had given the boys some passes to *The Mikado* and *The Vagabond King*. They were reported to have enjoyed the experience.)[15]

Reed noted that republic citizens were not "continually supervised in everything they did but were encouraged to develop individual initiative, were placed on their honor, and were encouraged to practice self-discipline; were given personal counseling and individual attention, received vocational and academic training from instructors who had interest in their personal welfare." The absence of bars, gates, and high walls sometimes caused elevated truancy figures. In 1940, 145 boys truanted 289 times and for the first six months of 1941, 73 boys 127 times. But in a program emphasizing responsibility for the self, this had to be expected, and the high figures were not a constant.

One important difference between the republic and more traditional schools was that boys were not "committed" for a specified time but were responsible for determining, to a large degree, the length of their stay. A rather complex merit system was instituted by which boys could earn their release. There were five areas of achievement covering the main phases of the program and a specific number of points necessary for fulfilling the obligations for each:

SPORTSMANSHIP	2
WORK	6
ECONOMIC	6
ATTITUDE	10
ADJUSTMENT	10

Upon accumulation of fifty points, a boy was eligible for dismissal. He could earn these points in as few as seven months, though usually he would need nine to fourteen months. Sixteen months was the maximum period for any stay, though without having accumulated the necessary points, a boy was considered "dishonorably discharged."

Points could be earned in numerous ways. The boys were not required to be the best, just the best they could be. Each boy was judged according to his own capabilities. He did not need to be a varsity star—he could be cooperative or sportsmanlike in gym. He was also rewarded for participation, completion of a task, reliability, initiative, prudent money management, and general good behavior.

In the 1930s and 1940s, the whole republic community was very much involved in the day-to-day operations. Few departments or activities lacked some degree of boy participation. The doing was the important thing—and the accomplishing. Said Reed: "Boys for the first time learn to work and many of them thrill to the experience of attacking and finishing a job."

There was always farm work, of course, growing and tending crops. But in the early 1940s a new dimension of self-sufficiency was added. Superintendent Reed began an extensive canning program. As chronicled by Ruth Colebank, the first year was disastrous. "Stored in the hospital basement, the cans of tomatoes in particular . . . exploded with a terrific bang sending forth the most putrid odors, all of which sent the resident nurse into near hysterics."[16]

Undaunted, Reed studied the situation and the next year was determined to do it right. Said Colebank, "Armed with a stop watch . . . he took over the canning of the green beans. We followed every direction meticulously, washing, blanching, packing, precooking, filling with the brine to within three-eighths of an inch from the top. Henry [Mr. Colebank] took over the sealing, cooking, and cooling—and we lost not one can either of beans or tomatoes. We also did tomato juice, dill pickles, and kraut." Harvesting the beans was a community affair, with everyone gathering afterward "on the lawn between the buildings" for snipping them. "In forty-five minutes to an hour" they could produce ten or twelve bushels of beans ready for canning.[17]

Reed was very much aware of the importance of good public relations. He paid regular visits to the Farmington Sheriff's Department. The yearly apple harvest always yielded a bushel for the state police at the Seven Mile Road and Grand River post. He kept local newspapers informed of events. The republic hosted a yearly baseball game between the probation officers from the juvenile court and the boys. He invited members of the outside community to use the Rollin H. Stevens Glen for picnics and swimming.

There were problems, times when good press was superseded by bad press, brought on by incidents involving the boys and on rare occasions the staff. These moments brought great disappointment, an element of trust having been broken. Reed thought there was only one way to handle it. "You talk to the investigator, you talk to the prosecutor, you talk to the police, and be as honest as you can, be as fair as you can, and let it stop right there." Offsetting bad publicity with good used to be easier back then, Reed noted in a 1985 interview.[18] Modern codes of confidentiality dictate that no pictures or names be divulged to the press. Articles from the 1930s and 1940s included pictures of the boys engaging in healthy, perfectly normal activities. There's nothing like the face of a well-scrubbed smiling boy to win supporters. Community and parental visits were encouraged back then, too.

Not all problems were a result of boys' misbehavior. Despite every effort to find help compatible with the boys, with the republic philosophy, and with the general thinking of the day, the republic occasionally erred in its judgment of character. Reed remembered one distressing experience with a young college worker. "Part of our philosophy . . . was to give young people . . . the opportunity to work, under close supervision, [with] disturbed children." Many of these college workers went on to successful careers in sociology and psychology. But one young man really stepped outside the bounds of acceptable behavior. Reed remembered that he seemed slightly out of step with the times, sporting a beard when being clean-shaven was the vogue, wearing shorts and knee socks when young men just did not wear that sort of thing. But he seemed to have good rapport with the boys and was hired.

In the middle of the night not long thereafter, Reed was awakened by a terrifying scream. "I was sure somebody was pulling somebody's fingernails out with a pair of pliers. I hit the bedroom floor and took the stairs eight by eight." The source of the screaming was a young boy who had been shaken awake by the young man, who held a flashlight against a skeleton he had taken from a locked closet and was dangling at the foot of the boy's bed. The child had to be sedated and the young man removed. Reed warned him that if he did not leave under his own volition, he might face some physical persuasion. Reed noted that inept handling of a child by anyone in any position could undo what was done in treatment sessions.[19]

On occasion Reed also had to deal with some staff bickering, though those problems were generally handled by department heads. He felt that regular, fully attended staff meetings helped ward off dissension and misunderstanding. Once a month alternate pairs of employees would tend to the boys assembled in the gym while everyone else went to the meeting. The benefits were that if a question or problem regarding meals arose, the cook was there; problems with maintenance could be addressed to those responsible for upkeep. And more important, reactions to policy changes could be aired.

Living arrangements also made it possible for many in the group to function as a family, or at least to be involved with one another. The professional people—dentist, doctor, and psychiatrist—and part-timers did not live on the grounds, but the superintendent, assistant superintendent, department heads, social worker, nurse, dorm matrons, and cooks did. Reed felt this gave them a closeness—and therefore a greater potential for success—that would be missing in a nine-to-five work assignment. As Sam Rabinovitz noted, "No where else can I remember a psychiatrist and a farmer working together to help a boy—and this happened while they were playing billiards [or poker], having lunch, having a drink, or formally discussing the boy's problem in the most formal manner. All were members of the team. The relationship between the boys [and their families] and all staff of the Ford Republic was real, human, and varied. The opportunities for the boy to 'find himself' were many."[20]

This sense of teamwork extended beyond the confines of the campus. During these years, two men worked closely with republic youngsters: Monsignor Edward J. Hickey tended to their souls; Harry August, the consulting psychiatrist, tended to their minds. Monsignor Hickey conducted Sunday mass, counseled the boys, and sometimes, as Ruth Colebank remembered, played a few sets of tennis on the courts that her father, her husband, and the boys had built. Harry August spent one day each week with some of the more troubled youngsters. On occasion the two would find themselves at loggerheads, particularly in regard to church liturgy and more relaxed psychotherapeutic approaches to human sexuality. Though each held to his own thinking about acceptable modes of behavior among their charges, they came to a swift gentlemen's agreement that assured harmony, neither stepping on the other's toes or tenets.[21]

Some of the republic's young college workers went on to very successful careers. Reed remembered one—John Guillaumin, a University of Detroit graduate and son of a master painter. He was assigned to supervise a small group. Knowing that the young man had learned his father's trade, Reed asked if he would be willing to pass on his skills to the boys. Guillaumin took on the assignment happily and probably for the first time began a project in which the element of time was no consideration. Reed told him: "This is where you start your vocational training with your crew. . . . Teach the boys about colors, about tools, about paints and how to handle the customer. . . . Take a week, take a month. . . . I don't care so long as the boys learn about painting." So he and the boys painted Doris Herron's schoolroom—slowly—with lots of attention to paint mixing, thinning, shading, surface repairing, brush strokes, and procedures. This instruction became a regular part of the pre-vocational training program. And according to

Reed, Guillaumin carried "many of the ideas learned and honed at the Boys Republic" into his later work at the Hannah Center for Boys in Sonoma, California, where he was eventually appointed lay director.[22]

Another young man Reed hired in the early 1970s later became his successor. Charles Henry showed an "extremely outstanding ability to get along with people, with children," according to Reed. When the war erupted, Henry enlisted in the Marine Corps where, as a kind of probation officer for corps prisoners being returned to the states, he was able to make good use of his talents. He then went on to probation work at the juvenile court before taking the helm. And in 1947 Reed hired Gordon Boring, the third of the "young men [he] employed fresh off college campuses." Boring joined the staff as a psychologist and stayed for over thirty-nine years, twenty-four of them as, in Reed's words, "an eminently qualified" superintendent.[23]

The 1941 Child Welfare League Report had noted some weak points in the organization. Some buildings and facilities were antiquated and gloomy. The board was not being kept up to date and some members and committees were not performing their duties as they should. Only six of the twenty-five board members had taken advantage of the annual tour of the grounds in 1940. The league suggested that if the board would not agree to more frequent meetings, active participation in committees, and regular tenure review and dismissal procedures, the republic should either get a new board or close down.

The staff was often overworked, and not everyone had the dedication, patience, and love essential for effective boy work. The social worker was far too overburdened to even be able to write comprehensive reports. She was responsible for gathering all case histories, which included conducting interviews with family and school personnel and checking all court and social agency records. In addition, she was assigned to public relations work, to transportation and medical care arrangements, and mail screening.[24]

The latter was very time consuming and, Reed felt, very important. He attempted to ward off problems by advising parents not to send their boys "news that will worry or disturb them" and to report "serious illness or other emergencies to the Superintendent rather than to the boy directly." He warned that he would not give the children any letters that might prove discouraging or upsetting. Still the need for screening was there, partially because upsetting news was broadly defined and included any contact from an individual with whom the boy had an "unwholesome relationship."[25]

Esther Meredith, staff social worker from 1934 to 1945, considered censorship a "protective thing, so someone would be there with the boy if a letter would be upsetting to him." It also helped if a boy was "writing home exaggerating something." They could talk the situation over, and she could ask, "What would this do to your mother?" Letters also gave the staff insight into what was going on in the home. According to Meredith, "Nine-tenths of the letters went through untouched."[26]

The Child Welfare League recommended the addition of another social worker to the staff and an increased salary for the existing one. It also recommended facility updating, particularly in the medical area. One of the researchers was especially offended by the swimming hole: "The water is extremely dirty, and most unpleasant in appearance. The writer was informed that each and every boy has to be inoculated for typhoid before he is allowed to swim. It is the writer's opinion that the boys should be inoculated for every possible disease before they should be allowed to swim in such a reservoir of surface drainage. The management is most fortunate that some form of epidemic has not run rampant as a result of the boys using this swimming hole." The same writer liked the recreation facilities, particularly the picnic area, but felt the Ford dorm needed drapes and colored bedspreads.

Some recommendations were unrealistic. The league suggested a forty- or fifty-mile move to a more rural setting since the area in which the republic was located was being built up. In addition, it felt that the boys needed "more advice and training in the choice of clothes." Although the boys had the option of blue, gray, brown, or khaki shirts and brown or blue pants, they usually chose a blue shirt and khaki pants, which made them look uniformed. The writer felt that the matrons should advise the boys that "their every day dress should not be determined by the fact that a certain type of garment does not have to be cleaned as often as another type" and that the matrons should extend their supervision of "clothing and shoes" to include fashion consultation. The boys should also be required to dress up more often, perhaps once a day, since the "morale" on Sundays was so high.

In terms of education, length of service, previous experience, attitude, health, temperament, and personality, the staff received acceptable, high, and sometimes excellent grades. Especially impressive was the low turnover rate: "The administrative officers are either fortunate, very capable, or both." Some staff members were lacking in extensive previous experience, but not to the detriment of the republic. Despite some problems, they also displayed a good attitude about their mission. And they enjoyed reasonably good physical health, though the league urged routine physical examinations.

The league also had high praise for the superintendent and his assistant. Reed, the report noted, "understands thoroughly the principles and problems of child welfare." At various points he was called conscientious, reliable, well-qualified, diligent, objective, able, devoted, capable, interested, personable, and efficient. The league thought that Colebank was indefatigable, efficient, and resourceful—and ought to be relieved of her widespread responsibilities so that she could devote her energies to the areas where she was needed most.

The league did question the suitability of self-government for the republic. It set up the following criteria for successful operation:

1. The boys must have a firm "moral or spiritual code."
2. They should be of average mentality and intelligence with "powers of rationalization, initiative, and willingness to accept responsibility, not only for themselves, but for the group."

3. They should be at least sixteen years old.
4. They should not be too handicapped physically.
5. The best of the boys must run the place.
6. There should never be more than 150 citizens.
7. The facilities must be in an isolated locale, far from a city, superhighways, and means of transportation.

According to these criteria, the republic was sadly deficient. Of all the average boys, most with little religious background, 20 percent were under fifteen. As for powers of "rationalization, initiative, and willingness to accept responsibility," if the boys had those qualities, they would not have been there in the first place.[27]

In 1941 Superintendent Reed saw a dream of his come to fruition. Throughout the 1930s he had, according to Ruth Colebank, worked "slowly but doggedly toward the establishment of a small clinic for therapy." Finally he was able to engage the services of Dr. Ernst Katz, a Freudian psychotherapist whom the Nazis had driven out of Vienna and who was residing in England when Fred Butzel arranged entry into the United States through Canada.[28] Counselor/social worker Esther Meredith recalls their first meeting and subsequent three-year professional association fondly:

> One fall afternoon in 1941, Sam Rabinovitz and I met Dr. Katz as he arrived in Detroit on a Trailways Bus. We both were immediately impressed by his warmth, understanding and general manner—a courteous, cultured, continental gentleman. Subsequent experience bore out those most favorable impressions: This eminently qualified [man] was exactly what Boys Republic needed to bring its treatment program to a high level of effectiveness. It was a unique situation: A therapist *living* and working with the boys and staff. His first apartment was on the dormitory floor of Ford Hall. Next door was the matron's apartment. Downstairs were the offices of Ruth Colebank, Assistant Superintendent,

Charles Perry, purchasing agent, myself as social worker, classrooms and a make-shift counseling room for Dr. Katz.

About this time, part of the staff began to serve as hosts of the tables in the boys' dining room and Dr. Katz readily assumed one of these positions, seeing it as another fine opportunity to develop his relationship with the boys.

With our consulting psychiatrist, Dr. Alfred C. LaBine, there was complete accord and mutual respect. Together they helped many a boy and his family to cope with their problems and conflicts. With the After-Care counselors Sam Rabinovitz and Earl Baxtresser, Dr. Katz was able to be involved in a boy's readjustment to home and community.

All in all, the years when Dr. Katz was an integral part of Boys Republic marked a particularly high point in the history of the institution; it was then the program as a whole reached an optimum level.[29]

Reed concurred: "The entire program really was in tune." However, four years later Reed's dream dissolved: Katz took a position in a Marquette prison; Guillaumin went to California to work with troubled boys; and Esther Meredith quit her job to have children. The loss of Katz hit Reed especially hard due to the unlikelihood of ever finding again a person of his "professional training and personality."[30]

As did most non-defense-related enterprises, the republic suffered from a shortage of qualified personnel during the war years. While republic salaries were not competitive by any means, money was not the real issue. And, as usual, there was an abundant supply of candidates for admission. The real problem was simply that there were not enough people to oversee the operation. In September 1943 the republic was operating with only 60 percent of the personnel it needed. By December of that year the figure had fallen to 50 percent. Some workers had taken defense jobs that were more lucrative and gave them the feeling of helping the country. Conscientious objectors assigned to civilian humanitarian endeavors were available, but they did not necessarily have a natural aptitude for boy work. But, of necessity, according to Rudolph Yanke, republic principal from 1942 to 1981, there was some relaxation of "qualification standards."

The republic definitely was suffering. At a special board meeting in 1943, Reed said that the republic had become a "very shallow shell with little real self-government work being done and a most limited amount of rehabilitative work." He feared it was becoming a custodial institution, a disaster to his mind, and questioned whether it could stay open. They needed a cook, two firemen, two kitchen helpers, three teachers, someone to work specifically with the boys, a social worker, and two night watchmen. There was a full-time staff of eighteen, not counting the professional staff, and only nine were meeting minimal expectations.

He cited the case of one woman who exercised in the presence of the boys without consideration of appropriate modes of dress. A male worker was given to bouts of profanity. Similar institutions countrywide had a staff/student ratio of a little over three to one, while the republic's ratio was over six to one. In response to a War Manpower Commission questionnaire Reed noted that the staff worked at least seventy hours a week.

The citizenry was down to 60 from 115 the year before, not from want of troubled youths but for lack of qualified people to work with them. Some regular staff members were recruited to help out in the areas that most needed personnel, particularly the heating plant and the kitchen. Henry Colebank took charge of the former, while Ruth Colebank was drafted to fill in as cook when the regular cook and her farmer husband simply failed to return after a weekend off.

When two boys came to the store to alert her to her new assignment and she expressed some dismay, they volunteered their services. And work they did. She sent them off with baking equipment and a cookbook and they "made ginger bread and plain cakes, unfrosted, which we serve[d] warm in big chunks to the delight of our boarders." Ruth herself "mastered the secrets of beef stew and soups and [they] managed to suit our clientele." Sometimes Ruth was also called on to help when the infirmary nurse, heavily burdened and emotionally exhausted, took to her bed.[31]

There was a sense of pulling together in those years, but the circumstances that created unity also exacted a toll. The whole purpose of the setting—adults and children living, working, and playing together—was being lost when Reed had to rush off for work in the fields, or when the psychologist was doing double duty in the office. There were few opportunities to be available to a boy who needed friendship, informal guidance, or advice of the kind that comes naturally when working together on a project or walking in the woods.

Enlisting more boys to ease the burdens of the staff did not always work either. In her writings Colebank tells of a youngster assigned to get breakfast on the table. His peers would not let him rest because he had the keys to the icebox and bakery, so Colebank had to be up at 6:00 each morning to get him started. In addition, she had to go over the menu with him every day so that he could proceed with as few mix-ups as possible.

Colebank complained that she was unable to perform her duties because she was "spending . . . time in the kitchen because there is no substitute cook, or in the dormitory because there is no substitute for the matron who is on her vacation, or in the truck garden because the gardener is on his vacation." There was not enough staff to oversee the boys, or at least make them aware of adult presence, should they be tempted to misbehave. Night watch and dormitory duty were particularly important. Dr. Katz told of a boy he was treating for bed-wetting. The lad was showing some real progress until another youngster, recruited for night watch, put water in his bed as a joke.[32]

Reed lamented the hurly-burly atmosphere: "There is nothing more important than answering a child's question when he asks it."[33] Noted Meredith, "We just aren't seeing the boys—we are bogged down getting the meals on the table. We are trying to live from day to day."[34] Something had to be done quickly. The board was urged to aid in the search for competent and dedicated people to work with the boys. Eventually help did come as the result of a massive advertising and publicity campaign.

By January 1944 the general outlook was a whole lot brighter. Once again the republic was fully staffed and after a low population of 57 boys the previous year, the republic was preparing for 108 in 1944. To its credit, the republic had emerged from the darker days with a well-stocked root cellar, canned vegetable and fruit shelves, and well-maintained buildings.

On January 14, 1944, the Ford Republic became the Boys Republic in the hope that the institution would no longer be thought connected (erroneously) with the Henry Ford family and hence thought to have access to his wealth. This false impression often hurt its fund-raising efforts.

Nineteen forty-four was a good year for favorable publicity. The boys won recognition for their outstanding raspberry patch. A Michigan Department of Agriculture inspector called it "one of the finest in the state." Reed commented that the boys needed that kind of activity, "something to do, something to take pride in, and something to hold their interest." Another reward for their labor was that "during and for several days after the picking season [they were served] individual shortcakes at . . . lunch, each short-cake surrounded top, sides, and bottom, with heaped up scoops of raspberries, the whole drenched in cream."

In an October 23, 1944, *Detroit Times* article, writer Vera Brown applauded the efforts of the chief cook, who wanted to be a professional chef one day: "He makes a fine meat pie and his sunshine cake is second to none."[35]

That year was also a good one in general for crops. The republic produced and canned 180 gallons of beans, 30 gallons of peas, 670 quarts of strawberries, and 50 gallons of sauerkraut. The 100 gallons of raspberries they canned included 500 quarts from a nearby farmer in payment for the boys' help with his harvest. In an observation sweetly reminiscent of an earlier superintendent, Reed said of the boys: "They aren't bad. Their energies are just misdirected." Homer Lane would have been delighted.

Reed recalled when Rex Nutten, recently retired vocational education teacher at Royal Oak High School, came to the institution and proposed a plan for having the kids build a "flat-bed" farm wagon. In conveying the good news that the plan had been approved, Reed said, "There's no time limit. Get the kids into planning, developing, and producing the wagon." Reed also remembered that this approach was "a bit far out for some of the other staff, but the wagon was eventually in running shape—all boy produced." He added: "Some of the skeptic staff were amazed, but the wagon did run to the satisfaction of Kate and Lady, the team of draft horses."[36]

Old Boys' Day that year was as successful as ever. Republic graduates, many of whom were now farmers and small businessmen, returned with advice for current residents and a large degree of hope. It was a gala affair. Old friendships were renewed and new ones made. They had a picnic, witnessed a court session, played baseball, laughed, and talked together. Sometimes visitors came from as far as three hundred miles away for these occasions.

Esther Meredith thought the most eloquent testimony was the return of these former residents, "often accompanied by their wives and children"—and those visits were not restricted to Old Boys' Day but occurred "every week."[37] Sam Rabinovitz treasured that continuing contact with graduates, saying that his most rewarding moments were when he was asked to "come to [a] birthday party or a graduation," sometimes to be with a boy "when he got married."[38]

The next few years were uneventful and good. In 1946 twelve boys established a 4-H Club called "Republic's Atomic Energy." Three members groomed Hereford heifers for a show, one began a flower project, three worked with pigs, four with gardens, and one with field corn to feed the pigs.

May 1947 saw the boys' takeover of the republic—a planned event. The citizens were put in charge of the day's activities and the management of the institution. The first thing they did was cancel school and order pancakes and fried eggs for dinner. Then they learned about "budgets, material shortages, schedules," and all that goes into operations. This practical experience was invaluable.

In October 1948 Clyde Reed accepted a position in Wisconsin and once again the republic was looking for a superintendent. Ruth Colebank was relieved when they were able to appoint an old friend to the republic, Charles Henry, a former counselor. Of the outgoing superintendent she said, "Clyde Reed was wonderful with the boys . . . really enjoy[ed] working with them. He frequently joined [them] on the play field and started some new game. But no . . . other activity had quite as strong an appeal for him as self-government and the state meeting." He would not say much at the meetings but would pay strict attention, "asking a question occasionally or making a suggestion in the form of a question." He tried to get them to "take some initiative for themselves. He tried to help them to help themselves." She added sadly, "He tried hard to revive the old spirit but there were [beginning to be] too many disturbed boys too preoccupied with their own problems to be able to feel concerned about community needs."[39]

To Reed, the job was enormously gratifying with the opportunity to watch boys who came to the republic "very disturbed and distressed with histories of upheaval and unhappiness in their personal and family lives . . . find a satisfactory way of life, adjust." These were the boys for whom experts predicted no more than a 12 percent reform rate. It was fascinating, he reported, to see "boys who [had] known no rule except the dictatorial rule of the street gangs, react to the fairness and equality found in our government program." He observed in 1948: "There are no college presidents listed among our old boys, but there are large numbers of stable citizens—factory workers, truck drivers, and small shop owners." When asked if the republic experience had changed him, Reed answered with an unqualified "yes." "You grow with your job or you deteriorate. You don't stand still in your emotions, your philosophy, your productivity when you are working with wiggling, changing, loving, repressed, withdrawn, explosive adolescents. The challenge is there in front of you every day and you have to grow with the years; cynicism [will only] erode your own enthusiasm for working with upset youth." Reed never lost that enthusiasm.[40]

Chapter 5

The Postwar Years: Charles Henry (1948–1953) and
Milton J. Huber (1953–1959)

THE POSTWAR YEARS WERE TRANSITIONAL ones for the republic, ones in which Homer Lane's turn-of-the-century idealism came face to face with twentieth-century pragmatism, with its advanced technology, improved testing methods, and new views on the causes, prevention, and "cure" for aberrant behavior. By 1957 the republic had a new physical facility and a new governing principle, one which called for viewing the troubled boy as well or unwell, rather than good or bad. The earlier emphasis on teaching, on showing a boy appropriate behavior with the hope that he would then behave appropriately was replaced by a philosophy that embodied psychological resolutions to delinquent actions. The arm-around-the-boy approach—the getting dirty together in a common enterprise, like building a dam or erecting a wall, the learn-to-do-as-I-do-by-watching-what-I-do philosophy—had to make room for one that entailed a highly sophisticated delving into the psyche to uncover the "whys" of misbehavior.

As explained by Gordon Boring, republic psychologist, juvenile institutions fall into three basic categories:

> One is custodial, which is primarily a housing type of facility wherein the basic needs are met; another is training, wherein youngsters are taught . . . educationally and intellectually what to do, what is right and what is wrong, and behavior

is judged in terms of good and bad; and the third type is
treatment . . . wherein the youngster's behavior is looked
at as being symptomatic of some underlying psychological
problem.[1]

The training phase of the republic's history was becoming out-
dated, needing to address a different sort of boy with different
manifestations of emotional upset. From a vantage point of over
thirty years' association with the republic, Dr. Bernice Izner bore
witness to these changes in the citizenry that necessitated changes
in operational concept. In the early 1950s, she said, the typical
boy needed "residential placement, some custodial care. He came
with minimal difficulties in the community . . . possibly not having had parental supervision." By the late 1950s, however, more
and more delinquent boys were being admitted, boys who were
given to displays of temper, to "acting out" their hostilities, to
stealing, drinking, and sometimes taking drugs. More often than
not these boys were anxiety-ridden, victims of poor self-images
and a lack of self-worth.[2]

The self-governing concept became problematic. Immature,
potentially explosive boys were poor candidates for having a major say in the lives of other distressed youngsters, a factor which
sometimes resulted, according to Boring, in forms of blackmail
and false charges.[3]

It soon became evident, much to the dismay of proponents of
the existing system, that such an operation was no longer viable
for the "new boy." Said Izner: "If boys cannot even function out
in society, it is unfair" to expect them to have an active role in
decision making. Too many are dependent and impulsive. They
"cannot even control their activities in school, let alone sit long
enough to think through a principle that might be involved in
trying to govern themselves."

Though increasing numbers showed a need for therapy, not all,
Izner hastened to explain, were prime material for "in-depth psychotherapy." Each case was treated individually and the determination of what sort of treatment seemed most suitable was made

as soon as was feasible. Some boys seemed best able to "accept" counseling and some behavior modification, with a focus on helping them develop a more positive self-image.

Izner felt that the importance of having an "open" program, a facility with no walls, should not be underestimated. Having the "responsibility of staying on the premises or leaving . . . helps [the boys] to develop self control and inner strength to deal with their own life style at the Boys Republic." And, she noted, "truancy as a whole has never been a great problem." A chronic truant would not be forced to stay.[4]

The citizen of the mid-1950s still went to school, worked on the grounds, engaged in recreational activities, and gained vocational skills, but he also had regular sessions with clinic personnel who administered tests designed to open heretofore closed avenues of the psyche. The causes of emotional distress were sought on the theory that if a boy understood the source of his dissatisfaction, he would be better equipped to deal with it.

A late 1950s description of republic operations nicely spells out the change in concept: Each boy had a treatment plan outlined by the "psychiatric team." The boy received "constant intensive individual psychotherapy" in the hope of aiding him in "examining his feelings and attitudes" and helping him develop "some insight." Rather than serving penance for a misdeed he was counseled, asked to look at why he did what he did. The broken window, often resulting from an attempt to prove to others that he was worthy of the hatred he felt for himself, that very act of destruction, became a tool for gaining entry into the troubled mind. He was not punished because with help he might understand the reasons for his behavior. Again, the boys were well and unwell— not good or bad. And bad behavior was symptomatic of internal conflict. The staff was tolerant of aggressive actions, believing it was better that such displays occur in a controlled environment than in a public setting.[5]

Alan Ternes, a *Detroit News* writer, applauded the republic concept in a 1957 article: "When a boy finds he is not slapped down or rejected by counselors, he turns to other adults to find something to oppose, as he has done most of his life. Finally, when the boy cannot find hostility around him, his thoughts turn to himself and he realizes much of the hostility is within himself. He has then taken the first step in a long struggle to escape his own tangled emotions and attitudes."[6]

Every employee was involved in the treatment process. A 1957 night watch job description shows that the position embraced the original definition of a custodian as a keeper or a guardian. In addition to sweeping, mopping, waxing, and cleaning windows and sills, the employee was asked to:

1. Become acquainted with how the boys are sleeping. Look in on the room. Correct any situation, such as boys sleeping in their clothes, boys not sleeping between their sheets.
2. Turn off all radios and night-lights which boys may have on in their rooms.
3. Note restless sleepers or anything out of the ordinary. Quietness will allow boys to fall into deeper sleep. Continue spot checks throughout the night.[7]

According to James Clatworthy, Oakland University professor, "The organizational transformation" during which "the fabric of self-government [was] slowly unwoven" had begun "under Superintendent Reed, but [it took] nearly twelve years and three Superintendents to complete. . . . The transition from a farm and training school to a clinical counseling facility was not surprising given the growth in clinical psychology following World War II and the changing social, economic, and political forces at work."[8]

Indeed, the whole country was enmeshed in change—in the family structure and in modes of dealing with young people. Government programs and youth recreation centers had mushroomed during the war, but many had proven ineffectual, suffering from factionalism, lack of public involvement, and an inability to get to the source of the difficulty. Youngsters might populate the recreation halls daily, but they returned to home environments that were little changed by programs or good intentions. Reassurances by scholars that the "family" was tough, had endured upheaval before and would continue to do so, did not assuage growing fears that the family was disintegrating and that old values were being lost. Families were losing their cohesiveness as women who had joined the labor force during the war were not returning to the home at its conclusion and as the divorce rate began to climb. This dramatic restructuring of the traditional family unit was at the expense of the children.

Many lived with two working parents, a single parent, or relatives or friends. Many were shunted from home to home to foster parents who could be exploitive and uncaring. Lucky was the child who found warmth, understanding, and lives worthy of emulation in a foster home. Some youngsters made their way to the Boys Republic, where caring adults were available for times of crisis, sadness, joy, or just ordinariness.

There they found an organization undergoing subtle but persistent change, experiencing what historian Alan Clive describes in the larger context as a classic conflict with roots long preceding the war: "On the one hand, psychoanalytic proponents [see] delinquency as an individual phenomenon, best dealt with by personal guidance and therapy. On the other hand, many social workers and their sociologist allies [perceive] youth crime to be the result of a bad environment, a problem susceptible to community-oriented solutions."[9]

Change of any sort, but especially in ideology, is bound to meet with resistance and a degree of suspicion. Older staff traditionalists feared what they saw as a growing tendency toward permissiveness in handling the boys. While not advocates of punishment for its own sake, they felt that sure and swift penalties for misbehavior best prepared a boy for reentry into the community.

Younger clinicians believed that punishment had already proven ineffectual with the type of boy who found his way to the republic. Despite conflicting philosophies in this and other areas, staff divisiveness never reached a critical stage because a boy's welfare was always the chief concern. Still, these were unsettling years and thus was the climate when Charles Henry assumed the directorship of the Boys Republic in November 1948.

Henry's Republic

Charles Henry was no stranger to the organization. In the early 1940s he had worked as a counselor under Clyde Reed. With a degree from Western Michigan University in hand, he had joined the Marine Corps where he served for four years, rising from private to captain, eventually becoming the officer in charge of general court martial prisoners and an instructor in military schools. Upon release he became a counselor at Jackson Prison, later working with the Wayne County Juvenile Court, the Boys Vocational School, and the Council of Social Agencies.

From the outset Henry seemed to have a definite plan for the republic. In the early months he worked within the existing operational framework, but he soon began imprinting the republic with his own personal signature.

A 1949 pamphlet points to clearly conceived and drawn lines of power or authority: "Through our program we attempt to develop a proper respect for the authority of God; a proper respect for the authority of the home; a proper respect for the authority of the school; a proper respect for the authority of the community." Therein lies a subtle shift from the concept of cooperation to obedience. How alien this would have been to Homer Lane, who, from his position of authority, could have commanded the boys to wash without caring about making them want to.

The same pamphlet attributes badness in a boy to "hunger: hunger for food, hunger for love, companionship, or understanding"; another pamphlet notes that "some boys are born to trouble—victims of bad homes, bad companions, bad environments." These views seemingly endorse the traditional ideas regarding the causes of delinquency, but a notation explaining the clinical aspect of the program shows a revealing departure: "We consider each boy who comes to us to be more or less emotionally sick.

Otherwise, he would not have committed acts against people or property to the extent that he had to be removed from society by a juvenile court judge." The writer adds: "Sometimes the causes of delinquency lie deeply covered. . . . A boy is much more complex than an automobile engine . . . and it takes carefully trained, skillful personnel to dig out the reasons." There are two schools of thought embodied here, the two philosophies whose adherents were being bound together in an uneasy alliance.[10]

A 1951 text hints at changes in self-government: "A program of student participation is fostered. Boys select their own officers, handle certain matters in their citizens' court, enact certain laws in their state meetings."[11] The board of directors' minutes show that Mr. Henry had spoken more directly on this topic at a February 26, 1949, meeting: "Mr. Henry informed the Board that since assuming the responsibility of Director . . . he and his staff have been de-emphasizing the self-government program in an attempt to build up a program of student participation. He explained that this was necessary if the agency is to do the job for which it is set up."[12]

In 1950 health, welfare, and fire inspectors from the State Department of Social Welfare visited the republic. Overall their findings validated what the staff already knew: the physical facilities were in sad shape. Gunnar Dybwad, superintendent of the Children's Division, described the situation aptly: "My visit . . . has left a very vivid picture in my mind: That of a lively spirit residing in a corpse, and at that, in one which is rapidly decomposing." He added: "It seemed to me that everywhere the program was strait jacketed by your physical conditions: You were trying to encourage informality, healthful surroundings, close personal relationships between the staff and the children, and yet everywhere the buildings seemed to interfere with those goals." He concluded that the lack of money for repairs had "brought about a situation which has made the buildings not only unattractive but definite hazards to life and limb." Dybwad also noted that the overcrowded dorms were "totally inadequate," constituting "a definite health hazard" and that the "presence of a toilet in the one dorm without any hand washing facilities" violated "even the most primitive of health and sanitation rules." He warned, "The Boys Republic is steadily sinking down to the bottom of the list in terms of quality care." The sanitation and fire officers concurred. The report contained such words as "menace," "unfit," and "unsafe" and threatened condemnation in the "not too far distant future."[13]

In an April 1951 follow-up letter, Dybwad spoke again of the "stranglehold" that the "vigorous on-going program" was in. He commended Henry's "efforts to work in . . . educational and recreational programs with small, carefully selected groups of boys" but feared the efforts would "go to waste" as long as the children continued to be housed in "inadequate mass living units." He concluded that "only a program which will completely supplant your present residential facilities with smaller units will do justice to the program upon which you have started so successfully."[14]

An earlier article in the *Muskegon Chronicle* confirmed what Dybwad found but did have something positive to say: "The Republic is not a fancy looking place. The buildings are old and drab, even if the lawn is well-kept and the signs neatly painted" but concluded that "a lot is being done, in make-shift workshops and on a warped gym floor, that doesn't show on the surface."[15]

The findings were not surprising to anyone. A January 1948 State Department of Social Welfare report had addressed the deplorable state of the facilities and contained specific recommendations for change, citing in particular the 1912 congested, hazardous building that was "literally falling apart," the Quonset hut replacing the barn that had burned, the kitchen roach problems, the general need for painting and refurbishing, the need for a swimming pool created by the sewage pollution in the "natural swimmin' hole," and the antiquated laundry. In March 1950 Henry had told the board that the republic was truly "handicapped," that something had to be done if they were to "retain, let alone improve, our standard of service." It would still be some years before a new facility would be built, but the gears had been set in motion.[16]

THE REPUBLIC AND THE COMMUNITY

From its beginning the republic had served as a vehicle for college students to gain valuable practical experience in youth work. Many of these summer and part-time employees went on to careers in social work and counseling. Ties with the community were especially strong in 1950 when the organization embarked on a joint enterprise with the Wayne State University School of Social Work that would produce four master's theses exploring the republic's overall effectiveness.

The initial study, conducted by Martin A. Adler, provides a solid look at the basic framework of the institution and chronicles day-to-day operations. His 1951 thesis shows a republic in flux, embracing some old policies, discarding others, and welcoming some new ones. Private case acceptance (as opposed to court appointments) had become a thing of the past; there were too many problems with in-arrears accounts and premature withdrawing of boys, which misleadingly increased the institution's failure statistics. Staff meetings at that time were sporadic, mostly in the form of individual conferences as the need arose. Most notable was the uneasiness among the staff as new philosophies mixed with old ones, as training concepts came face to face with treatment ones.

Adler nicely illuminates the problems and the tensions experienced among the staff:

> There seem to be two major groups existing within the republic framework. One . . . favors a less permissive attitude toward the boys [and has] ambivalent feelings toward the clinical staff and its program. This group generally consists of the personnel with longer employment service. The second group, comparatively young in age and seniority, and smaller in number, favors the clinical approach to the treatment programming of the Republic. There exists within this group a feeling of insecurity and lack of experience in the face of the verbalized experience of the older or non-permissive group.

Henry saw it as his responsibility to mesh the services, to make the therapy and teaching aspects of the program interdependent. To this end, he breathed new life into the clinical program, appointing Bernice Izner and Gordon Boring directors and increasing the clinical staff. This staff would be very much involved in policies, procedures, and treatment plans for the boys.

THE BOYS OF THE 1950S

In February 1951 the republic had 82 citizens, 39 of whom had committed no previous recorded offense, and 21 with just one count against them. Only eight had been in trouble three or more times. Most of the crimes were the same as in previous years: breaking and entering, truancy, and incorrigibility.

The "model" or composite republic boy, notes Adler, was a fifteen-year-old, white native-born American Protestant resident of Wayne County with a ninth-grade education and a low normal IQ who was a first offender truant and/or thief. He had been given a progressive achievement test or differential aptitude test, possibly a Rorschach or Thematic Apperception Test, to help determine his school placement, program of study, and possible treatment plan. His dorm placement, in part, depended on his general discernable attitude. Aggressive and well-developed boys were assigned to an older, sports-active, respected Big Brother and to Ford Hall. Relatively passive, withdrawn, and underdeveloped boys went to the Baldwin dorm and would be supervised by a calm, easily approachable Big Brother who would not make demands. In general, Baldwin housed the more emotionally disturbed.

A TYPICAL DAY

The typical day in 1951, as chronicled by Adler, began at 6:40 A.M. for the boys assigned to kitchen or dining room detail. The others had an extra ten minutes before being expected to get up, go to the bathroom, wash, and dress for the 7:15 breakfast.

The boys followed the same seating and eating procedures for all meals. They entered the two dining areas singly or in groups and sat in assigned seats, three or four boys at each table. A boy chosen by a kitchen staff member led the group in grace. The table showing the best deportment was called on first to line up for food served from a portable steam table by a kitchen staff member and two or three boys. The staff, having a separate dining room in the centrally located kitchen area, served itself, though one or two boy waiters were ready for orders of coffee, milk, or tea. Within several minutes the entire group would be served. Despite the lack of regulations regarding noise, mealtimes were generally orderly.

A dietitian came in weekly to prepare menus for the following week. There were frequent State Health Department inspections, and "wash ups" before meals were supervised by health officers and staff who also were responsible for sanitation maintenance.

After breakfast the boys returned to the dorms to make the beds that had been left undone to "air them out" and to clean up the sleeping area. Bedding had to be uniform and neat. The house parent and boy officer in charge of each dorm conducted daily inspections. Afterward the boys were permitted to smoke, the Ford boys in the basement, the Baldwin ones in either of two recreation rooms. Smoking was allowed, with parental consent, because it seemed that the boys would do so surreptitiously otherwise.

The cleanup and rest period was followed by a morning assembly all boys were required to attend, except for kitchen workers and hospital patients. They separated into their dorm units on either side of the gymnasium and the boy officer in charge of each dorm checked the roll and called his charges to attention. A staff member then usually gave the command to rest, advised the boys of their job assignments, and made general announcements. After the assembly the boys would do some sort of work on the grounds or in the dorm until 9:00, at which time they were given a smoking break. By 9:15 they had to be in school or at work.

The morning session lasted until 11:45, at which time the boys returned to their dorms for a few minutes of recreational activity before the noon lunch. After lunch some boys returned to their dorms for a nap while others played cards, basketball, or pool, or smoked.

Supper was ready at 6:00 every evening except Saturday, when the hour was moved up to 5:30. The boys were free afterward for active participation in games or sports like kite flying, ping-pong, and marbles or for sedentary pastimes like model building, supervised television viewing, radio listening, or reading.

After an 8:30 snack of cookies and milk, the boys washed and got into their pajamas. At 9:00, after attendance was taken, they kneeled beside their beds for the evening prayer and then voted on what radio show would be tuned in for the lights-out hour. Usually a mystery or music program was favored. At 10:00 the boys were expected to go to sleep and many did. A few engaged in quiet conversation.

The boys had more free time on Saturdays. Special activities included hikes, cookouts, ball games, and movies. Five companies allowed on-site viewings of their films, which, during one three-month period in the early 1950s, included: *Scudda Ho Scudda Hay*, *The Boy with Green Hair*, *Rachel and the Stranger*, *Fancy Pants*, *The Yellow Cab Man*, *The Stratton Story*, *Body and Soul*, *The Green Grass of Wyoming*, *Tarzan's Magic Fountain*, and *Intrigue*. Comedies and shorts were regular extras.

Major holidays were celebrated with special events, programs, and entertainment. Boys in good standing might go to a Tigers game or to the circus. Saturday was store day. The boys would line up, those wanting candy first. If not in debt, they could choose two kinds of "popular nickle [*sic*] candy." Debtors were limited to one. The store was too small for clothing displays, so the boys only knew about what they saw on others and what the supervisor, who made a real attempt to keep up with the latest styles, would show them. During this period parents could bring clothing to the boys, a practice that sometimes encouraged competitiveness and thievery.

Sunday mornings revolved around religious observances. Catholic boys attending communion could eat a late breakfast. Protestant boys could put in their work during mass. Catholic boys would do their chores during the Protestant service. After a noon lunch the boys showered and put on their Sunday best for the 2:00 to 4:00 visiting hours.

There were few visiting restrictions, though each boy was allowed but a single pound of candy and one comic book. Fruit had to be eaten right then and, while the boy could accept money, he had to turn it in to the office where it was kept until he was released. In good weather the boys and their visitors usually gathered in the "Visiting Woods," where they had picnic lunches or sat around and read the funnies. In bad weather they would meet in the gym. The boys had to wait in the dorms until called, individually, to greet their guests. A few boys sold nickel pop.

The response of parents and families to the boys varied. Sometimes there appeared to be little communication. Some gatherings were relaxed and happy. Sometimes parents took the opportunity to praise the republic staff; once in awhile a parent would look for signs of physical abuse of his child or for signs of prison-like procedures. Mostly visitors were quiet.

A boy in good standing who lived more than thirty-five miles from the republic could spend one weekend a month at home. A local boy could also go home for two days, but he had to return at night. Boys could earn bonus days.

That Charles Henry doubted the validity of pure self-government for these boys is clear by 1951. Noted Adler, "Administrative supervision in the direction and control of the boy government activities is exercised within the state meetings." Indeed, they were "patterned after Town Hall meetings." The assemblage aired grievances, made suggestions, and all subjects were open to discussion, but petitions requesting changes in policy had to be signed by the boys ahead of time. Requests for earlier release time were not considered.

The court system functioned much as before, but punishments were restricted to fines, the range of which were predetermined. The judge had only to consult a chart that listed the minimum and maximum amounts that could be imposed for each offense and then make his determination. But there was a great deal of ceremony in those days, with the judge in full robe, with the court standing until being bid to sit, and with a pledge of allegiance beginning each session. All verdicts could be appealed and the supreme court was available for tough cases. Some cases were heard in private. All cases were checked first to see if they would be embarrassing to the boy if aired publicly.

The boys still elected officers and conducted vigorous campaigns. In the year of Adler's study, election posters urged that the voters not "be sad—be bad. You saw the rest—now vote for the best" and suggested, "This is the weather for a gentle breeze, and if you don't vote for me—you darn sure will freeze."

In addition to modifying the court and government features, Charles Henry also oversaw the change from a fiat economic system to a record-keeping one. As noted by Adler, "All records of earnings, savings, court fines, and purchases [were] kept on a work card under the supervision of an executive staff member."

His tenure saw the abandonment of the farm animal program and the shelving of the three-tiered luxury, regular, and economical meal plan. Reed's root cellar became an air raid shelter and a squad system, in which boys were broken into groups of six to eight, six per building, was instituted as a safety measure in case of enemy attack or a tornado alert.

The boys did general maintenance and cleaning of the facilities, and sometimes ran errands, washed staff cars, or set pins for a bowling club. There were regular kitchen and dining hall helpers. Laundry operations included washing, drying, repairing, and ironing clothing. Under the direction of a supervisor, several boys ran the washing and drying equipment and then sent the clothes to another unit, also under supervision, where they would be designated for repair or ironing. Three boys were stationed at ironing boards and two boys were trained in operating the sewing machine.[17]

Henry inherited a school program in some trouble. A 1948 warning from the Children's Division of the Michigan Department of Public Instruction of the Department of Social Welfare that the school was a "borderline case for approval and had a very low rating" only reached his attention in May 1949. He quickly responded that he was in the process of setting up a program for special courses for republic faculty at Wayne State University and the University of Michigan and was attempting to get special teachers from the Detroit Board of Education. (Reed had made a similar attempt back in May 1948). He promised to change the situation and by the end of 1949 the school was fully accredited.[18]

The education program at the republic was very flexible. If a boy seemed negative and hence ill suited to structured classes at first, he would be set up in a work/vocational instruction program. If he was deficient in math or reading skills, he would be given remedial work. Those who could function in a regular classroom setting were taught how to accept the fact that they had to go to school and display respect toward authority figures, such as the teacher and principal. Learning, cooperation, and good group interaction were stressed. Anyone could have a period of grace but all were given a great deal of encouragement to attend school and change unhealthy attitudes. Boys were placed in classes according to maturity and personality rather than age. Aggressive, maladjusted boys would be teamed up with young, more permissive, and energetic teachers. Immature boys would be assigned to a female teacher who might become a mother figure. Many different subjects were taught, with the emphasis always on learning practical or meaningful information. The teaching staff worked in close cooperation with the clinical one.

In the 1950s the republic began correlating its school program with that of the public school system. Each boy had a "salmon card," which was a record of his progress up to the time of his admittance and gave an ongoing account of how he was faring in the program. He would take the card with him when he went back into the public school system.

Most classes were about an hour and fifteen to thirty minutes long. Generally the morning groups, meeting two times a week, kept abreast of the news through reading the newspapers and *Current Events*, a weekly school publication. Reading and math were also taught in the morning. Afternoon classes, meeting three times a week, covered art, spelling, and English. Nature study classes were geared to the emotional maturity of the boys, with younger groups concentrating on simple identification of plants and animals, intermediate groups delving more deeply into studies of their environment, and the more mature groups learning textbook concepts.

The nature classroom was always a special treat for the boys, housing stuffed animals and display cases and live exhibits of rats, skunks, possums, snakes, turtles, fish, or whatever the woods and glen yielded on a given day. Nature classes were especially popular in the summer when the whole outdoors became the classroom. Shop classes were held less for vocational purposes than for acquainting the boys with tools and helping them gain technical skills. The recreation program offered a full slate of activities, including traditional sports and games. Supervised recreational periods were used to encourage withdrawn boys to participate and more aggressive ones to control their outbursts. The boys also had time for board games, reading, napping, marbles, and crafts.

The republic had an active youth choir, which served the organization well in public relations. The group appeared on television and radio shows and performed for various clubs and associations. At the conclusion of the February 21, 1950, board of directors meeting, the twenty-five-voice choir sang a hymn, "Fairest, Lord Jesus," a hunting song, "John Peal," and a Negro spiritual, "The Old Ark's A' Moverin."[19]

In a follow-up study of the boys, Wayne State University graduate student Harold Bissett concluded that despite the fact that over one half of those in his sample (a sample restricted to boys released after January 1, 1949, and before September 1, 1950) returned to high delinquency areas and 67.5 percent to broken homes, 72.5 percent had no further run-ins with the law.[20] Observed thesis advisor Norman Polansky in a letter to Henry: "With the number of strikes against them environmentally, the boys don't do badly at all."[21] And again to Henry: "Any institution can easily improve its success statistics by limiting intake only to the most hopeful boys."[22]

In response to a further study that showed a high percentage of boys not making it through the program (171 to 51) in a sample taken from December 1949 to January 1951, Polansky suggested that "perhaps the disparity is more an index of the devotion of the staff to an ideal of trying to help even very upset boys than it is a lack of success."[23] Noted thesis author Edward Moscovitch, "The staff at the Republic has definitely shown its willingness to accept, and take many chances with so-called 'marginal' cases. Perhaps then, this is part of their function, to attempt to help as many delinquent boys as possible." Other factors helped inflate the nongraduate figures, such as early or medical discharges.[24]

Early in 1953 Henry submitted his resignation, effective March 15. He had decided to turn his attention to the National Children's Home of the Veterans of Foreign Wars in Eaton Rapids, Michigan, as executive director. Though he had told Ruth Colebank at the outset that he would only stay five years, she had hoped that he would become too enthralled to leave. His replacement was an ordained Methodist minister.[25]

MILTON J. HUBER

Milton J. Huber was a handsome, affable man with a ready smile and a flare for public relations. He envisioned himself as the republic representative, the one who would establish good community relations, who would draw the republic to the attention of the state, perhaps the country. Indeed, he called himself "Mr. Outside" and Gordon Boring, assistant executive director and de facto head of the program, "Mr. Inside," sort of the "Blanchard and Davis days of the Army football teams," observed Boring later. Huber saw as his primary job the handling of "court relationships, United Community Services relationships, [and] other placement agency relationships."[26]

Huber did make a good impression. As a minister, he knew how to attract an audience and keep its attention. All of his youthful training pointed toward "holding forth," toward teaching or preaching. He received an AB in 1943 from Western Maryland College, a Bachelor of Sacred Theology from the same institution in 1946, and a degree from Boston University in 1949. As assistant secretary of the Boys Division of the Huntington YMCA and from working in Boston's tough South End, he gained valuable experience in dealing with atypical youths. Between 1946 and 1949, he held pastorates in Massachusetts and Connecticut. Before coming to Detroit in 1952 as assistant minister of the Central Methodist Church, he taught criminology at Western Maryland College and social ethics at Westminster Theological Seminary. He saw his appointment to the republic post as a marvelous opportunity to use his skills to enhance the organization.

He was perceived by some people to be a man of action, not satisfied with small-scale achievements. His tenure would bear witness to the establishment of a full-scale camping program; the birth of Youth Anonymous; a change in facilities; and a more definitive adoption of a new treatment concept.[27]

Right from the start he provided the press with just the sort of drama it wanted. A *Detroit Free Press* story from May 2, 1954, began with an alarming statement: "A new way has been found in Detroit to prevent a potentially 'bad' boy from turning to delinquency and crime: Give him a dog to raise." This absolute was followed by the story of Carl, a youngster seemingly beyond hope who even the clinicians at the republic doubted could be helped: "He's truanted too much already; he'd probably run away from here the first night," they declared. Enter Huber, his plan, and an "against all odds" tale. Said he: "He has come to distrust people. But he might attach himself to a dog and there find the love and security he misses." Would that it were so simple, but apparently the boy did establish a closeness with the animal, did show improvement, and somehow did manage to muster the strength to accept the terms of the alliance: when the dog reached maturity, he had to go into training to be a leader dog for the blind.[28]

Huber strongly believed that a boy could learn to love others through the care and feeding of animals. Nature study was a very important part of his program and at one time residents included Blondie, the Raccoon; Onery, the Butting Deer; Ouch, the Porcupine; and Snoopy, the Badger.

On August 9, 1954, the *Detroit Times* carried a long article, complete with a picture of the new director and his boys, in which Huber explained his thinking on the nature, treatment, and prevention of delinquency. He did not feel that rounding up delinquents and incarcerating them was the answer. Incarceration was quite different from rehabilitation, which seeks a cause, helps the offender understand that his behavior is not acceptable, and helps him gain reentry into society. He observed: "You can't whip, imprison, or punish a boy into being good." He explained that most troubled youths are products of broken homes, and some parents simply do not pay close enough attention to their offspring. He told of an incident that would always remain in his mind. The police visited him one day bearing a shoe belonging to a thirteen-year-old. "The boy, hurt in an accident, was dying in a hospital and for a day and a half nobody had been able to find out who he was. That is, some parents somewhere hadn't been concerned enough to report his absence."[29]

In December 1954 Huber met with a graduate psychologist and an ex-convict and laid plans for a rehabilitative program that would bring together delinquents and alcoholics with police records. Some youth workers were apprehensive about any kind of alliance between young lawbreakers and older ones, but the program creators had a clearly defined mission and some evidence that it would be effective.

YOUTH ANONYMOUS

Dr. Albert Eglash, psychologist on the staff of the Detroit Youth Commission, had served on the Mayor's Rehabilitation Committee on Skid Row Problems where he had seen "the simple program of Alcoholics Anonymous bring to an end the supposedly fixated behavior of compulsive drinking." Earlier experience in University of Michigan lab classes had shown him that the maze behavior of rats could not be changed through punishment but through gentle nudging. He began to wonder if the nudge that AA provided for the alcoholic could be designed to work for juveniles who continued to break the law despite suffering penalties. If drinking was a compulsive act, maybe antisocial acts were, too. The idea had been germinating for some months when Eglash found an ideal candidate to help him implement it: a rehabilitated offender with a burning quest to dissuade others from following a path leading to a wasted life.

Ernest "Tip" Rumsby grew up in the Purple Gang district of Detroit where, as *Free Press* writer Warren Stromberg noted, "as a boy on the streets . . . he drank with the men . . . was always looking for a fight and always found it." By age thirteen he already was a regular at the police station and had been arrested for drunkenness. At seventeen he joined the Navy, hoping to break the pattern, but within a year received a dishonorable discharge. Thereafter followed armed robberies, car thefts, attempted murder, and kidnapping charges with one stint in Leavenworth and two in Jackson Prison. For the last year of his imprisonment he was sent to the Detroit House of Corrections and it was there that he discovered Alcoholics Anonymous and the Reverend H. Ed Weinzierl, pastor and founder of Radio Temple, Berkley, Michigan. AA taught him how to take one day at a time in stopping compulsive drinking and the reverend, he said, gave him "a better understanding of . . . God."[30]

Rumsby was determined not to wind up in prison again, so, upon release, he secured a job with White Star Trucking and began to see what he could do to help others avoid his mistakes. He spent some time with the inhabitants of Skid Row, a "throwback," he said, to one of his father's jobs with the Salvation Army. He met Eglash during this period and, at the latter's suggestion, went to the Youth Commission office to see what he could do to help stem the growing tide of delinquency in Detroit. The summer of 1954 had been especially bad for the city, so Rumsby persisted, returning to the office time and again to ask: "What can I do to help?"

Eglash, the man with the idea, decided to take on the man with the mission and see if, indeed, the simple principles of AA, of mutual help and self-help for controlling impulsive, compulsive behavior, would be effective with troubled juveniles. They needed a testing period in a controlled environment. Milton Huber of the Boys Republic was able to provide them with that. The three men worked out a juvenile delinquent version of AA in which former alcoholic offenders would talk to the boys in their own language about problems they, boys and men alike, had in common. Through open discussion the boys would learn that others had the same problems and they, together, could work on resolutions.

On the first Thursday in January 1955, "Tip" told his story to eighty somewhat skeptical, world-weary boys. The response was phenomenal. According to Huber, "a spasm of spontaneous questions following his presentation . . . delved into everything from the kind of 'rod' he had used on his 'jobs' to the kind of 'ole lady' he had." The boys related to Rumsby, he felt, because he had been "through the mill. He knows their 'beefs.' He's from their side of the tracks. Stigma, rejection, guilt, defiance, bitterness, and all the other terms applicable to boys in trouble are more than professional phrases to such a man." It helped, he said, that Rumsby was a "brute of a man" with a "magnetic personality that can turn adversity to advantage." Stromberg called him a "strapping figure of a man . . . with a handsome face."[31]

When Rumsby told the boys that he could only return if invited, he was mobbed by youngsters wanting to shake his hand— and Youth Anonymous was born. (The boys had rejected the name Delinquents Anonymous, noting that alcoholics did not call themselves "Drunks Anonymous.") Though the Youth Anonymous program was relatively short-lived, it made an impact.

Every week for the next several years boys gathered to discuss their own problems or to listen to the stories of ex-offenders who had "been there." The boys elected their own officers and chaired their own meetings under the guidance of Rumsby and, later, other reformed convicts he had recruited to counsel boys. Rumsby liked the fact that he was "doing a job of rehabilitation at both ends." Meetings were patterned after those of AA and were guided by its Twelve-Step Program, which, according to a Detroit Commission on Children and Youth brochure, called for "an admission that one needs help; a willingness to seek spiritual help as well as help from the group; an attempt to be honest with oneself and to make appropriate amends or restitution to others; a willingness to share the program with others who have problems similar to one's own." Meetings began with a prayer and ended with the AA credo, which was printed on wallet-sized cards and distributed to each boy: "Grant me the serenity to accept things I cannot change, courage to change the things I can, and the wisdom to know the difference."

The Twelve Steps
1. We admitted we were powerless over our behavior—that our lives had become unmanageable.
2. Came to believe that a Power greater than ourselves could restore us to sanity.
3. Made a decision to turn our will and our lives over to the care of God as we understood Him.
4. Made a searching and fearless moral inventory of ourselves.
5. Admitted to God, to ourselves, and to another human being the exact nature of wrongs.
6. Were entirely ready to have God remove all these defects of character.
7. Humbly asked Him to remove our shortcomings.

8. Made a list of all persons we have harmed, and became willing to make amends to them all.

9. Made direct amends to such people wherever possible except when to do so would injure them or others.

10. Continued to take personal inventory and when we were wrong promptly admitted it.

11. Sought through prayer and meditation to improve our conscious contact with God as we understood Him, praying only for knowledge of His will for us and the power to carry that out.

12. Having had a spiritual awakening as the result of these steps, we tried to carry this message to others and practice these principles in all our affairs.

The tenth of the twelve steps brought on many lively discussions among the program participants. Admitting to a wrong might be okay unless you "rock" the guy's "jib," offered one boy. "He'll waste ya. How ya gonna tell him you're sorry?" Or, offered another, "Suppose you clout some guy over the head. You go up to admit you're wrong and he'll let you have it." At any rate, admitting to a wrong, they agreed, "took guts."[32]

Huber noted that "boys who are formerly withdrawn and suspicious in the usual clinical setting seem to relate more readily and to participate more enthusiastically to this type of counseling program."[33] Eglash concurred: "You can't beat good into a boy. Neither can you preach it into him. But if you can bring him face to face with himself he can usually figure out what's wrong."[34]

Staff members as a rule did not attend these meetings. Under Tip's guidance the boys were doing nicely without them. The Youth Anonymous idea caught on and soon there was a program at the Brighton Correctional Facility and there was talk of neighborhood groups. Tip was still driving a truck five days a week and working with church and other programs. He needed funds so that he could devote himself full time to his project. The Detroit Rotary came through with a $10,000 grant and Tip was able to set up office and work with a nine-person advisory board made up

of three Rotarians and six professionals involved in work with
juveniles.

As coordinator, Tip was approached by people of all ages, people
who had gone wrong and hoped to make something good of their
jumbled lives. One letter expressed the feelings of many:

> Dear Tip,
>
> Like you, I too am a graduate of Jacktown, a 4-time loser. I
> too have wondered what I could do to help others keep out of
> there. But never tried to approach the authorities, because I
> figured those bastards aren't interested in helping. Tip, I guess
> I was wrong.

Warren Stromberg cited Eglash's story of a Belgian priest, the
Rev. Father Damien DeVeuster, who worked in a leper colony in
the late 1800s, to explain the value of having ex-prisoners counsel
potential prisoners: "Father Damien, as he was called, was unable
to fill the spiritual needs of the lepers as long as he referred to them
as 'you.' Once he had become a leper himself and referred to the
others as 'we' it was recorded by Father Damien 'all of us found
peace and all of us found understanding in God.'" Reductio ad
absurdum, perhaps, but it is clear that some of the boys benefited
from Youth Anonymous. As Huber recalled:

> The boys who have difficulty in forming a positive identifica-
> tion with people are receiving the most help from the Youth
> Anonymous program. Possibly Tip and his fellow-workers
> epitomize this type of boy's basic feelings of rebelliousness
> toward society and accordingly such a boy is attracted and
> identifies himself initially with the negative or criminal past
> of Tip and others. Over a period of time through continuous
> association the relationships of these boys are strengthened
> and gradually the socially commendable values for which
> Youth Anonymous stands are assimilated and become an
> integral part of their personalities.[35]

In 1955, in an effort to determine the impact of the total program on the boys, Huber once again teamed up with the Wayne State University School of Social Work to produce a master's thesis that explored the lives of seven republic graduates. As explained by author Alfred I. Palmiere, its purpose was to "get at [their] inside lives" and achieve some understanding of whether their republic experience effected change in them. To help determine the degree of success in his sample, Palmiere needed to take a close look at each boy's family, neighborhood, school, employment record, social conduct, and the extent to which he seemed to have picked up desirable modes of behavior or thinking during his stay at the republic.

The boys were selected from those who had been admitted after 1953 and had been graduated for six months or more, in the hope of getting a glimpse at the effectiveness of the new treatment program begun in 1952. Palmiere made clear that the boys were in no way representative of the whole population and that the selection may have "inadvertently" leaned toward more "poorly adjusted" boys who had a "poor prognosis" for success upon leaving; that is, their failures would not be indicative of the republic's failure.

Of the seven boys studied, only three attempted to return to school and they dropped out quickly. Only four were able to get a job and only one still had it. Palmiere suggested that this pattern was typical of the whole teen population at that time, where youngsters were employed for short-term, part-time work to fill in as needed.

Of particular note were the boys' reactions to the republic experience. All discovered that the place was not as bad as they had anticipated. All appreciated the open setting, one observing, "I felt I was trusted and knew I could leave if I wanted to." They had ambivalent feelings about the staff, which represented authority. Said one youngster: "Some treated you like dirt; others were helpful." But the staff was credited with being accepting, understanding, and fair. Five thought the counseling program was good, one saying that the vocational testing helped him define his interests and abilities, others saying that they could "talk over personal problems" with the counselors. One boy, noted Palmiere, "thought the cathartic effect of the contact 'released a lot of tension and kept a boy from truanting or starting a fight.'"

Palmiere concluded that in many respects the boy court was more real to the boys than the real one:

> To almost all of the boys, the court seemed to represent the strength and voice of society and there seemed to be some appreciation and learning of the fact that it was a sensible and logical thing to avoid being punished through it. . . . This suggests the interesting hypothesis that the real legal manifestation of societal authority in their lives, the Juvenile Court, did not have the deterrent influence on them that it is supposed to have, but that the Boys Republic court was the real court, while the natural court was the play court.

He also observed that "many of the boys in post-institutional lives do practice regular saving, pay room and board, and recognize the need for budgeting." Five of them thought they had "grown up, were more serious and thoughtful now"; four thought that being "treated and given responsibility" had helped them "accept the rules and rights of others." Noted Palmiere: "All seven said they had learned their lesson, that they realized now the consequences of anti-social activity and were afraid of being sent to the vocational school in Lansing or to the adult court; however, two of these demonstrated by their behavior that this was only lip service." Though the sampling was small and may not have been representative, the study does provide a glimpse of the type of boy served by the republic.[36]

THE MID-1950S

Throughout the mid-1950s Huber continued to pursue his mission: To cement ties between the republic and the community and to draw national attention to his program. In March 1955 he appeared on Dennis James's national television game show *On Your Account*. He won $300 and James's gratitude by working out priority shipment of a Chrysler Motors boat that would not otherwise have reached the noted host until mid-summer.

Huber also branched out into the community by allowing one young drummer to appear on the talent segment of a two-hour television show for teens called *Saturday Party*. He called this action "another reflection of the type of programming possible with the new type of boy." In the summer of 1955 he embarked on an ambitious camping program that led the first group of boys to northwestern Michigan and to the Governor's Mansion in Lansing. They cooked and ate outside every night on this successful venture.

A year later he took all the boys to the University of Michigan Fresh Air Camp for two weeks, along with several staff members. Huber reported at the September 13, 1956, board meeting: "The impact of the experience is still being felt at the school in the form of less disciplinary problems and higher morale among the both boys and the staff." Apparently the boys impressed the camp manager and were commended for "good deportment."[37]

In 1957 Huber earned his spot in heaven. He conducted a seventeen-hundred-mile camping trip with two staff members and fifteen boys across the Upper Peninsula and as far as the Porcupine Mountains. He returned aglow with praise for and pride in his charges. The event received considerable play in newspapers throughout the state.

The internal workings of the republic were not as illustrious during those years, however. The spring of 1955 brought trouble. A hypodermic needle was found, there was evidence that some boys were using marijuana, and a boy was discovered smoking aspirins and tea. The September 16, 1955, board meeting minutes contain some disturbing information. Racism was cited as a factor in planning summertime recreational activities: "Swimming facilities have become a serious problem. Only a special appeal made Kensington Park available to our interracial group and it is twenty miles distant and offers but wading depth."[38] Not noted then was the fact that the boys had to stand in the republic truck for the whole trip.

January 1957 proved to be, Huber reported, "as difficult a month . . . as has been experienced" by his administration. Many of the boys were engaging in aggressive and destructive behavior; some had to be removed from the program. There had been two attempts to break into the office and safe. Huber urged the republic to work on a screening procedure. The board responded quickly and instituted one; the Wayne County Juvenile Court withheld sending boys while they determined their reaction to and "acceptance of the new screening program."[39]

In May 1957 the republic suffered a mass truancy of nineteen boys, bringing the total population down to fifty-three. Huber had prided himself on low truancy, often citing the numbers and comparing them with those of earlier administrations. He lamented that the episode followed a six-week truancy-free period and suggested that it was brought on by the "belated awareness of contagion among the boys of what the new [six-month screening] program means to them in terms of a longer stay at the Republic." Said Huber, "the transition from old to new, though gradual, will arouse anxiety and tension among those boys committed earlier under the non-screening six month program" and it was after a couple of the boys "who thought under the terms of the old program that they were due to go home shortly became aware they would be here longer" that the mass exodus took place.[40]

Some of these boys had backgrounds that were predictably sad, bearing evidence of abuse, both physical and mental, by parents, relatives, and siblings. The boy whose father had a tendency to expose himself in front of the children and make filthy remarks would bear no recognizable scars, but he suffered psychic pain and after the third placement in a foster home tried a sexual attack on an adopted daughter. This child had an IQ of 132.

The board minutes tell of children, covered with impetigo and lice, suffering whippings, usually from drunken fathers. One youngster acquired a deformed finger when he was four years old from helping his brother put a dead rat through a meat grinder. Another youngster inflicted his own physical pain by swallowing a tack and a pin.

At one time Huber was forced to return "three boys . . . to the Court so seriously disturbed that they [had] been since recommitted to mental hospitals." Judge Kaufman had apologized for the kinds of boys he had had to send to the republic, citing serious overcrowding at the training school in Lansing as the reason.[41]

By the mid-1950s relations with the juvenile court had become more strained. In June 1957 Huber reported to the board that there had been almost no referrals from the Wayne County Juvenile Court. He said: "We have not been successful in getting across to that agency the value of our new program and the services we are offering the community."[42] Boring noted later that the republic and the court had been so close for so long that they had been thought of as a single unit. Some people at the court had come to believe that placements were made at their "discretion," that the "Republic had very little to say." It came as a shock, therefore, when the republic "developed an intake procedure and criteria" for accepting youngsters. It took many hours of deliberation for court staff to accept "that that was the case."[43]

Relations with the court had been uneasy for some time, partially because of policies, partially personalities. From its inception the republic had been primarily a private organization, receiving most of its funding from private sources. State and county involvement was minimal—too minimal according to those responsible for paying the bills. While the court had an obligation to contribute toward the care of boys it committed, the "county and state were unwilling to bear the full cost," according to Richard Huegli, former executive secretary of the republic, assistant secretary of the Downriver Council of Social Agencies, and longtime United Community Services director. Therefore, he said, private sources "had to make up the difference between the actual cost and the amount paid by the county and state." Records show that as far back as 1916 to 1917, for example, Wayne County only contributed $7,896.38 of the actual operational costs of $16,465.57.

And as former President of the Board of Directors Gaylord Gillis remembers it, "We had many financial problems, particularly with Wayne County, since they would never give us very much money per day for each boy. One time it was two dollars and twenty-five cents per boy which was back in 1957–58. Our cost at that time . . . was about fifteen dollars to twenty dollars per boy per day."[44]

To some at the court it didn't matter how unrealistic their payment was since the deficit would be picked up by charitable foundation monies. This attitude created some bad feelings. An institution serving the public deserved greater public support.

Problems with funding had made the out-of-state boy especially welcome, since with him came the money needed to cover his care and treatment. These placements became a source of controversy, however. According to attorney Don Harness, president of the board in 1958, "We only took them because it helped to balance the budget," since "we only got one-fourth to a half of what it cost to keep a boy for a day" from local Michigan courts. He added, "People did not understand how tight we were for money." A newspaper headline announcing that "United Foundation money was being used to support out-of-state boys" was bad publicity, and the republic eventually stopped accepting placements from other states.[45]

A January 1954 United Community Services meeting addressed the question of whether the republic should continue as a private agency. In attendance were, among others, Judge George Edwards of the probate court, Harry Winston of the republic, and Louis Miriani of the City of Detroit Common Council. Judge Edwards stressed the importance of keeping the republic a private institution, thereby being assured of the "freedom and flexibility in programming" that was so successful in erasing the commitment stigma and in maintaining an "atmosphere . . . more typical of normal living conditions." Mr. Miriani reminded the group that the "problem of relieving the community of the expense of the care of the boys had been under consideration" four years earlier. Since schooling was such a major cost, he suggested that they press for legislation that would relieve the community by turning the responsibility for the boys' education over to the public school system.[46]

One participant advocated public support for the republic, as "post-court care is increasingly being looked upon as a public responsibility" and "larger financial support through the Juvenile Courts and County and taxpayers [would allow the United Community Services] to put some of its money into preventative programs." Another participant countered this argument, saying that such funds would have to be spread so thinly that they would have little impact—and the "Republic would still be needed."

Another speaker asked the assemblage not to "fall victim to a trend already too prevalent of turning over too many of traditionally voluntary responsibilities to government." He added: "Private sponsoring . . . is in accord with American tradition." The general feeling was that "it would be most serious to consider discontinuing an agency or converting it into a public institution when Wayne County already is carrying a major portion of the financial load of child caring treatment through taxes," and the assemblage voted unanimously for the republic to "continue as a voluntary organization under private control."[47]

Sometimes problems with the court had to do with personalities, not procedures. A particular judge might resist the idea of institutional placement for a youthful offender or react negatively to republic administrators. As far back as 1937, the minutes of the Budget Sub-Committee on Protective Services meeting had forecast the problem: "During Judge Healy's administration there has been a decline in commitments of Wayne County boys, both in quantity and quality. The agency has interested probate judges of other courts throughout the state in sending boys. As a result, twenty percent of the present population is from out of Wayne County and represents a [less troubled boy] than a Wayne County one." A 1939 State Welfare Department Report reinforced the idea that "Judge Healy does not approve of institutional care for children and is not in sympathy with the Ford Republic."[48] Whether true or not, this allegation points to some definite

tensions between the institution and the court. Problems also developed between Huber and Judge Nathan Kaufman. These two
strong-willed men often found themselves at loggerheads.

In the 1950s the republic was also under pressure to increase
its intake to accommodate the county's burgeoning preteen population, the postwar phenomenon known as the "baby boomers."
The old facilities just could not hold an increased population and
certainly were not conducive to the kind of treatment the staff
was beginning to envision for its charges. In order to successfully
implement the total care philosophy combined with a small-group
approach to therapy, the institution needed a new facility. As Harness recalled, "The old place was pretty crummy. It was a pretty
depressing sort of place and nothing in it . . . would tend to acti-
vate [the boys] into thinking of better things."[49]

A 1955 Detroit Sunday Times article drew attention to the deplorable state of the facility, noting especially a building "cracked
from ground to roof . . . patched with three huge strap-iron angles bolted to the walls" and a single upstairs toilet for forty boys.
The poor ventilation and cooling systems, inadequate showers,
and broken-down laundry were also cited as disgraces. A later Detroit News article noted that "no matter how fine the staff, the
school needed a roof over its head that did not leak, and buildings
that were not hazardous."[50]

The facility problem had long haunted the republic. During
the war years licensing agencies had tended to overlook physical
plant deficiencies, understanding problems with funding and being satisfied simply in having a place that was run competently
and lovingly. Changes had to be made, however, and with the aid
of its influential director, the board was able to commission noted
architect Minoru Yamasaki to design an uninstitutional-looking
facility in a new location just a half mile west of the original one.
Housed on eighty acres of woody, hilly countryside, it would include three cottages for twenty-five boys each. Most rooms would
be large enough for three boys, though each cottage would also
have two single rooms. The cottages' "natural counseling units"
were perfect, providing, according to Professor Clatworthy, for

what Huber termed a "more intensified program which will in-volve a longer period of service to the boys under our care." Huber planned to upgrade the cottage counselor classification and double the cottage staff, hoping to attract graduate students to the "total treatment team."[51]

The million-dollar facility, $513,000 of which came from the Metro Detroit Building Fund, included printing and automotive shops, classrooms, a nature study building with cases for animals, a gym, a swimming pool, a school building, an auditorium, a kitchen, and a dining hall.

The day of the dedication in September 1957 dawned bright and clear. The boys followed their usual morning ritual but by afternoon were dressed in their Sunday clothes. At two o'clock the guests started arriving—board members and their wives and friends; Van Patrick, popular local sportscaster; Red Barber, na-tionally known and loved sportscaster, who would give the key-note speech; Lieutenant Governor Phil Hart; Mayor Miriani; Bishop Crowley; heavyweight champion of the world Floyd Pat-terson; young Tiger right fielder Al Kaline. Lots of pictures were taken, and lots of hands were shaken. Then the assemblage gath-ered at the main building where dinner was served.[52] What fol-lowed was a highly charged, multifaceted program filled with drama and a few theatrics.

It began with a staff- and student-designed slide presentation that took the guests on a journey from the old republic to the new. It introduced them to a boy who "nobody seemed to want," who was "too sick now for us to help." His loneliness and frustration were brought to life through glimpses of the old facilities from angles that were sure to make them look deserted and abandoned. The scene then shifted to the new republic and to a new boy testing the waters. The presentation followed him through the first days of meeting his counselor, the athletic director, the school principal, his teachers, and program personnel, and concluded on a realistic, somewhat melancholy note: "There really is no happy ending to this journey of ours. The happiest thing we can say is the worst of some our boys' loneliness and paralyzing fear is gone."[53]

The script, rather Spillane-like with its purple prose, was nevertheless effective. It spoke of the "sad and permanent finale of a prison cell" and of the "steel and mortar and glass" reflecting only the "brightest of community compassion" and of the "healing of our children" and of the only alternative being a "headlong tumble into disaster." The dramatic scenes were reinforced by the language: The "constant probing at the delicate threshold of violence," "the tumblers of the human mind," "the infinite corridor of despair," "the ominous tracks of hatred and frustration," the "peeling away [of] crusted layers of attitudes and emotions" and the "sloughing away [of] barriers of emotions and attitudes." In one final flourish the narrator asked the audience to envision the "thousands of those children who lie sleeping somewhere tonight in impoverished little rooms, in cold fugitive garret holes and in a rotting bed."[54]

Red Barber indicated that that was a tough act to follow, but follow it he did. His speech was filled with words from notable "sports figures: St. Paul, Branch Ricky, Bob Zuppke, Enos Slaughter, and Zip Newman." The inclusion of a saint was intended to awaken even the most foggy-headed and Barber justified his choice by quoting two lines that seemed to him the epitome of the credo that should be followed by anyone engaged in athletics—or life: "Let us run with patience the race that is set before us" and "as a man thinketh in his heart, so is he." Barber stressed the importance of thinking and acting "cleanly," of not giving in to adversity. He used examples of sports figures overcoming the odds. He urged the boys to "learn from . . . mistakes, accept counseling, accept guidance . . . get up and go on." He ended with a sort of lay prayer: "God created it all. Science has never created anything. Science is merely busy discovering additional parts of God's creation." In a dramatic gesture, he turned on a small hand radio to show the boys that a thing could be real without being visible and asked them to "tune Him in."[55]

People remembered that day well. Gaylord Gillis recalled it as an "elaborate affair," made possible by having Public Relations Chairman for Ford Motor Company Charles F. Moore on the

board of trustees. Don Harness remembered Floyd speaking in-
formally to the boys about "straightening out and the importance
of living a good life" and all those who were there impressed him
"very, very much." In noting the enthusiasm of the boys he said,
"You wouldn't think they would be impressed by the same things
[as] a Board member."[56]

The move to the new facility was not without unanticipated
problems. Despite intensive counseling in groups and individually
in preparation for the move, the boys were unsettled. Rudolph
Yanke remembered that there were more truancies then, both in
response to the change in locale and to the change in concept,
which, as one board member noted, really went into effect with
the move. It is unlikely that the boys were aware of the ideological
changes, noted Yanke. The new program evolved slowly enough
for those "staff members not comfortable [with it] to transfer to a
different field of work." But according to Boring, the "differences
in the training staff and treatment staff" had become "more and
more pronounced" and certainly "climaxed most precisely when
the Boys Republic moved from Nine Mile Road and Inkster to the
north side of Nine Mile."[57]

By this time Gordon Boring, Huber's "Mr. Inside," was overseeing most of the internal operations. And under his guidance
change was inevitable. According to Boring, the program needed
to change because it was "under considerable attack by many professional groups and by the court systems and other people who
were placing youngsters at the agency." The new breed of student
was not being served by self-government, he felt. The process was
turning into one of bribery and blackmail. And as Clatworthy
pointed out, "without strong advocates for the self-government
and training programs on the Board of Directors and a Superintendent whose background was the ministry and who was willing
to allow his professional staff to develop and implement program
policy, it was reasonable that the Director of the Clinic would
assume greater leadership."[58]

Boring noted later that the counseling staff at that time "was
an insignificant force in the agency and did not have much au-

thority." Therefore, it could not assist the boys in resolving their
conflicts. Under his leadership, the newly hired showed a pro-
clivity for the treatment concept. Therein lay the problem, he
said: The older staff, the "old guard," was training oriented; the
new, treatment oriented. Some older members of the staff who
did not like the new procedures moved on to other jobs and were
replaced by people in tune with Boring's vision. When the treatment staff nearly equaled the educational training staff, says Boring, they went through "a stormy period" during which they "had
a split. . . . Many, many problems and some conflicts" arose and
continued to grow until the transition was complete and the staff
was heavily weighted in this clinical direction. The staff, and consequently the boys, experienced some stress during this period.

The dance was an astonishing success, receiving even more
Although not oblivious to the problems, Huber moved right
ahead in the public relations department. Riding high on his successful summer camping experience and dedication day and ceremony, he embarked on a program that was marked for failure. On
October 17, 1957, he drew the board's attention to a pioneering
event, one that had "not been tried in similar institutions anywhere in the country to date." He had organized a dance for his
boys and the girls from the Redford YWCA and the Lutheran
Home for Girls in Detroit. He boasted that all but two of the lads
were involved in preparing for the event. Scheduled for the Friday
before Halloween, it was to "reflect the possibilities of programming in our institution now that we are in control of our intake
and the selection of our boys."[59]

The dance was an astonishing success, receiving even more
news coverage than the dedication. Some young volunteers had
taught the boys basic dance steps in preparation for the big event.
Most were students and wives from Wayne State University. Many
of them brought dates to the dance and attendance totaled over
one hundred and fifty. Huber happily noted that "the boys have
a whole new group of friends to exchange letters with" because
many names and addresses had been swapped.[60] Huber could not
have foreseen the problems in what he saw as the innocent forming of new friendships. Some people feared that this address ex-

changing could lead to further contact—and this was not what the dance co-sponsors had in mind. They envisioned their girls as USO entertainers. It was all right for them to dance with the boys but not to date them.

A YWCA directive was issued telling the girls not to go if invited to future dances. But plenty of other girl groups asked to attend and for the next one, held on November 22, 1957, girls from the Redford Avenue Presbyterian Church and the Franklin Settlement came. Huber informed the board of the many letters from the girls attesting to the "gentlemanly conduct of the boys."

But concerns grew and board member Harry Winston questioned the "limit to which the school can control the relationships that develop between boys and girls." Though the youngsters were required to remain inside and control at the dances was good, there was no way to supervise future meetings and the "extent of liability of the institution . . . was the main point of concern." The board proposed a somewhat curtailed dance program of two to four events a year, properly spaced, "preferably during the cold season when there would not be the temptation to go outside, in spite of regulations to the contrary."[61]

In his 1957 annual report Huber announced that although improvements in the quality of republic life, both "functionally and aesthetically," were "beyond description," the "honeymoon . . . is definitely behind us." Within seven months, the extent of the problems in design of the facility was fully realized. Aluminum doorknobs and hinges were easy to bend, dent, and remove altogether. That delinquent behavior does not necessarily go hand in hand with lower intelligence became clear as the boys worked out ingenious ways to sabotage the place, using the very ingenuity that Lane said kept them alive on the streets. They showed a great acuity for using bits of wire to rig locks, thus limiting staff members' access to many rooms. And according to Huber, "door knobs have been yanked off hither and yon all over the campus." In addition, a door had caved in on impact with a shoe and "one plaster wall has been fallen through as well as two of the large plate glass windows." Hardware replacement would cost $2,000 and glass damage was running about $50 a month.

There also were numerous problems inherent in floor-to-ceiling glass windows, aesthetically pleasing though they may have been. Anything below knee level seemed fair game for breakage—and more sturdy material would need to be installed. Also, intact windows needed washing and the many tiled floors special attention. Another problem had to do with temperature control. The south side of the administration building experienced tremendous temperature variations "between cloudy and sunny days regardless of the temperature outside," though usually it was unbearably warm, as was the reception area. However, Huber concluded, "Considering the type of boy we are serving, the plant has been bearing up very well."[62]

But that was the problem, according to some former board members: They had not considered the "type" of boy. Gaylord Gillis observed that the design was "more suitable for a girls' finishing school."[63] Commented Don Harness: "The Board [thought] it looked great . . . on paper" and no one realized that "we'd have to replace . . . a lot of windows with steel plates because the kids were going to kick the windows out. We just never realized how disturbed some of these children were." He added: "We didn't get furniture that was strong enough and hard enough to pick up and throw around."[64] Clyde Reed concurred: "Two-by-fours bolted together are much more durable than flimsy one-by-twos."[65] Concluded Harness: "We . . . were thinking more in terms of providing a nice, pretty location . . . than thinking in the practical realities of it."[66]

In the 1957 report Huber also pointed to some staffing problems, resulting from only being able to offer noncompetitive salaries: "Many apply but few can afford to serve." This leads, he said, to a situation in which a "poor man is better than no man at all," which was certainly antithetic to the treatment philosophy. Huber also noted the dearth of women on the staff and conveyed the feeling of several child guidance centers that had suggested a balance would give the boys the "feminine association" they required. But, Huber explained, so long as the limited staff short-ages required using "teachers and clinicians" in the cottage areas, men would need to predominate. "Women cannot move freely among teen-age boys in their bedrooms and washrooms where trouble very often occurs."[67] Harness remembers finding cottage monitors as one of the biggest problems: "We couldn't pay them enough. They could make more money on welfare. . . . We had a very, very difficult time finding suitable people who would stay there overnight and keep these kids in tow."[68]

Huber noted happily that the "new referral program is generally accepted today, whereas for a while it was merely tolerated in some quarters." He observed that more referrals were being "initiated by child guidance clinics such as the Children's Center, Lafayette Clinic, Hawthorne Center, and various visiting teacher offices and the Wayne County Court [entered] the case following tentative acceptance of a boy to give formal approval to the placement plan and to underwrite the financing of his stay at the Republic."[69]

He found it interesting that an attempt to increase the per diem rate for Detroit-area boys to four dollars resulted in an actual increase from two dollars and thirty-one cents to two dollars and forty-two cents, especially in view of the fact that the republic was then "offering treatment services to the Wayne County Juvenile Court at a much lower rate than it pays for custodial care at the State Training School . . . where the per diem rate paid by the County is four dollars and twelve cents!" At the end of the report, Huber reminded the board members that he had intended to highlight problems that needed rectifying and they should be "careful that in examining the individual trees [they] do not lose sight of the forest itself." He added that "adversity is the stuff men and institutions grow by" and that, in toto, the "view is a satisfying one" and "the best years are yet before us."[70]

A 1958 pamphlet written by Huber titled *Which Way Is Up?* describes a typical troubled boy thusly: "Confused and frightened by failure, he becomes tangled in his rejections and loneliness. Twisting and turning, looking for release, he finally strikes out at his imagined enemies by breaking society's rules. He's like a man circling blindly in the snow, his emotions out of control, endlessly leading himself deeper and deeper into the darkness." Huber goes on to explain the republic's stand on punishment: "The re-education process starts by throwing the whips away. . . . Punishing only teaches a child how to punish; scolding teaches him how to scold. . . . The consistent moral standards of the adult staff are daily laboratories of training to many of these youths to whom any such standards were previously foreign."

For the particularly maladjusted youngster, "The traditional treatment of a month in the country, with model airplanes and a cow, would hand him a silent, if secret, laugh." A hyperbolic statement, certainly, but attention-getting. Such a boy was "tough [but also] sick; his unhappy ailments are emotional." He had "no deposits of love, understanding, recognition, or social acceptance in [his] emotional bank account. . . . Behind him are old familiar pressures, confusions, and impermanencies of the detention home, the police, the social agency, the broken home, the angry neighbors, the hostile parent and the stern impersonality of the law. Before him is the first of the men who will attempt to reshape his life." Throughout, the handsome boy is pictured in consultation, paging through a magazine, watching the others play from behind a door, sitting sullenly in a chair, going to church, and finally, broadly grinning.[71]

Throughout 1958 Huber had frequent speaking engagements. He had been invited by the State Department of Public Instruction, along with only forty-nine other specialists, to attend a special conference on working with emotionally disturbed children in the public school system. He noted to the board in April 1958 that public relations had improved and that there was high morale among the boys who had been active in weight lifting, fishing, and newspaper clubs. Six boys had been approved for jobs in the Farmington community.

The records mention some experimental hypnotherapy with "a patient whose basic pathology suggested that he would not respond to current practices." The alternative, to Huber, seemed to be release to his agency with a recommendation that he be hospi-

talized, "knowing full well in advance that he was not an admis-
sible patient." Huber had hoped to use hypnosis with those who
were not receptive to the "specific clinical procedures [of] individual counseling and therapy, group therapy, discussion types, and
role playing" and were "continuing to manifest symptomatic behavior in the social group setting to indicate that no basic changes
were taking place."

Board minutes from May 1958 to October 1959 contain evidence of continued problems with the court system, new successes,
and new tragedies or near tragedies. Some thefts were reported,
one boy nearly succeeded in hanging himself, another attempted
suicide by iodine consumption, and a third attempted homicide
by incineration.[72]

The republic did receive some good publicity, however, through
Mort Neff's television program *Michigan Outdoors*. He first showed
film taken at the republic and then had a three-week feature
showing boys cutting Christmas trees and preparing them for sale
on the lot in front of the school. Huber explained that the "overall
purpose of this project is to give the boys something to focus their
minds upon as the holiday approaches." The proceeds from the
sale of trees and wreaths would enable them to buy presents for
loved ones, the balance going in a special outdoor and camping
fund. The boys made the wreaths in the Nature Center, produced
Christmas cards in the printing shop, and did handiwork in the
crafts room.[73]

In February 1959 Huber reported on receiving funding from the
Helen Joy Foundation to begin a program of post-treatment care
and presented a tape recording of a hypnosis therapy treatment
indicating that it was a "promising new technique . . . being used
experimentally."[74]

Meanwhile, Huber's outreach program was in full swing. The
July issue of *Sports Afield* described the republic's outdoor program
and the Michigan Outdoors Exhibit at the Detroit Boat Show
included a spot for the republic's nature program. Huber hoped
this would acquaint Detroiters with the existence and purpose
of the school. Autumn brought more talk of possible additional

state funding. The director noted that the population being served was more statewide than citywide. One hundred and forty-five boys had come from other sources than Wayne County Juvenile Court and of the thirty-five recommended from the latter, only fifteen were accepted, five of whom proved unworkable after a trial period.

Huber suggested that the reasons for the "continued limited number of referrals from the source having wardship over the largest number of boys" were "bigger than either the personalities or agencies involved." He added that "another source of support is needed if this trend continues" and asked the board to consider:

1. Foundation grants
2. Splitting the budget into segments assumed by various interest groups
3. Cost sharing—Board of Education, United Foundation of Metropolitan Detroit, and the Michigan United Fund—on the basis of boy residence
4. State agency operation[75]

The October board meeting minutes note that Boring had been offered an administrative position with another boys home. The threat of losing Boring unsettled the staff. He had long been the leading force in program redesign and implementation. In a way he was the new republic, and the new republic's guiding philosophy was his.

There had also been a growing dissatisfaction with the overall operation of the republic, whether it was being run as efficiently and effectively as it needed to be. The staff was certainly not in a state of rebellion and relations were not exactly hostile, but many simply did not like Huber's way of doing things. Board member Don Harness was charged with dismissing Huber, and he left the Boys Republic abruptly at the end of 1959. Meanwhile the administration had found a way to dissuade Boring from accepting another job: It appointed him executive director, a title he was to hold for the next twenty-four years.

BRIDGE LEADING TO THE REPUBLIC (Warren Stomberg, *Detroit Free Press*, 1963; Boys Republic Collection).

THE FARMHOUSE REPUBLIC, C. 1907 (Boys Republic Collection).

"FORD HALL," from 1909 Ford Republic brochure
(Boys Republic Collection).

FRONT COVER of 1909 Ford Republic brochure
(Boys Republic Collection).

HOMER LANE, C. 1909
(W. David Wills, *Homer Lane*).

BOY JUDGE AT WORK, from 1909 Ford Republic brochure
(Boys Republic Collection).

"Twinney I and Twinney II," from 1909 Ford Republic brochure
(Boys Republic Collection).

LADIES AND GENTLEMEN IN FRONT OF GREENHOUSE
(Ford Republic Collection).

BOYS MOPPING THE FLOOR, from 1909 Ford Republic brochure
(Boys Republic Collection).

ICE MAKING ON THE LAKE AT THE FORD REPUBLIC, December 1925
(Detroit News Collection).

THE ICE HARVEST, December 1925
(Detroit News Collection).

TALLYING THE VOTES, election day, October 1927
(Detroit News Collection).

VOTING DAY AT FORD REPUBLIC, October 1927
(Detroit News Collection).

OFFICERS OF THE FORD REPUBLIC, from 1914 Ford Republic brochure (Ford Republic Collection).

"GUILTY OR NOT GUILTY." The court in action, from 1940s Ford Republic brochure (Ford Republic Collection).

HAYING, September 1927
(Detroit News Collection).

THE BOYS REPUBLIC STORE, c. 1940
(Boys Republic Collection).

"HARVEST TIME," from 1940s Ford Republic pamphlet
(Boys Republic Collection).

FORD REPUBLIC
FARM

120 acres under cultivation
50   "   in the Rollin H. Stevens Glen
20   "   of woodland

Our farm population

20 –   [cow]
3 –   [horse]
3 –   [goat]

10 –   [pig]
27 –   [pig]
10 –   [chicken]
3 –   [duck]

Many boys are given farm training
at Ford Republic, and are placed
on private farms after release from
the school.

Our farm, truck gardens and
orchards produce enough fresh
vegetables and fruits for the boys
and staff, and enough food for
the farm stock.

FORD REPUBLIC FARM, sketch from Clyde Reed
(United Community Services Collection).

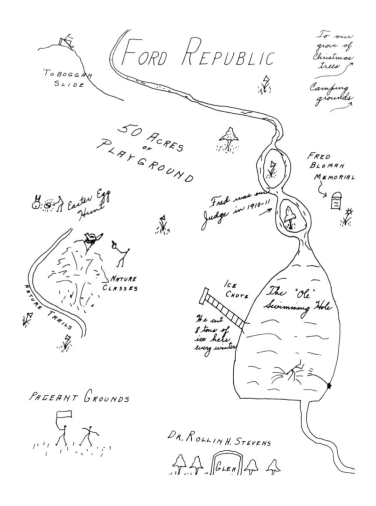

FORD REPUBLIC, fifty acres of playground, sketch from Clyde Reed (United Community Services Collection).

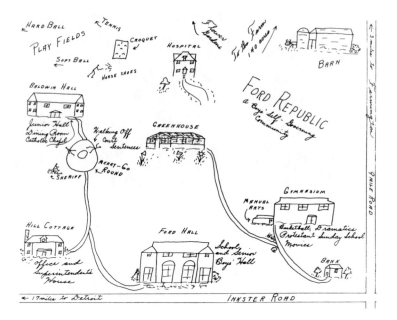

THE FORD REPUBLIC, a boy's self-governing community, sketch from Clyde Reed (United Community Services Collection).

"The Citizens' Court," from 1909 Ford Republic brochure
(Boys Republic Collection).

Shoe repair at the Boys Republic from 1948 brochure
(Boys Republic Collection).

Chapter 6

Gordon Boring and the Politics of Change: 1959–1983

THE 1960S BROUGHT CHANGE TO the nation and, consequently, to the republic. Long-haired musicians from England were singing thinly veiled songs about LSD, and "mind-expansion" and "personal guru" had come into the public vernacular. Strange youngsters, called "flower children" or "hippies," were dancing in the streets, shedding their clothes, extolling the virtues of marijuana—if not in all hometowns, certainly on national television. Many elders thought the clothes should be shed, if in greater privacy. These scraggly haired, anomalous beings wore leather and denim, beads and feathers, dashiki shirts and headbands. What had happened to Peter Pan collars, bobby socks, saddle shoes, and DAs? And what exactly was the "altered state of awareness" that two respectable Harvard professors were singing praises to?

By 1967 a race riot had erupted in Detroit, leaving the city in an uproar and bitterly divided. A war was also dividing the country into hawks and doves. The rather pro forma objections to *any* war registered earlier in the century by pacifists seemed in sharp contrast to the vehement, boisterous, outraged protests, with burnings of draft cards. The euphemistically termed "conflagration" in Vietnam was enraging a large segment of the population, rather than drawing anticipated support or more characteristic indifference. Later the soldiers, many of whom never really understood why they were fighting in the first place, were to return to silence—if they were lucky. There were no parades, no tributes, no banquet dinners. Some of them were spat upon and labeled "baby killers." The tenor of these troubled times would have a far-reaching impact. The fighters and the flower children alike would have children, and some of these children would be the republic residents of the 1970s and 1980s.

Retrospective commentary suggests a clear connection between the upheaval in the country and the emergence of a new citizenry at the republic. Former Board Director Fred Auch believed that these disruptive times may have been directly responsible for the boys being "much more disturbed, more educationally disadvantaged, and substantially more prone to acting out violently." Phyllis Griffin, who joined the staff in 1969, becoming executive director in 1987, noted that some of the boys of the 1970s and 1980s had parents who had not been able to find themselves in the 1960s and were still searching, a state not conducive to imparting parental wisdom and guidance.[1]

Certainly the citizenry reflected the outside world. The confusion, the disgust, the elevation of the "if it feels good, do it" approach to life, and of "seize the day" and to hell with the corrupt conventions of a corrupt power structure forced youngsters to bear witness to a world trembling on its axis. Janis Joplin urged them to "get high," as did the denizens of Haight-Ashbury. And many children did.

Gordon Boring can attest to that. His twenty-four-year directorship witnessed the emergence of a new sort of boy, tougher, streetwise, and more prone to experiment with drugs. He was also emotionally scarred and disturbed. Boring was prepared for the new boy. He had seen him coming.

GORDON BORING AND THE REPUBLIC

By the time Gordon Boring was called upon to assume the directorship of the Boys Republic in 1960, he had already established himself as the leading figure in the organization. As a thirteen-year veteran, he fully understood the guiding philosophy and, indeed, had been directly responsible for many policy decisions. As assistant director he had handled internal operations.

His qualifications were substantial. With a degree in psychology from the University of Michigan and his studies in clinical psychology, he, perhaps more than anyone, knew what made the organization run. That knowledge, combined with the respect, admiration, and loyalty of his colleagues, ensured a strong leadership.

Boring had been intrigued with the republic right from the start. A very good friend's father, a retired schoolteacher who worked at the republic, had told him about a newly opened counseling position. Within ten days, Boring had applied and on June 15, 1947, he began his four-decades-long association. Boring recalls that a boy named Jack "was directly responsible for me taking the job." During a tour of the grounds, the boy had shown such enthusiasm, had seemed so anxious for Boring to work there, that his decision to accept was not long in coming.

Boring's special interest in working with disadvantaged children may have evolved from his own unhappy childhood. Family circumstances had made it necessary for him to live in foster homes for several years. He remembered those years as the worst in his life, filled with "some rather horrible experiences." It was only many years later that he realized that his conception of what kinds of care boys needed was in part formed by the care he had not been afforded. He said, "I probably got more education when I was only a boy about what kids needed than I did in all of my professional training." One thing he learned was that an aggrieved child in a foster home has no one to complain to, no one to talk to about personal things. For that reason, Boring felt, residential treatment or group home treatment was often better than foster care: "When a youngster is depressed, when he's anxious, when he is frightened, when he is confused, he has someone to go to" and sometimes the problem can be resolved immediately. Sometimes, said Boring, just "getting the two kids together in a face to face interview" brings about peace. There was never a time, he added, when he could not "find something in the 'life-space' of one youngster that the other youngster couldn't identify with."[2]

Group work was invaluable for that reason. If one boy revealed his fears about his mother's health, for example, he was sure to find others with similar fears. Common bonds could speed up the process of healing. So great was Boring's conviction that group and individual therapy needed to work side by side that when he became executive director in 1960, he sought a marriage of the two disciplines. He had once believed, and had predicated the 1956 program he was asked to develop on this belief, that "if we could resolve all of the individual conflicts within all of the individual youngsters, we would have the problems beaten and would live happily ever after. It was a beautiful thought," he noted later, "and it began to work in part; but it undid itself when the youngster walked out in a group." Accomplishments in individual therapy did not always translate into group situations; and progress in the latter did not assure carryover.

Believing that compartmentalized therapy had severe limitations, Boring was determined to mesh the services by bringing all staff together in a total milieu approach. The appointment of Carlton Peters, a social group worker, as assistant director facilitated the implementation of the new concept.

Boring involved everyone in the therapy process, including cooks and maintenance men. Each staff member was given at least some insight into each boy's particular problem. While the boys' records remained confidential, enough clinical material to facilitate handling was uncovered. Boring recalls: "We had a social work staff, a psychological staff, and a psychiatric staff [and were moving] into the dimension of social group work with great enthusiasm and tremendous support from the University of Michigan."[3]

Boring knew that the staff had to have the same frame of reference so as not to confuse the youngsters. He also saw the value of having therapy take place in nonclinical settings, such as the kitchen or the shop. He tells of some close therapeutic relationships that evolved between cooks and boys and maintenance men and boys. This is why he wanted to provide enough of a boy's history to all employees to help them work with the clinical staff toward the healing of a boy. Said Boring: "We began to teach [all staff] clinical concepts, various treatment concepts." Non-clinical staff was then able to capitalize on the closeness and responsiveness of certain boys and "correct the youngster in a non-professional manner [that allowed the boy to] accept that correction on a very positive basis." Surrogate mother/child relationships and role-model relationships became invaluable to the republic.

Sometimes the accepted therapy mode of discipline—one which was antithetical to punishment—gave rise to debate, especially with staff members used to the old crime-and-punishment dictum, but eventually all were "woven into the entire cloth, the entire fabric, that made up the Boys Republic system."

This period of transition, though, of an emerging treatment philosophy, was one that Boring called "stormy," one in which old clashed with new. It was not unusual, he said, for him to work "sixteen to eighteen hours a day, day in and day out," in order to "keep the thing going in one direction," to keep it from being "blown to smithereens." He remained encouraged, however, by the ongoing republic credo that if you "simply remain client-centered . . . you cannot go wrong."

The treatment concept grew out of Boring's belief that the republic boys had become "emotionally hurt by the forces brought to bear on them by our own society." It was predicated on the theory that an "emotionally hurt" child could not control the "forces brought to bear" on him in an environment he did not make. The purpose of treatment was to "eradicate the effects of the hurt and damage [the boys] had suffered [and] to help them . . . return to society emotionally sound and secure, in harmony with themselves and their community."[4]

Therapy of this sort would only work with boys of normal intelligence whose psychic makeup seemed receptive to personality change. It would be of little value to those with severe mental or intellectual limitations, problems, or impairments. Therefore, the republic looked for "psycho-neurotic boys whose lack of emotional and/or social adjustment to the normal vicissitudes of life [were] reflected in high levels of anxiety and strong feelings of guilt." These were boys who revealed "varying degrees of aggression or passivity and emotional immaturity which [were] reflected in their poor esteem for self, their conflicts with others, their seeming lack of realistic aspiration, and their inability to internalize social values."[5]

For these boys, said Boring, "no single treatment method or technique can be utilized with success. Each youngster must be approached on a totally individualized basis." Some have "strong needs to rely on others and are extremely reluctant to become involved in self-determined activities; others may show tendencies to be stubborn, but are ineffective in their self-determined activities. These boys may possess a low tolerance for frustration and they may react on an impulsive, hostile basis in order to obtain their goals." How vastly different are the perceptions here of "bad" boys from those which led to candy-making as a resolution to "badness."[6]

A program of this sort demanded careful and thorough personnel training. According to a 1960s republic handbook, new staff "constantly have supervisory and clinical personnel available . . . to help them learn sound treatment methods and techniques." Once a year all staff received official evaluations, which made note of their "professional interest, enthusiasm, originality, and competence; and their ability to learn new treatment techniques and apply them." Boring saw a "direct relationship between therapeutic gain and the professional competency of treatment personnel." A rather lengthy probationary period of six months allowed staff, clientele, and trainees to determine if the new alliance would be viable.[7]

The offenses that brought boys to the republic in 1961 were more extensive than those of earlier years: stealing; threats of murder; sexual activity with younger girls or siblings; truancy; incorrigibility at home and school; voyeurism; school phobia; disorderly conduct; drinking; and sexual experimentation.[8] Boring recognized that many of these boys felt intensely guilty and sought punishment. They acted on impulse; if something frustrated them, they struck out instead of looking for the core of the frustration and trying to find ways of dealing with it. Counseling sessions attempted to "create a larger time gap between the time they feel the impulse—let's say it's anger—and what they think about it and how they act on it. If they simply feel and act, they're going to do something assaultive."[9]

In 1961, in the hope of attaining boys' involvement in republic operations while at the same time stemming the manipulative behavior so often in evidence at state meetings, Boring began an experiment with an honors group called the House of Representatives (HOR). The plan was to show the boys model behavior, hoping that it would catch on. The HOR constitution called for developing "an attitude [of] trust, setting an example for other boys [and] helping them . . . develop [a personal] sense of pride." This proved to be a little too lofty for the clientele. There were resolutions about making adherence to an honor system seem worthier than bragging about thefts. There were attempts to revamp the honor system. And the group agreed not to use strong-arm tactics to coerce compatriots into good behavior.

But it soon became clear that "many boys just don't seem to care about an honor system" and the proposal was tabled. At one point the group censured itself for not taking itself seriously. They did agree upon and eventually implement family-style dining, though not without some fears that the "larger boys would take too much food and the smaller boys wouldn't get enough to eat." After some questions about cottage monitors taking bribes, some discussion about the possibility of having two milks at dinner, the observation that "an honor system where House Members need to set the example creates too much pressure on the individual members," and a general awareness of a serious loss of interest in the organization, the HOR disbanded.[10]

In 1962 Boring attempted to give his professional staff an idea of what group therapy sessions were like for the boys. He organized what were later referred to as "Administrative Skull Sessions." Frank Harris, who joined the staff in April that year, remembered the first meeting well: "He set it up in such a way that we had the inkling that we were going to be talking about ourselves. As soon as we got together, there was that resistance, that hesitation, and the whole thing. That was a way of kind of assisting us to see what the kids go through when it comes to talking."[11]

The guidelines for the skull sessions were clearly established and followed, somewhat in accord with the confrontation sessions that were becoming so popular in the 1960s. Nine rules prevailed:

1. All professional personnel and supervisors would be there;
2. There would be no hierarchy;
3. All suggestions would be considered important;
4. Any questions would be okay;
5. Professional demeanor would be maintained at all times;
6. No one would have to implement a recommended change;
7. The meetings would be secret;
8. Meetings would last forty-five minutes;
9. Participants had to be "mature enough to be professionally attacked by their colleagues and open-minded enough to try to profit by any interpretations of personality flaws or blind spots as . . . pinpointed by colleagues."[12]

In the early 1960s the republic needed to address the problem of upgrading and increasing staff training. With the new program in full force, teachers needed training and/or a substantial awareness of the features of special education for atypical youths. The job called for more than the ability to teach; the teacher needed to be in tune with treatment concepts and had to have enduring patience. Observed Boring, "Not everyone can absorb the verbal abuse nor deal professionally with the acting out behavior some of our clients project in attempting to express the turmoil that exists within themselves."[13] A staff upgrading bulletin noted that three teachers had been released because of their inability to "absorb the pressure of a treatment program. They [had] put an emphasis on formal teaching, [letting] the chips fall where they may . . . rather than concerning themselves with student learning."

Once again the need for increasing teacher salaries became apparent. Republic educators were dealing with an "academically retarded" clientele, "ninety-five percent [of whom had been] expelled from school or were on the verge of expulsion," this despite having a "higher than average I.Q." Teachers were expected to work one evening a week and every fourth weekend. They had to learn "social group work, psychiatric and psychological concepts, be able to utilize them, and communicate with other personnel." Despite these heavy demands in 1962 they were paid on average $1,100 less than public school teachers. With this gap, the program was beginning to lose some very good people.[14]

In November 1962 Boring wrote to United Community Services official Cleve Mason regarding problems with the teaching program. They had lost eight people, with one threatening to go, since September 1961. Personnel were becoming demoralized and the boys sensed trouble. There were two main causes for the loss: in addition to needing more education to work in special education, the teachers also worked an eleven-month year instead of the traditional nine-and-one-half one for public school teachers; and the maximum salary lagged by $2,000 to $3,000 compared with that of the public school teacher. One teacher left with a promise of $2,500 more a year, another for $2,000, and two for only $450 and $250 respectively "because long range earning power is so much greater in the public school system."[15]

While Boring had a firm grasp on his role as executive director, he admitted he was more interested in working directly with the boys than in attending to administrative details. Because he wanted to be easily available to them, he adopted an open door policy. It was not unusual for a boy in distress—because of a real or imagined hurt—to show up in his office while he was conducting some matter of business. Boring always found time for him—the time that he had been denied as a child.

To compensate for all the hours devoted to "direct service," he often had to see to "administrative planning" at 4:30 or 5:00 in the morning. That was a price he paid willingly to be able to devote his "time and attention to their concerns and their worries and their fears and their anxieties." He wanted them to know, he said, that "at any time, they could see me."[16]

But administrative details also vied for his time and he never shirked a responsibility. There were problems with the boys, with staff, and in the community. Over the years he had to deal with boy trespasses in the community, with discontent among the staff, with interpretations of policy, with public relations, and with increasing external rules, controls, and paperwork.[17]

Department head meetings in the fall of 1962, for example, revealed problems with the thoroughness of nightmen's cleaning, continued furniture breakage, and poor school attendance and bad study habits. In November there were problems with towel distribution and handling, with leftover food being "piled on the carts," rendering it "not re-usable," and with boys "ripping sheets for shoe rags."[18]

Many organizations, foundations, and private benefactors donated money and material. When the noise in the dorms became a problem that could no longer be ignored, Boring turned to the board for help. Fred Auch, chairman of the Buildings and Grounds Committee, arranged for a local company to contribute tiling. Boring made certain the company was duly thanked: "Those who made this contribution possible will undoubtedly never have the opportunity to see how their generosity will affect our clients, but . . . noisiness in the cottages has been one of our major problems. Loud noise is particularly stimulating to emotionally disturbed adolescents and frequently results in serious group problems."[19] Monetary donations made off-property birthday celebrations, camping, and roller-skating trips possible. These extras held boredom and routinization at bay, which may have reduced the turmoil in the program.

In 1964 Boring suggested that board meetings on campus with members arriving and walking the grounds be discontinued because "they tend to disturb the boys and disrupt the program." This, said Boring, "did not at all satisfy all Board members at all times. Some were very open and honest with me about their wanting to be involved more directly in services to youngsters." Boring said that though he was concerned about that—after all, people on the board were in that position by virtue of their interest and concern for the program and boys—he nevertheless felt that a close relationship was unwise, given the penchant of boys of this sort for fomenting trouble. They "have had to learn to manipulate to survive" and "are quick and really tremendously successful in turning people against one another. It requires real understanding, real training, and real preparation to do the job day in and day out" and for that reason he encouraged the board to "keep an arm's length posture from the everyday operating procedure."[20]

There were flare-ups in the community on occasion, though Boring claimed that in thirty-seven years he had witnessed only nine or ten severe problems. In fact, he said, it would be easy to verify with the Farmington police youth division that they had "more trouble with local youngsters themselves." He remembered one instance of a neighborhood robbery. When a police officer stopped in to query him, he said he was not aware of any trouble, but told him he would "put out a couple of quick feelers." Within a short time he had extremely cooperative kids piling up their illegally gained goods on his desk, probably because there was no sense of "trying to getcha," he said. The kids knew that the police "were not being nasty but were trying to resolve the problem."[21]

Boring noted, "If there's ever [anything going on] which is dangerous to the welfare of the kids, we will know about it in no time . . . because of the anxiety in the group. We may not know exactly what is wrong but we will know something is wrong. Believe me, it will not take very long for that information to get to us. One youngster will find a way of letting a staff member [he trusts] know what is going on." When a boy stole a 357 Magnum from his stepfather and brought it on campus, republic staff was able to confiscate the weapon in short order. Occasionally there were false accusations; when something bad happened in the neighborhood, a few people were quick to charge the republic boys. Most neighbors were positive and supportive, however, throughout Boring's employment.[22]

The implementation of a walkie-talkie system helped considerably in curbing trouble in the republic community. No matter where staff members were on the eighty acres, they could keep in contact via these devices: "They know when Johnny goes to the gym; they know when he leaves the gym; and they know when he checks into the cottage . . . so there is very little room for someone to be missing without it being known," noted one employee. As the staff saw it, the boys did not consider this as surveillance per se. They realized that this was also for their protection. They could not be wrongly accused.[23]

The citizens recognized that it was in their interest to remain on good terms with the outside community. In many cases, said Boring, the youngsters wanted the "perpetrators . . . to be treated much more sternly than they are treated." They did not want any single boy to "jeopardize their privileges or their relationship with the community." The community treated them well, especially with gifts at Christmastime, and they knew that. Said Boring, "[W]e try to get a little superego involved, a little conscience . . . in each and every situation, and try to make some gain out of it. Each and every experience which occurs here is an opportunity for some treatment gain for some kid in the group."[24]

In the early 1960s Boring oversaw the establishment of a classification system. Each boy was given a monthly rating dependent on the degree of his progress during that month. Cottage, recreation, school, clinic, and administrative personnel classified boys according to the following:

"New Boy" (no score)	New boy just beginning the program. Too soon to give further classification.
"Primary" (0–3)	Boys not responding to program. Indicate poor behavior and attitudes—very poor adjustment and response to program and counseling.
"Secondary"	Boys making moderate progress in program and counseling.

(4–7)   Fair attitude and behavior. Moderate effort.

"ADVANCED"   Boys making good progress in program and
                        counseling.
(8–10)   Good attitude and behavior. Good effort.

A cover letter explained his new system: "Each student must be classified carefully [and realistically] in regard to [what he] can do plus what he will do; his learning ability, behavior and motivation. A boy's classification might change if behavior and motivation change and gains are made." Monthly reports were posted so that each boy would have "an idea of his general improvements and progress." Each department head was responsible for securing from his staff a list of boys with their corresponding ratings of 0 to 10 points.[25]

Boring's administrative duties sometimes led him into sensitive areas. Because he wanted codes of conduct and behavior clearly spelled out, the records are filled with carefully worded and precise memos dealing with infractions, staff discontent, and misunderstandings. When he learned that six sleds had been destroyed, he fired off a memo to the effect that boys had lost sled privileges and that use would have to be supervised from then on. There were regulations for attendance checks, rules for swimming pool use, and memos regarding telephone abuse by the staff. One memo reads: "It has come to my attention that some ill feelings may be caused by you irritating each other about parking procedure. It is imperative . . . that all of you avoid such situations. These things can affect your working relationships."[26]

With regard to smoking, he advised the staff not to force the boys to go underground: "To attempt to absolutely and rigidly enforce the law . . . could only cause us to lose many cases." He bade them not to interfere with or impede the process of psychotherapy. At one point he threatened a fifty-dollar fine for losing one's keys and once advised that "those employees who do not reach work during inclement weather will be charged with a vacation day."[27] Noted John R. Schaupner, clinician from 1971 to 1979, "Once

Gordon hit his stride, no one, staff or boy, dared say a word unless asked."[28]

A problem that Boring called "too bizarre to even describe" created by an ex-employee prompted him to recommend that the credit union refuse loans to staff not on the payroll for at least three years and require written job evaluations of those who appeared eligible.

An ever-prevalent problem during these years as in earlier ones was how to facilitate a boy's transition from institution life to life in the community. All too often rehabilitative efforts were for naught when a boy reentered a basically stagnant, unchanged environment. Republic Administrator Mark Sperling recalled his frustration when learning of the suicide of a boy he had worked with diligently: "His progress . . . wasn't complete" and within nine weeks of going home to "the same situation," he was dead.[29]

Psychotherapist Bernice Izner observed that each new citizen was viewed in terms of where he would go upon release: "There is no point in keeping him if we cannot make a plan." The whole treatment program revolved on preparation for a return—to a community, to a home, a halfway house, or an independent arrangement.[30]

Too often follow-up efforts were stymied by inadequate funding and insufficient staff to oversee an intensive program. In 1959 the republic had embarked on a five-year experimental aftercare program made possible by funding from the Helen Joy Newberry Foundation. Under program guidelines, boys, parents, teachers, and administrators were counseled before, during, and after a boy's release. Statistics had shown that very few boys had succeeded upon reentry into public school systems and experience indicated that the culprit might be a system that appeared too overwhelmingly complex to a boy who was not so much hostile as afraid. Boys and parents, to whatever degree possible, were prepared for the day of release. Schools, which normally might see the returned offender as the troublemaker who left, would now see him hand-in-hand with a person who could serve as interpreter for each side. Boys came to realize that when there was a problem they neither had to strike out nor flee. They could make a telephone call. Often the aftercare counselor was asked to clear up mistakes in records so that a boy could be placed at the proper grade level or so that he could compete in athletics.

An early study of the aftercare program's effectiveness showed a surprising change in dropout figures, the rate going from 80 percent to 20 percent. Boring doubted its accuracy at the time, but the results of a study nearly two years later showed that more boys were staying in school longer (77 percent).

The program certainly was successful in allaying some of the fears of the school personnel by keeping in close personal contact, by being there when problems arose. The boys had somewhere to turn. One lad asked his counselor, "Will you talk to my teacher? She thinks I'm lazy, but you know how hard reading was for me." Noted one aftercare counselor: "Interviews with boys, class sessions, visits with schools, attendance directors, visiting teachers, principals and teachers, school counselors, probation officers, home visits, phone calls from the boys themselves, all add up to continued treatment for our boys—and a sixty hour work week."

When the state assumed financial responsibility for the boys in the 1950s, the republic aftercare service was shortened to ninety days. While staff members understood the necessity for the state's overseeing of state wards, they regretted the loss of contact, which they had come to believe was essential.[31]

Throughout the years attempts had been made to determine the success rate of republic graduates. Said Boring: "There are problems with oversimplifying a measurement of success." James Clatworthy had told him that with his dissertation work there had been "no particular model he could develop which would determine success." Some kids got in trouble, but "the things they had gotten from the Republic system—its way of operating, the way of dealing with people, the way of talking with people, the way of handling their feelings and expressing them—subsequently proved to be extremely beneficial to them." And a "youngster who might not be in any trouble might not be making any significant headway and he might be staying on a fairly level plane. Although he might be avoiding difficulty with the law, he might not be a well-functioning person in society." So which one is successful? A kid who is returned to a home "loaded with pathology" probably will become "contaminated" again: "This is not a measurement of the program and its success, but a measurement of what society has to offer."[32]

According to Boring, group home placement should not be viewed as a sign of failure. People may think of institutions and group homes as bad things, as evidence of failure, but often they are the best thing for kids. The only way to measure success, Boring felt, was to talk to individuals, to ask them how they are getting along. He realized that the cost would be prohibitive.

He told of an experience camping with the boys. Some trustees from Jackson had been assigned to haul the trash from the camping site. A fellow with a big "PRISONER" stamped on his back called to him. He was a former republic boy and was delighted at having run into Boring because he had wanted to tell him that if he had not been at the republic he surely would be dead. He said: "I learned how to do a lot of things that I never knew about before I got there." He was going to be paroled the next week. Boring asked, "Are you going to be all right?" He responded, "I'm going to be O.K." Failure or success? Although he had ended up in jail, he probably had learned some things and hoped to use this knowledge to become a productive citizen. Said Boring: "I don't think it's fair to say that you can take a youngster for a year and a half or so and change everything that happened to him the previous fourteen years."[33]

The executive director's report of December 15, 1966, noted an increase in referrals, and the average daily population for 1966 was seventy-two boys, or 96 percent capacity. It also made reference to a situation in which eleven boys had needed to be segregated from the rest of the group in a special class because they were "constantly creating havoc" and to a boy with a "severe psychosexual disturbance" who was believed responsible for an "outbreak of sexual activity in one cottage."[34]

Clinician John R. Schaupner related an amusing tale that high-lighted the conflict that arose during the anti-establishment days. A boy "whose appearance epitomized the 60s radical look" needed to see the local podiatrist. The doctor could not conceal his dis-gust with the boy's entire demeanor. Said Schaupner, "Before I knew it, I was standing between a 6'2" podiatrist and a defiant representative of the 'hip' generation, both uttering profanities and threats. I thought the best course was retreat and pulled the angry adolescent into the car, leaving the doctor still shaking his fist after us in the parking lot."[35]

In the late 1960s, when boys' psychiatric problems began to overshadow their social problems, counselors in a newly created afternoon program started submitting regular reports outlining day-to-day happenings, successes, failures, and potential prob-lems. Counselor/psychologist Gordon Sokoll observed gladly that one boy was in a good frame of mind, but wondered about an-other who had become unusually (perhaps suspiciously) friendly. Of one youngster he said: "He's too comfortable. Can't we make something happen?" He said of another boy: "[He] feels all is closing in on him. Good! Maybe can lead to important interview material."[36]

There were some boy fights, one involving the picking up of a brick and a coke bottle and another resulting in a rumored knife threatening. When kitchen staff complained about a boy swearing, Sokoll asked for a little latitude because "he's so tied up inside, ventilation is important to his progress." One boy had several sexually oriented books confiscated and another needed to be confronted about his fantasy of having spent the first eight years of his life in a "primitive north woods" and never having used a knife and fork.[37] Counselor Thomas Gearhart reported on a boy wielding what he called a "pimping stick" and a few boys jumping on a damaged locker that contained another boy. There was also a lighter fluid–sniffing incident.[38]

A 1967 Child Welfare League of America report outlined the basic changes in republic philosophy, though its assertion that "the approach to each youngster is determined by the diagnostic category to which he is assigned, rather than by his specific experiences and needs" was misleading and too formulaic. Though it was true that a youngster diagnosed as suffering from a "personality trait disturbance" or as a "passive aggressive type" would receive "predetermined" treatment, his particular circumstances would be very much a part of his case history and would be considered in determining an approach.

The league report was generally favorable, though it recommended changes in the meal format: "Tables are not set prior to the serving of meals, the serving platters usually lack silverware, milk is served in cartoons [*sic*] and in the rush to get through with a meal, the food is literally hurled on the table." The resultant confusion and lack of acceptable manners led to "opportunities for playful attacks and attack planning."[39]

By the late 1960s United Community Services announced that it would no longer assume two-thirds of the cost of caring for public wards. While understanding that the Wayne County Court could only work with funds released from the Wayne County Commissioners and the Wayne County Auditors, the UCS decided to force their hand by withdrawing private monies.

Having been "put on notice," the republic met with a coalition of agencies in the Wayne County area to seek a way to increase public funding so that there would not be "such a heavy drain on the UCS" and so that the Republic could continue offering services to children in the area. According to Boring, "The county officials said, 'Go to the state,' and the state officials said, 'Talk to the county.'" This "ring-around-rosey" situation prevailed until 1970, when the Michigan Federation of Child and Family Agencies was "finally able to get the State Department of Social Services to assume the full cost of care for each . . . child, providing the Wayne County Court would agree to commit the child to the State Department of Social Services." This was a monumental change, considering that the cost had risen from five or six dollars a day per child in the 1960s to sixty dollars a day in the early 1970s. The importance of having state funding for a private agency should not be underestimated. Observed Boring: "Private children's agencies can do a quality job of treating youngsters at a lower cost than public agencies can provide. This is one of the reasons clearly why it's profitable for the state tax money to be spent in this way." As a result, the clinical staff began working directly with the state social work staff and ties between republic workers and court workers were all but severed.[40]

In September 1969 Boring reported on an "unbelievable amount of stealing . . . much teasing and arguing but not as much fighting as usual." In a display of good humor, he added, "The . . . boys are enjoying more unstructured recreation activities. They much prefer playing in the creek to baseball or football. Playing with small cars on the floor and sidewalk is a popular activity right now, and stealing the cars to play with is another popular activity." He concluded, "This is a fascinating group of youngsters. In short, they hate school, love the glen and the creek, argue constantly, hide, steal and seem to remain in perpetual motion. . . . The staff does well [when] they can just get the youngsters' attention."[41]

The city of Detroit was experiencing its own problems in the mid- to late 1960s. A race riot in 1967 had left the populace shaken—and afraid. During this period republic boys displayed a great deal of acting out behavior and engaged in considerable fighting, stealing, and arguing.

The spring and summer of 1971 marked just the beginning of a rash of unpleasant incidents at the republic. A series of robberies was followed by some racial unrest, the result, Boring thought, of allowing too many new boys into the program after June. Arson, drug possession, and drug use became common problems as well. In January 1972 one-quarter of the population was involved in a drug roundup, which yielded "everything from capsules of heroin to marijuana," all of which had been accumulated during Christmas home visits by boys both wishing to sell and just impress.[42] In March 1972 clinic director Allen Ablitz reported that the republic was "receiving many seriously socially maladjusted boys who are overly aggressive and hostile and fearful of forming close personal relationships with adults."[43]

In November eighteen boys were enrolled in the vocational program of the Farmington-Walled Lake Schools, but ten were simply unable to handle the traditional setting. Boring observed, "We have a large number of very immature, impulsive, acting out youngsters [and] staff alertness, involvement, and intervention are constantly required."[44]

In January and February 1973, Ablitz reported "seeing many seriously disturbed adolescents . . . who are twelve or thirteen and virtually have no home to return to or visit." So much stealing had occurred in the early months of the year that the director noted: "We seem to be unable to really keep anything secure. This leads to accusations, arguing, fighting, and more stealing, if for nothing more than retaliation."[45] By May things had not improved; the population was reported to be "very unstable." Six fires were set in different buildings. One boy boasted about his part in the setting; another from Ypsilanti State Hospital used gasoline to start his fire; a third boy stole gasoline to sniff. All three were removed from the program. Boring observed that the "entire incident was weird and frightening" and questioned the republic's "ability to contain, control, and successfully treat" as many boys as it did.[46]

The September 1973 director's report noted a much more disturbed population than on that date a year earlier. "They have much more difficulty responding to simple directions, concentrating in school and in counseling [and display] impulsive, defiant, quarrelsome, hostile, and destructive behavior."[47] Boring's report two months later revealed that the population was low because the program was not "accepting youngsters . . . who are apt to be a serious community problem or who have a history of serious assaultive or destructive behavior [indicating they needed] a closed setting." Several boys had been returned because of behavior that seemed to "threaten the welfare" of others. Though by no means excluding more seriously disturbed boys, the republic could not "become a dumping ground."[48]

Most of the boys were operating at such a low level academically that the school program had turned into a tutorial service. In addition, the 10 to 15 percent of the boys who were "demanding, hostile, aggressive, and manipulative" needed the most time, to the detriment of the other boys. To meet the needs of all and handle the increasing paperwork, some staff members were visiting boys' homes on their own time, in part to accommodate the growing numbers of parents who were unable to afford the bus fare to the republic.[49]

In 1974 legislation forced the republic to relinquish control over the schooling of the boys. The law read that the school district was responsible for the education of all school-age children residing in that district. Thus began a period of emotional strain, hurt feelings, and tension created by conflicting ideologies—and by regret at having lost a major part of the program. But even in that year of upheaval, the boys did enjoy movie trips, toured the Ford plant, saw Pistons games, went bowling, and visited a haunted house on Halloween. They also formed a photography club and joined a Christian Brigade.[50]

It was during these years, in the late 1960s and early 1970s, that the republic had regular campouts for the boys. According to Mark Sperling, this was before "our population became a lot harder to contain in one place for that many hours." He remembered one particularly grueling experience, just before the program was phased out, during which a boy threw a mattress into the campfire and then the kids chased each other with shovels.[51] Frank Harris remembered these outings as times of invaluable exchanges, times when kids, huddled around a campfire, were less guarded and more eager to talk about what was bothering them. The atmosphere was conducive to relaxed, seemingly nontherapeutic conversation. In the midst of discovering that some boys had been physically abused, among other things, there were lighter times on these campouts, too. One of these took place after the boys and staff had heard reports of flying saucer sightings in the area. After they found some dead cows in a field, Boring, with no explanation, ordered the campers to pack up and head home. On the road back to the republic, they passed a convoy of army trucks and the streets of Ann Arbor were almost devoid of activity. Cut off from any contact with the outside world via radios, or short waves, a few counselors were certain that there had either been a Martian invasion or World War III had been declared. Imagine their relief when they learned they had been summoned home because of a threat of a major storm.

Harris remembered how foreign country woods seemed to tough city kids. They were used to noise and activity. At campouts everyone would stake out a section of the tent, but in the morning he would find kids sleeping all around him. Said Harris, "At campouts, we'd do some thing to lighten up the tone, atmosphere, get the kids laughing, smiling a bit." Closer relationships sometimes developed because the staff and boys had to overcome adversity. They cleared areas for pitching tents, built campfires, and cooked their own food, some of which, according to Sperling, turned out very raw. Said Harris, "Out there we live together, and stay together, we cry together, we laugh together. We eat the same food, with the sand in it."

Harris also remembered one particularly unruly bunch that he attempted to coerce into settling down in the tent late one night by telling them that there was a mad dog in the area. Boring, who happened to be passing by at that moment, boomed: "You're damned right there's a mad dog out here. Now get to sleep!"

He also recalled one camping incident that could have had a more serious outcome. The boys used to take large truck inner tubes and roll them down a hill with a "good one-hundred yard slant." Boring agreed to get in a tube one day and the boys aimed him at a tree at the bottom—the "one tree in the whole meadow. I couldn't believe it," said Harris. It was like "they had some kind of guidance system on the inner tube or the tree—it just went right to it." Boring hit the tree and "tubes went flying. Everybody said, 'Oh, no,' but he got up, was all right."

Harris believed that the camping trips were equally if not more valuable for the staff. They proved an excellent training place for new staff. Their "psychic makeup won't allow you to wallow in pathology." Staff had to treat problems as they arose; there was no time for research, for looking things up in books. They had to rely on themselves and find ways to "intuitively treat kids." Self-reliance was a natural by-product of nine days, twenty-four hours a day of close contact. At 11:00 the counselors would meet to have a critique of the day's events, happenings, boy progress. Sometimes these sessions would go until two or three in the morning and everyone had to be up at eight o'clock. Harris said that the campouts "created a natural dependency . . . in a short time, something that was harder to come by back at the republic." They "created conflict and disharmony from a natural standpoint because conditions were such that they weren't fabricated or made up."[52]

The camping program had to be disbanded, not only because of the new breed of boys but also because of more strictly enforced camping regulations regarding the proximity of bathing facilities and running water at each site. In addition, staff overtime pay became too hard to come up with and the Wage and Hour Act made the general cost prohibitive. For a while staff tried to run the program on the grounds, but when adversity struck the boys could not understand why they could not just walk back to the cottages.

THE MID- TO LATE 1970S

The mid-1970s proved problematic. A serious gang fight toward the end of 1974 resulted in four boys being removed from the program. There were a number of robberies in the neighborhood and the boys were natural suspects since five of them had been caught off property at night and a nearby store had been robbed of wine. One culprit had experienced substantial difficulties with the police prior to admittance to the republic and the police were reported to be angry that he had been admitted at all. He later was convicted of armed robbery.

A 357 Magnum scare created some anxiety in the program, but the 1975 summer session promised to be a good one, with Director of Recreation Frank Harris requisitioning among other things a projector, a movie camera, rowboats, bikes, costumes for the talent show and movie, track club jerseys, roller skates, hockey sticks, craft kits, and a mini-bike.

Some new teachers at the Farmington school were having problems with the boys, but the republic was not aware of any out-of-the-ordinary difficulties until one of them resigned. A "sizable group of boys got out of control, intimidated, and physically abused" her. Harris and Boring went to the school to reestablish order and control.[53] The boys were still adjusting to the new school arrangement by November 1975 when a reported "fourteen percent of the boys were suspended . . . every day," with one day totaling 25 percent. At that time stealing and fighting incidents had lessened, but an "increasing number of youngsters [had] home situations [that were] so deteriorated that they don't care to go home, even for a weekend visit."[54] Boring's reports in 1976 confirm this. Efforts to reunite kids with parents were stymied because some families simply did not want anything to do with them anymore. Several boys asked permission to stay beyond the release.[55] Severe racial problems toward the end of 1976 consumed Boring's time as well, and paperwork was becoming increasingly burdensome. He noted: "Our clinicians are now required to do an exhaustive intake evaluation because referral material contains such a sparsity of information." The referral agency might not have had much information or they might have withheld some.[56]

A 1977 in-depth study by three program placement specialists from the Department of Social Services documented the republic's program of "ego support and development" and individual, group, crisis, and family counseling. It noted that some families resisted involvement, but the "clinicians continue to contact [them] by phone, mail, or direct home calls." At that time, they were establishing family involvement with 50 percent, maintaining contact with 40 percent, and being rejected by 10 percent.[57]

While most of the facility impressed the social services team, the cottage area was called "very dimly lit, gloomy, and depressing, lacking warmth and cheerfulness." The study noted that "Farmington personnel [were] somewhat insensitive to the needs of the client population, had difficulty relating to the educational flexibility needed in the Boys Republic," and sometimes expelled as many as twenty-five students for "disciplinary reasons." The remainder of the report was filled with praise and concluded that the "relationship, both cordial and warm . . . between staff and young people . . . [and] the familiarity of all observed staff with *all* young people was simply impressive."[58]

The year 1977 began with the republic's still failing to meet state licensing health and safety requirements. An Oakland County Health Department visit in July 1976 had revealed deficiencies in "protection from insect infection" and restroom maintenance, as well as housekeeping and lighting conditions that promoted the potential for fire. The republic took steps to comply with the codes, but a reinspection in August 1976 had revealed ongoing problems with ventilation and lighting.[59]

A January 27, 1977, fire inspection report noted problems with an inadequate system for alerting and evacuating boys during a fire, the use of electrical extension and makeshift light cords, exit door functioning, and the maintenance of fire extinguishers and alarms. A plan for remodeling was assessed by the board in March 1977, as it was clear that health and fire violations had to be rectified if the institution was to continue to function. On May 5, 1977, the regulatory consultant to Children's Agencies, finding that the problems were being addressed, recommended that a license be issued. (All buildings were renovated and corrections made in 1978.)[60]

A particularly insightful earlier United Community Services report (November 20, 1970, for the 1971 capital funds campaign) noted the special and unusual circumstances surrounding the need for repairs:

> The agency's emphasis on psychological aspects of the boys' problems has resulted in the agency seeming to let the boys "act out" their feelings more than would be customarily expected. This acting out takes its toll on the physical facility. Some of the repair and replacement items would enable the physical plant to stand up better under strong physical use; for

example, the replacement of pine door jambs with oak jambs and the replacement of gym lights with a new type which has guards.[61]

In response to the State Department of Social Services Licensing Consultant's notation in the spring 1977 report about the "school suspension policy and bathroom scheduling periods for students," Boring fired off an angry letter to William Miller, principal of alternative education in Farmington Hills. The consultant had reported that a student had told him that bathroom visits must conform to a schedule, "a specific time in the A.M. and P.M. [and] any deviation [was] cause for suspension." Boring thought this inhumane and said: "We cannot regulate, or legislate, our viscerogenic functions." Though he realized that some children used the bathroom for avoidance as well as voidance, he urged that the teachers be sensitive to their needs. Miller responded angrily that the republic ought to check out "hearsay" with school personnel before jumping to conclusions. Boring had earlier addressed the problem of boys being suspended for "rebelling against some of the rigid codes of conduct expected of them in school."[62]

A tragic incident occurred in 1977, one that was followed closely in the newspapers. A twelve-year-old boy who agreed with his mother that he should not visit or live at home again was spending weekends with a foster family, with the hope of turning this into a permanent arrangement when he was released from the republic. Unbeknownst to anyone, the twelve-year-old was left in charge of three youngsters, ages two, three, and five, all foster children from a different Department of Social Services worker, and the woman's own seven-year-old while she went to work. Following instructions to bathe the two-year-old, he filled the tub with hot water, causing the child to die of scalding. The youth was charged with "brutal scalding, beating, and drowning," but the charges were dropped because of insufficient evidence and the boy was readmitted to the republic.[63]

Phyllis Griffin remembered two other incidents in particular, one that was unsettling, the other downright frightening. One time there was rumor of an impending sexual attack on her. The rumor had reached Boring, who said to her, "God damn it, you get out there, and you walk through that program right now. [Let] them know you're not afraid. And show them you will *not* be intimidated." Griffin recalls looking at him "like he'd lost his mind," but she went "down there" because "Gordon is a fabulous person" and she knew she really did not have anything to fear. The boys were awestruck at her boldness in directly confronting them. One immediately apologized because, said Griffin, "he knew I had his whole life in my hands." Another boy's mother came out and knocked him right out of a chair. To Griffin's amusement, she heard him say, "What would I want with that old woman?" On another occasion Griffin had to physically struggle with a boy who assaulted her. Even though the boy was penitent and Griffin shaken, the republic allowed him to remain. There were no further incidents of this nature.[64]

Trouble did not always come from within, as Mark Sperling remembered all too well. One day in the early 1970s, a heavily intoxicated man who seemed to hold staff and boys alike responsible for troubles he was having with work, his wife, and life in general created havoc as he attempted to enter one of the cottages, his little girl in tow, and then wandered around the ravine. Some kids on the bridge, obviously sensing his state of inebriation, began spitting at him. Incensed, he charged into the canteen area, grabbed a kid, and began choking him on the pool table. A counselor crashed a chair against the wall, causing the man to run off in the direction of the pool, where Sperling was: "This guy at the fence [started] swearing at me—words that I don't think our kids have ever used and, without exaggerating, I swear this guy came over the fence with one hop! I had never seen anything like it. . . . I hit that . . . door in maybe two seconds . . . went through the locker room and fell on my face . . . because my [shoes] were all slippery . . . and the guy was behind me." Luckily for everyone, the state police were waiting. When the man saw them, he sat down and cried.[65]

Commented Griffin: "Sometimes you really begin to question whether or not all that you go through, day in and day out, is really worth all of it. [But then] kids come back and let you know how they've been doing [and you know] it's all worthwhile. It only takes one [success story] to let you know that the last five years were worth it."[66]

Chapter 7

Toward the Centennial and Beyond: 1983–

As THE BOYS REPUBLIC CENTENNIAL approached, staff, board members, patrons, and boys alike were taking the time to assess the institution, to look at what it had been, what it was, and what it would be. Summoning up the past brought some heartache, memories of boys who could have been helped but were not, of boys who were helped but returned to an unchanged world, of boys who died—in wars, in accidents, by their own hand, or at the hands of others. But there was joy, too, and pride in remembering the successes, in recalling the laughter, the companionship, and the camaraderie.

AN OVERVIEW OF THE STAFF

The caliber of the staff has remained constant. Indeed, part of the republic's uniqueness through the years has been its ability to attract dedicated staff for less illustrious salaries than they might get elsewhere. Some do a period of service and then go on—often to "jobs at important state levels," said Gordon Boring. Others become agency directors and college instructors. Added Boring, "Almost everybody . . . who worked in the clinic in the beginning days ended up with their doctorate degree."[1]

Qualified staff was always easier to come by during Republican administrations, observed Frank Harris. Democrats had a tendency to augment the numbers of social assistance agencies while Republicans often sent social welfare professionals out looking for jobs.[2]

There were periods of severe staff shortage, most notably in the war years, and there were some problems with misconduct and unprofessionalism. Former Superintendent Clyde Reed remembered one instance in which two staff members with "exemplary" relations with the boys simply could not stand the sight of each other and whenever they "came within speaking distance, sparks began to fly." One of the combatants, a matron in a maintenance area, had high standards. She expected her charges to adhere to strict rules and regulations—and she never wanted for volunteers to work in her department. The boys liked and respected her. Said Reed: "She did not have an education degree in anything, but she did have lots of warmth for the boys." The other combatant had the "brawn of . . . a Detroit Lions' lineman" and "an ebullient personality that attracted and intrigued the boys." When apart, each served the republic well. Together, they "broke down the good they were doing. They irritated each other. They challenged." The situation grew so ugly that they had to be counseled by Reed and staff psychiatrist Alfred LaBine, but to no avail. The boys began discussing the "open antagonism" between the two. Finally Reed invited them to his house, where he "served coffee and cookies in an amicable setting." Reed discussed the important roles they played in the organization and their obligation to the boys. Then he issued an ultimatum: "The next time [they] had one of their open, hostile, caustic, confrontations in front of the staff and boys, both would be dismissed." Said Reed: "With the sword of Damocles hanging over their heads, the pair did control their animosities." Staff members, concluded Reed, were "human beings with their own quirks and foibles" and, as such, sometimes "go quite contra to administration policy."[3]

In general problems have been minimal and staff harmony has been more the rule than the exception. This general amicability has been true among clinical, line, and service staff. Executive directors' reports through the years have contained numerous tributes to maintenance and kitchen workers as well as to professional staff. Boring reported in 1971, for example, that there had been "real progress in maintaining facilities," the ease possibly attributable to the maintenance crew's having made "bed side tables and footlockers for all the rooms in the upstairs cottages," which allowed the boys to protect their belongings. Boring found the maintenance crew's improvements remarkable.[4]

In a discussion of the full staff involvement in the treatment process, Boring said of the kitchen workers: "These gals took on the role of mother figures most often . . . and were tremendously loved. . . . They were fascinated with the clinical concepts we taught then, and took this on with great gusto. Lady after lady for years did a tremendous job of working with the kids." He added, "Similar kinds of constructs occurred in the maintenance department. They worked with [the boys] and they helped them and they taught them. . . . They [were] integrated and interwoven into the whole treatment program."[5]

In 1976 Boring said that that year's staff was the most conscientious and competent group ever assembled at one time during his employment. Forty percent had been there for over five years. Even in the late 1980s, according to Frank Harris, of the fifteen to twenty new people hired yearly, fewer than half left. Board member Frank Parcells noted in the 1981 historical survey, "A more dedicated group of people I have never met." Sam Rabinovitz called them "all members of the team," adding, "Just as I respected each and every one of the Ford Republic staff, so did they respect me. None of us threw our weight around. We just joined together, each of us contributing what we could." Bernice Izner concurred: "In the over thirty years I have been here, I can't conceive of any agency where there could be a more homogeneous, compatible staff. There have never been any problems with interpersonal relationships of significance except on occasion. . . . On the whole, everyone has a great deal of respect for each other . . . and never has there been any feeling of real rivalry." Said Harris:

"It is the staff itself that keeps people here." The fifty hours of in-service training also prepared staff members for their responsibilities, thereby cutting down on surprises that might cause disgruntlement.[6]

The staff of the 1980s and 1990s carried on the tradition of cohesiveness, almost to the point of being "incestuous," said Phyllis Griffin. Bill Burgess, supervisor of operations, agreed: "We just love the Boys Republic. I worked two jobs to stay here when I wasn't making enough money." By the late 1980s, Director of Group Work Bill Robertson had been there for seventeen years; Griffin, over eighteen; Frank Harris, twenty-two; Sally Owen, sixteen; Dave Hamil, nine; Frank Norah, twenty-three before leaving to open some adult foster care homes in 1985; and "Bill Burgess—forever," noted Sperling before going on to other endeavors himself after eighteen years.[7]

Staff cohesiveness is essential for getting to know and understand the boys and determine an effective course of action for each. And this whole staff knew a great deal about the total population, thereby ensuring greater control and less tendency on the part of the boys to try to play one member against another. In addition, the boys felt free to see anyone. Said Sperling: "There is ongoing . . . communication between the clinicians and the supervisors and the clinic to discuss concerns and constantly review cases." Though formal meetings are essential, staff members confer all the time. Also, observed Griffin, when one goes on vacation, others divide the caseload and "that way we get to know each other's cases fairly well."[8] Griffin also noted, "Sometimes there just isn't enough of one person." Some kids were so demanding that they would be shared or "handed off . . . to give a little relief" to the clinician. She concluded, "If the kids can wear you down, they've got you beat."[9]

Burgess also believed that the staff was "responsible for tone setting" and was convinced that "how we relate to each other is contagious." Boring had told them often, he said, that "once you pass the sign, try to leave everything that is bothering you behind because by you being upset or angry you may deal with something the wrong way."[10]

Harris confessed that sometimes staff set the "tone" with behavior as bad as that of the kids. He remembered sitting in the dining hall looking over at the bridge, monitoring the coming and going of the kids, and seeing Frank Norah across the ravine. Knowing that Norah could not see him, Harris summoned him on his walkie-talkie to a spot on the hillside behind upper east cottage. Norah, assuming trouble of some sort, rushed out back and stood there. Harris then engaged him in the following exchange:

> Harris: "Frank, put your walkie-talkie down."
> Norah: (obliging) "Like this?"
> Harris: "Yes. Now hold both your hands in the air."
> (Norah held both hands in the air).
> Harris: "Touchdown!"

Said Harris: "We did a lot of that because . . . if you carried a good tone, if you were in a good mood, or if you were happy, a lot of times it would be contagious to the other kids. In fact, a lot of times we purposely joked around just to 'contag.'" He remembered the efforts staff used to make, usually in the form of practical joking, to lighten up the tone at the republic and loosen everyone up. Sometimes they would lock someone up in the dark power room for a few minutes or jump out and scare someone. Then there was the gorilla suit incident in which an appropriately attired person chased Mark Sperling across the grounds. When Sperling injured his foot, staff decided to restrict itself to less elaborate antics.[11]

Phyllis Griffin said that during her long tenure at the republic (she eventually became executive director) she never had a dull moment. "I've been angry, and I've gone home and said, 'What . . . am I doing here?'" but she has never been bored or discouraged for any length of time. The job does call for constant reassessment, but a sense of humor helps with that. And, she added, "You can learn from mistakes." She was not certain at first that she was interested in working with boys with the kinds of problems those at the republic had. Therefore, when she accepted a position at the republic, she took advantage of her employer's three-year leave-of-absence plan that would allow her to return to her job if her new one at the republic did not work out.[12]

A Profile: Phyllis Griffin

Phyllis Griffin's undergraduate work had been in education and social work at Western Michigan University. At that time, in the early 1960s, a certificate could be issued after a period of field placement. Though her mother had offered to support her financially through her master's degree, Griffin had decided she wanted some practical experience and signed on as a probation officer for delinquent boys and girls in Alegon, Michigan. Later she worked with step-parents preparing to adopt their step-children. When an employment opportunity arose at the Wayne County Department of Social Services, Griffin took the civil service exam and spent the next four and a half years working with ADC (Aid to Dependent Children) and Aid to the Blind and Aged.

When she transferred to the children's division as a foster care worker and supervised the placement of children at facilities like the republic, she realized that she was interested in "a hands-on approach to helping people with their problems."[13] She was placing a youngster at the time of her interview with Gordon Boring and Tom Hughes. Within two days, in February 1969, she began her long-term association.

The early months of employment entailed twelve-hour days of great intensity. She worked from 9 A.M. to 3 P.M. in the clinic screening all kids, carrying a caseload, and being a counselor, and from 3 P.M. to 9 or 9:30 P.M. in the Group Work Department with line staff, getting a feel for what the work was like. Because she trained in both areas, she became very familiar with treatment concepts.

Griffin was not long in discovering that she did not know how to relax. She found that she was getting worn down. She had been accustomed to seeing friends frequently, but found that she needed some time by herself. She stopped scheduling as many activities on the weekends; she learned how to pace herself. She maintained that you had to stay ahead of the kids and if you were not up to it on a given day, it was better not to come in. She encouraged the staff to be honest, and mental health days were not frowned upon.

Griffin found that on occasion parents were more difficult to work with than the boys because they "sometimes have very delinquent values themselves." And all too frequently parents expressed concern that their boys were being coddled, were not being punished enough. Said Griffin: "If punishment were the answer, none of these kids would be here. If the kid could be spanked or frightened or punished or locked up—all that kind of jazz—they wouldn't be here. We've got to do something different."[14] A lot of the boys, she said, had a constant fear of being crazy, a feeling that most people experience one time or another. The important thing was to help them understand their feelings.

The good days far outnumbered the bad, she observed, telling the story of the youngster who visited her office one day, saying, "I came up to raise a little hell." It seems he was angry about a soap blob on his shirt, which he mistakenly thought had ruined it. Noted Griffin: "He didn't call us a bunch of names." He calmly complained. She took the shirt home, laundered and ironed it, and the next day, in the presence of some staff and boys, returned it to him saying: "This is my way of expressing my appreciation to you on how you handled your anger because you could have been cussin' and screaming and stomping like a lot of kids do, but you handled it like a mature young man." When he said, "Thanks a lot," she responded, "No—thank *you*." She mused that they too often get "caught up in responding to negative behavior." Her act of appreciation took no more than five minutes, but it undoubtedly made a strong impression on the boy. This particular youngster already felt in debt to her. He had truanted earlier and had been gone long enough to be dropped from the rolls, though, said Griffin, "not from our minds." He had called her one night from the police station. He was "scared, cold, and hungry," having lived in abandoned buildings and cars, and was afraid his mother would not come if he called her. Griffin got him back into the program, and he saw her thereafter as "the one who had rescued him."[15]

Griffin said, "When [boys] leave here and get in trouble, that's devastating. When they leave here and wind up destroying themselves, that's debilitating." But more boys succeeded than failed, and many who returned for a visit could attest to that.[16]

Phyllis Griffin was a no-nonsense lady—a tough yet tender woman who brimmed with honesty and good will. She left plenty of room for fun in her treatment philosophy.

A Profile: Bill Burgess

Phyllis Griffin's coworker Bill Burgess, chief of operations, grew up in a home that welcomed children. He remembered the place crawling with neighborhood youngsters and friends, all happily playing, smiling, and sharing his mom's freshly baked cookies. The younger kids had always seemed to gravitate toward him and he enjoyed organizing their play across the street at the park. Thus, when after an eight-year Air Force stint he learned of an opening at the republic from a friend, he applied. It was March 1965 and he remembers his interview well.

He had expected a lot of questions in a long interview, but within a short time Gordon Boring said: "Keep smiling and go out and hit the line." Said Burgess: "It was kind of in the back of my mind—what is hitting the line?" He was tested the very first day at lunch. The six boys at his table seemed uncharacteristically quiet for troubled youngsters. He attributed their silent watchfulness to curiosity about what manner of person this new cottage counselor was. They were probably trying to figure him out, just as he was them. He'll never forget the menu—hot dogs and beans—and with good reason. When he asked one youngster to pass the ketchup, the quiet grew more intense. One squeeze of the plastic bottle was all it took to cause the jimmied cap to fall and the ketchup to explode. The whole dining hall erupted in laughter. Burgess did not recall his exact response, but he knew he joined in, saying something like: "That's pretty good" or "I'll get you back."

He remembered being hard put to stay indoors during the summer months when there was so much playing to do outside. He loved being with the boys, both supervising and taking part in their play. Eventually he got into full-time recreation work, going from supervisor of recreation in 1967 to group work supervisor. He was instrumental in starting the on-site Learning Center for remedial tutorial work in 1982.

Burgess felt that his job had brought him greater self-awareness and was invaluable in helping him rear his own children. Sometimes his kids thought his ability to discern a problem before it even fully developed was almost uncanny. Said Burgess: "You learn to notice things—expressions on faces." He remembered Saturday afternoons when, exhausted from a morning of work at the republic, he would return to his home right across the street and find his son, ball and bat in hand, waiting for his turn at play. The boy had a good vantage point for witnessing Burgess "running around in the recreation program" and would say, "I told you if you can go over there and play you could come home and have fun." So Bill would forego his Kool-Aid, his lemonade, his rest, and would "drag" himself out for an afternoon workout.

Burgess's sensitivity to signs of distress also served him in inspiring trust and in developing close relationships with the boys. He noted, "Our relationships have a goal—to bring about change— to be nice, care about, and love them, too, but we want to help them to change." He understood the underlying motivation that drove the boys. A new resident who truanted, for example, might not be resisting placement as much as filling a need to see family or a girlfriend after what might have been a lengthy incarceration at the juvenile home while waiting for hearings and placement. "They'll come back," he said. There were some days when Burgess wondered what he was doing there, why he would be "beating [his] head against the wall." On those days, when the kids were "bouncing off each other," he would get tired. But then a day would come when everything seemed to fall in place, when the kids would get along and allow therapy to take place, and he would leave work elated.

Though Burgess's involvement was intense, he came across as easygoing, thoroughly relaxed. He was warm, likable, accessible, and was able to put others at ease. He said that if he were to win the lottery, he would get new cottages for the boys, ranch-style ones, each with its own dining facility.[17]

A Profile: Mark Sperling

Mark Sperling felt that his life was bound inextricably with that of the republic. He would not have guessed from his first experience at the republic on February 10, 1971, that would be the case one day. He was there for a job interview and by the time it was over, he was thoroughly confused. Three people talked to him in succession, each one picking up where the last had ended. He learned later that an employee had struck a child and an emergency administrative meeting had been called. All he knew then was that this seemed to be a "very mysterious place with people running in and out of offices." That did not stop him from accepting the position two days later.

Sperling had always been interested in teaching and working with kids. He was a graduate of Oakland Community College and had a bachelor's degree in sociology and social work from the University of Detroit and a master's degree from Eastern Michigan University and envisioned getting back into the classroom eventually. He thrived on personal involvement and felt it was essential for administration to keep in touch with the kids.

Sperling said that the "only constant at the republic has been change, change as the type of clients have changed and varied in degree." He felt that the major factor that had made the republic such an "outstanding residential treatment center has been its dynamic director Gordon Boring and his and the institution's ability to change along with its clients." He thought it essential to keep a very thin piece of glass between himself and everything else. Not to do so was to become emotionally and physically drained. But the good days were so satisfying that, "as the kids call it, you're all geeked up." And those days were more numerous than bad ones.

The memory of one tragic experience would never leave him, however. He was enjoying much success with a Boy Scout chapter on the grounds. The boys were enthusiastic and therapy was going well. During one troop outing, however, despite admonitions from a water safety instructor and close guard, a youngster leapt from a dock into treacherous weeds beyond the marked-off safe swimming area. His body had to be dredged out by the emergency squad. All the boys went to the funeral and Sperling always makes a side trip when his visiting his father's grave to Roseville Cemetery where the boy is at rest.

Sperling said, "I have made significant changes in myself, my outlook on the society at large, my personal relations, my ability to discern the importance of the type of work that I do as compared to that which is done in other programs. I have been proud of my accomplishments with clients." Sperling was a competent, analytic person who showed great concern for and interest in his work and in his boys.[18]

A Profile: Frank Harris

When Frank Harris was promoted to administrative assistant in 1975, Boring said of him: "He does an excellent job with boys and personnel alike. He is highly professional, energetic, and innovative. He has demonstrated the potential to handle the . . . position. My level of confidence in [him] is extremely high." It was because of these qualities that Harris was asked to assume the executive directorship in 1984, a post he held until December 1986.

Harris, a certified social worker with a master's degree in clinical psychology, did not feel ready for work with troubled youths back in March 1965 when his cousin told him of an opening at the republic. Interestingly enough, Frank Norah, another stellar figure in republic history, applied and took the position. But when another opening became available in April, Harris took the single most important step in his career.

His interview took place during a crisis. A youngster had fallen from a truck, bruising himself from head to toe. Harris remembered staff running hither and yon, excited and anxious, the boy screaming and crying—certainly an inauspicious moment for a career decision. He had no question, however, that his decision was the right one. In the ensuing twenty-two years, his enthusiasm for his calling never wavered. He remained as committed to working with boys as he was when, as a cottage counselor, he met his first group of twenty-five boys.

Harris saw his relationship with the boys as mainly therapeutic, not too "mushy," not too "palsy," certainly not that of father and child. He "enjoy[ed] their stories" and that helped in "getting along with them." He firmly believed that there was "generally something good in every kid." If at any time there were difficulties, they "invariably [found] the source of the problem."[19]

A Profile: Sally Owen

Sally Owen recalled that it was Frank Harris who first asked her how she would feel if a boy called her a "bleep-bleep." She assured him that as a public school teacher she had already been called just about everything. She found it amusing that the boys initially checked her out to see if she would "fall into a dead faint" at what they said. She noted that she had "learned more about [herself] from this job than any other experience" she had ever had. One thing that always bothered her was the boys' destructiveness. She would have liked to have seen the "incorporation of vocational and trade skills into the school program" and a "more sophisticated work detail operation for the boys on grounds that would encourage more positive upkeep of the Republic."[20]

Owen noted that despite the destructive tendencies of the boys, she "never felt threatened" in her work. According to Griffin, Owen had phenomenal intuition: "She gets these premonitions that 'something's going to happen,'" adding, "Nine times out of ten, she's pretty accurate."[21]

CHANGES IN THE POPULATION

Felicitous staff relationships were not always enough to relieve the strain of working with disturbed youths. Although vastly satisfying, the job was never easy. And in more recent years, boys have had longer histories of pathologies than those in the 1960s. Griffin attributed this to a number of factors, among which was the phenomenon of the troubled children of the 1960s having the troubled children of the 1980s. Too often the 1960s children never did find the "self" they were looking for and hence still were caught in a limbo of indecisiveness, searching, ambiguity, restlessness, and ineffectiveness. They were unable to guide their children effectively because they never gained the confidence and authority to do so. Said Griffin: "They have not yet adjusted to the disturbances and storminess in their own late adolescence and early adulthood. . . . They can't, in terms of the nurturing process, bring their own youngsters any farther along . . . than they themselves were brought." She added: "You have to also treat the parents in terms of helping them to develop more effective parenthood techniques. So it's focusing on the whole family."[22]

Families of the 1960s were generally intact, much like those of the child workers. The children of the 1980s, however, often came from broken homes, with a single parent, usually the mother, trying to raise three or four youngsters either on her own or with a live-in boyfriend. One boy resident had twelve brothers and sisters. Bernice Izner observed, "Often the families are [those] where there are multiple siblings of many fathers—three and four. This is not an exaggeration."[23]

The climate was also altered when the republic stopped accepting private placements, boys who according to Burgess, "were not necessarily street-type kids." Griffin noted that with this change in policy, potential residents had to "go through the whole commitment process: Commit some kind of delinquent act, be adjudicated, committed to the state and then placed at Boys Republic." The road to the republic was strewn with all sorts of misdeeds: property offenses, shoplifting, breaking and entering, and burglary (armed and unarmed). Murderers, sexual deviants, and arsonists were not admitted. The boys generally had an average to low-average IQ, had suffered emotional or physical abuse, and had come from a delinquent family structure. They also likely had been getting away with so much for so long that it was hard for them to understand the seriousness of their actions. Some boys, said Burgess, sold drugs at the behest of their impoverished families. Some stole to provide the family with one of life's niceties, like a radio.[24]

Sperling noted that the kids were not more delinquent but were certainly more disturbed. "The thinking processes seem to be less together." And the 1960s "classic delinquent" was not as hard to deal with. Burgess added that residents of the 1980s had experienced a lot of "emotional trauma." Griffin concurred: "Those kids came with a longer history of delinquency because of the community's tolerance for acting out behavior . . . [and] the longer the history, the more damaged the youngster seems to be."[25]

Early intervention was hampered by the financial crises experienced by so many families those days. Parents who might have been willing to seek help from guidance clinics simply could not afford to and by the time their children went through all the preliminaries toward republic placement, they felt very much removed. When private placement was the norm and families had to bear a percentage of the total cost—about seven dollars a day—they were much more a part of the process, if only, at two hundred dollars a month, to ensure getting the "most of the investment that [they possibly could]," said Griffin.[26]

But the costs of private placement had become prohibitive (seventy dollars a day) and were no longer underwritten by United Community Services funding. In addition, there was no Blue Cross coverage since the facility was neither totally medical nor totally psychiatric. Therefore most client families were on some sort of welfare, noted Sperling, and all the boys were state committed. "Getting parents involved," said Griffin, "is sometimes like pulling eye teeth." Efforts were hampered by "transportation problems, distance from the republic, the working situation, being afraid to travel this distance alone if it's going to get dark." Staff often had to make elaborate arrangements for conferences, sometimes at night in the client's home.[27]

Burgess was saddened by the growing number of boys who came from financially deprived families lacking the wherewithal for providing even adequate meals. Every year the republic sent home Thanksgiving baskets with turkeys and trimmings with particularly needy boys. This simple act gave the boy comforting reassurance that he was not being a burden to his family.

Burgess remembered kids who gobbled down large quantities of food and drink when they first arrived at the republic. He saw one youngster down eighteen small boxes of cereal; some boys drank as many as four or five pints of milk. Because most came from families "in which there is only just so much milk to go around, where meals might be limited to one a day," these kids were hungry. He worried about their being released and returned to homes where the financial situation remained poor.[28] All staff members who were on the grounds during breakfast, lunch, and dinner ate with the boys because mealtimes often provided opportunities to talk with the boys on a deeper level.

Breakfast time was a lot quieter than most meals, perhaps because, as Sperling observed, "kids aren't as awake." While there were fewer at lunch during a school week, that could be the "most anxious meal" said Griffin. Sperling added, "Certain meals will set kids off" if they do not like what is being served. Griffin added: "The meals are interesting because there's a different side of the kids that comes out . . . a lot of times kids' food really triggers a lot of very unpleasant memories." She continued: "They are remembering or thinking about some of the kids at home that may not be eating as well. That may be the kid that is making the most complaints about the food because he has some guilt feelings about eating three squares a day. At home, he may not get but one meal a day." Some were so angry about getting food that they would throw it away. Anger, said Griffin, might also be the result of "bad experiences . . . during the nurturing process." Added Sperling: "Food is love." The boys looked forward to their bedtime snack of Hostess cakes and milk or juice.[29]

Griffin recalled a youngster who always had to have a full plate of food. The minute there was a dent in his serving, he'd fill the plate up again. Then he'd throw the whole thing away. Griffin put an end to the practice by one day making him clean his plate. She remembered that this boy, a republic citizen for two and a half years, cried constantly. She often had him in her office just so he could sit down and cry.[30]

Sperling observed that the "population of youngsters in residence at any one time appears to be reflective of the events in the outside world [that is, the ending of the Vietnam War in the early 1970s, the experimental drug culture, economic trends]." The recessionary trends of the 1980s "caused many of the parents . . . and clients not to be as anxious [to have] home weekend visits. Parents had . . . verbalized their concern about the quality of life that they are able to provide in view of the economic hardship they experience," he said.

The republic's population in the 1980s was a little more heavily black than previously—about 65 percent—but demographics were constantly changing. Generally when an institution reached a fifty-fifty balance, racial tensions increased, but for the most part this had not been so at the republic, observed Griffin.[31] Staff stressed the importance of leaving behind prejudices and working together on their common problem. In addition, the republic made a serious effort not to segregate the population. If, for example, a black coalition seemed to be forming in a particular cottage, the boys would be reassigned.

Fewer boys were accepted in the 1980s, making caseloads much more manageable. In the 1960s, the population soared to 102, but in the 1970s, dropped to 75. In the 1980s, the population was stable at 65, with the upper cottages housing 14 or 15 boys each and the lower 13 each. The population saw a 50 percent changeover every year, said Sperling, with 100 percent renewal every one and a half years. In the 1960s boys might have stayed as long as three or four years, but a later state mandate called for getting the boys out as quickly as possible, usually within nine months to a year. Short-term therapy was realistic, concluded Griffin, a sure measurement of a facility's "credibility and viability." In addition, "most kids need to see that there is an end to the 'time' they do." They wanted to know when they were going to "get out." It was hard for them to conceptualize the treatment concept. Some were eager to learn, some had a superficial interest, and "some never buy it at all." Another problem with long-term commitment was that the boy might get too comfortable, which, of course, was antithetical to the republic's goal of getting him to the point where he could function within his own community. Griffin had no trouble with the pressure to show results within a year. Some boys stayed longer if necessary; no one would have been released if he seemed unready.[32]

When bad things happened, the staff got together, providing support and comfort. But they had open case conferences every day. Overlapping work days helped in communicating information about the boys. Group work staff came in at 3:00, and clinicians were there one and a half to two hours longer. Also a clinician was on duty during the week. Each gave one evening a week. Many used that evening to talk with evening staff about problems with particular boys. Staff meetings were also held regularly. Griffin attributed much of the staff closeness to Boring because of the "way he handled himself around us. He called us the kid's family, the only family he has."[33]

THE BOARD

An organization is only as good as its board of directors, those overseers who must provide guidance and support but know when to step back; who must be responsive to the needs of staff even if these needs do not coincide with their own vision of the purpose, function, and operational direction of the organization; and who must be ready for emergencies, for times of upheaval, and for putting their resources toward projects that benefit the institution and the community. The board of directors of the Boys Republic has always met these criteria, often exceeding expectations. Through the years it has figured heavily in the program and has served the community well.

Right from the start the board monitored operations without interference, trusting the integrity, commitment, and competence of its staff. It stood behind the republic concept in times of uncertainty and adversity, providing advice, reinforcement, and the monetary wherewithal to ensure quality care and effective programming. Noted Gordon Boring: "This group has been, in all my experience, an outstanding, caring, considerate, supportive group of people who are attempting to do whatever they can to help more unfortunate people in their community." In that capacity, they provided the first temporary shelter for juveniles apart from adults, gave funds to establish the first psychiatric unit at the Detention Home, later known as the Wayne County Clinic for Child Study, gave funds to provide dental care at the Detention Home two days a week, and allocated $13,000 to secure a psychiatrist to direct the clinic and funds to conduct a survey of the Cleveland Juvenile Court to compare with the survey completed in Detroit. In 1931 they sent police to study at the University of Chicago. The police established the Crime Prevention Bureau, later called the Youth Bureau. Throughout the years, board members have represented many walks of life, often appearing a microcosm of the urban area. Corporate executives, bankers, clergy, journalists, housewives, community leaders, service employees, attorneys, and law enforcement officers have served. At one time the membership included the secretary of state and the lieutenant governor of Michigan. But always it has included persons of wealth and modest means, of both widespread and modest influence, some of national or statewide prominence, some known only to the city or their own families. All have shown a generosity of spirit and a determination to help those who would one day lead—or fail to lead. The board has always been dedicated to the idea that many youngsters, afforded a second chance, will follow the path toward respect for the laws of the community, toward respect for themselves and all members of the community.[34]

THE PHYSICAL PLANT

The physical facilities have changed throughout the years, most notably in 1957 when the entire operation was moved to its present site, but one thing remains constant—the need for repairs and updating. In 1979 the cottage area was renovated, with carpeting replacing tiles, with night-lights, privacy screens, and dressers with drawers added to each room, and with a television and living room in each cottage. The three upper cottages had game rooms and living rooms with a television and the lower, smaller cottages had combined television and game rooms. Each cottage had three showers, one room with three showerheads. Boys were no longer separated according to maturity levels.

Other repairs and renovation were definitely in order. The offices were too small—and kids needed room, although, as Sperling observed, most therapy took place elsewhere. The administration building was inadequate—indeed antiquated. Griffin remembered that back in 1969 she certainly was not impressed with the looks of the place. And ten years later the place looked the same. The buildings were sadly in need of work. Still, there was a gym, a swimming pool, arts and crafts room, a table game area, a learning center, and an infirmary in addition to the cottages and administrative/clinical building—certainly enough room to meet the needs of the boys. There was also on-grounds housing for a few staff: a counselor, a program coordinator, and five supervisors. In addition, Harris and Sperling lived nearby. These people served well as back-up. When the weather was bad and staff had trouble getting in, they were there, sometimes even cooking breakfast for the kids.

The boys had a laundry service provided by an extension of the kitchen staff, but they were responsible for washing the walls and cleaning around the cottages. They could earn small amounts of money by trimming the bushes, cutting the grass with a push mower, and picking up paper. The residents did what they could to keep the place in order, and the outward appearance did not reflect the inner operation.[35]

THE BOYS AND THEIR TREATMENT

The Boys Republic of the 1980s was still a dynamic organization devoted to helping troubled youngsters adjust to and function effectively in a troubled world. The boys came with a full referral packet, containing a social history as well as psychological and educational information and review. Sperling called the institution an "eclectic agency with an analytic base." It was neo-Freudian, neo-analytic, but "not pure anything." It looked at all possibilities before determining the kind of therapeutic approach for a boy. Said Sperling: "Our kids aren't perfect neurotics . . . we can't use a classic Freudian mode." Therapy "happens at meals, bedtime, wake-up time."[36]

As reported by Phyllis Griffin, Dr. Izner took all new boys off medication, feeling it was important for staff to see their "raw behavior." Without access to the real boy, they could not make intelligent diagnoses or determinations. Staff monitored behavior and progress closely, and many times medication did not have to be reintroduced. Bed-wetters might have been treated with Tofranil, but it was coupled with behavioral treatment—being awakened two to three times a night to "increase muscle control and capacity of the bladder."[37]

In the 1980s the average boy probably received over one hundred and fifty hours of office therapy during his stay, but staff agreed that some of the best therapy occurred outside the confines of a single room. Hallway conferences, noted Sally Owen, often yielded "as qualitative a contact" as any. Sperling concurred:

"Sometimes the best interviews happen spontaneously on the lawn, walking around, sitting down with the youngster, sitting on the side of the bridge, going to the gym." He added, "Offices are not necessarily made to do therapy." He told of one boy whose inner demons led him to curl up in a fetal position in a construction pipe. His counselor would crawl in there with him and conduct the session.[38]

Some kids needed this kind of therapeutic contact three or four times a day, said Griffin. They might have seen either Izner or Boring in addition to the clinician. She said: "There are several people giving several hours to one kid. . . . It could be several staff members, several hundred hours."[39]

Most of the boys were released after they had completed nine to twelve months. The exact time was carefully determined by all staff members who had been involved with a particular boy. The most important factors to consider were as follows: How did the boy relate and respond to peers, adults, school? How had the boy changed during his residence? How did he handle family visits? How did he act in a group? Were his relationships with other boys, staff, and family getting stronger? Did his family seem to understand him better, and did he seem to understand them better? Did he identify and respond to feelings appropriately? Was he adaptable and flexible? How did he handle crises? Did he display good judgment? What kind of success had he had with his particular kind of therapy? The determination of the boy's readiness for the outside world came mostly from observable behavior. Said Griffin: "We try to make an assessment from every aspect of the kid's life." She found it interesting that so often the staff could conclude "spontaneously" that a particular boy was "ready" to leave.[40]

Bernice Izner noted that she looked at each new boy with an eye toward where he would go from there: "There is no point in keeping him if we cannot make a plan." The first choice would always be the home, but often that was not viable. Second choice might be a group home or halfway house. If the boy was old enough, staff members might recommend independent living. By thinking of the end at the beginning, staff could determine which boys could "benefit from [the] facilities" and which boys did not "have quite the inner controls to deal with such an open setting."[41]

"Inner controls" were developed and monitored through an elaborate, somewhat complex merit point system that, once mastered, served as an effective way of keeping the boys apprised of their standing. The boys were awarded points, or hours, for positive behavior. These hours applied toward home visitations. A youngster earning ten points a day with fifty hours a week would have been doing exceptionally well. He needed fifty-two points for a three-day visit and after reaching forty hours was given a two-hour credit. Boys were awarded points daily for interaction, cooperation, effort in school and treatment, and attitude by the staff members who spent the most time with them. They could earn four hours daily from 7 A.M. to 3 P.M., five hours from 3 P.M. to 11 P.M., and one hour from 11 P.M. to 9 A.M. the next morning. Behavior that was not positive would not be awarded points; negative behavior might also be fined, though a consistently poor attitude might be an indication of a lack of "psychic strength" necessary for residency. Such a boy would receive a placement review hearing. Necessary action might include return to the detention home or referral to a more structured institution.

DOCUMENTATION OF BOY BEHAVIOR

The republic of the 1980s, though state supported, was still very much a private agency with its own board of directors. It was not subject to civil service rules and at no time needed state approval for any policy decisions. The board appointed its own director. The state did, however, affix per diem rates.

With state involvement came an increase in paperwork, but Griffin had no quarrel with that. Despite quarterly statistical reports, quarterly reports on each youngster for his state worker, written treatment plans, release summaries, a sixty- to ninety-day summary of adjustment, and interim paperwork and letters, Griffin did not feel unduly taxed. She welcomed these controls

and checks, remembering all too well the tales of abuse and misuse during the early years. One thing that worried her about a
program being mostly state funded was that if the "state runs out
of money, you are in trouble," having put "all your eggs in one
basket." Griffin and Boring were instrumental in developing the
state rules, seeing a need for rigid standards: "Regular monitoring
is essential. It's a pain, but it has to be done. You get some clowns
in the system that you have to get out."[42]

The republic still had a Big Brother system, but a shorter term
one, a couple of days at most, to acquaint the new person with
supervisors, staff, boys counselors, and cottage routine. The Old
Boys' Day and periodic Open House Days had been discontinued,
primarily because family financial situations had changed. Some
families did not have cars and others could not afford public transportation. The Jaycees came out once a year and served the boys
a hot dog lunch and played baseball with them, but generally the
boys had few visitors. In a way, many of the boys needed that protected time away from the outside world.

Bill Burgess observed that home visits were often problematic
and sometimes followed by "regression" because the home "environment had not changed." If the boy changed but everything
else was in stasis, trouble was inevitable. "A lot of times when they
[come] back, they . . . either displace on other kids, on the staff,
or even the buildings."[43]

Sperling said he would rather have them break a window or
put a hole in the wall than hurt someone. He said the boys dealt
with their feelings by acting out. And it was better for them to
"beat the heck out of the physical facilities . . . than beat each
other up." Eventually they learned how to channel their anger
differently. In the meantime, they had some responsibility for
replacing or repairing the object of their destruction and the act
itself was used as a tool toward gaining greater understanding and
self-awareness.[44]

Griffin told of a time when boys in one cottage were creating
all sorts of chaos, swearing, acting belligerent. It was a little while
before staff discovered that a night man was bringing in drugs for

the kids—not selling—just trying to make them happy. That, said Griffin, was "his way of relating" to them. In regard to the response of the kids when the man was found out, she said, "No matter how rough and tough they want to present themselves, they still are very dependent, very frightened, and need to know that the adults responsible for them are actually in control." They responded with relief that things were back in control. They needed to feel protected. "These kids have missed out on so much nurturing. The biggest and toughest can be the biggest and softest." Therefore, while "their code won't let them narc on anybody," they are happy when the secret is out.[45]

Burgess spoke affectionately about the boys and was particularly amused when they complained about "too many trees, not enough noise, too much quiet." He recalled one particularly immature twelve-year-old he thought would not last two days. He came upon him "literally bouncing from one bed to another and hollering and screaming." Their eyes met and they both laughed, forming an immediate therapeutic relationship. One day, the youngster queried him: "Burg—don't get offended when I ask you this because I haven't related to black people a lot, but do you have a little tail?" Burgess smiled, said no, and asked why he had ever thought so. The boy responded: "Where I come from they think black people have little tails." The relationship between the two continued to develop and the boy stayed on for two years.

Burgess said that the boys themselves taught him how to work with kids. His greatest thrill comes from meeting an ex-resident, seeing him functioning effectively in a more traditional and normal setting. He most often meets former residents in the shopping centers during the holiday seasons. He told of one who dragged him "all over Northland" so that he could introduce him to his wife: "You don't get the rewards today. You get them down the line."

He recalled a computer analyst, wearing a three-piece striped suit, stopping by to thank him. He remembered meeting an ex-resident at a 7–11, which turned out to be an unnerving experience. A large, husky member of a crew working on the parking

lot had followed him into the convenience store and was watching him closely. Not many black people lived in Farmington at
the time and Burgess was apprehensive. When the man grabbed
and lifted him off the ground, he "thought [he] was being attacked." The ex-republic boy was bouncing him up and down,
saying, "Burg, Burg—that's my crew out there—this is my business. I want you to meet these guys."[46]

A "Typical" Day

There was no such thing as a typical day at the Boys Republic
in the 1980s. "The word 'typical,'" said Sally Owen, "is a real
misnomer around here because of what we're dealing with. . . .
Things aren't typical around here [as they might be] in a business
office." It was possible to come in with an agenda, but chances
were something would have happened the night before to alter
it. Monday mornings following weekend home visitations were
often tension filled. She said: "Terrible things happen. There's a
lot of spontaneity involved in this job, and you've got to be flexible
enough."[47]

Group worker Larry Rashad agreed that a typical day would be
a carryover from the night before. Afternoon staff coming in at
2:50 P.M. had to check to make sure all were accounted for, get
updates from the A.M. staff, go through the cottages, and get a
damage report.

For Griffin, the ideal day would have run thusly:

> The kids would get involved in some wholesome recreational
> activities, interact with each other harmoniously, get along
> really well, and do what they're expected to do—in terms of
> going to the dining hall and having a peaceful meal. Instead
> of saying "pass me the blink-blink potatoes," [they'd say] "pass
> me the potatoes, please." Then they'd go to bed at 9:30, sleep
> until 7 A.M., get up, wash [she noted that many of the kids
> were allergic to soap and water], clean up their rooms, make

their beds, go to breakfast, be ready for school at 9:00 with *all* kids in good enough shape for school, return at 2:30. There would be no kid crises, no staff crises, and daytime staff would be able to go home some time that evening.[48]

But it was not like this at all. This is why, observed Owen, they avoided setting up tight time schedules that might have to be broken. Sperling remembered thinking at first that the program was too flexible, that the boys were given too much freedom. It did not take him long to see the "necessity for flexibility in setting up a viable treatment plan allowing the youngster to achieve maximum emotional growth."[49]

Group worker Tom Palmer also thought initially that the "boys had too much freedom and the staff was too lax." He realized later that freedom was necessary if the boys were to get their anxiety out. Group work supervisor Greg Chapman was similarly concerned about the seeming casualness in the program: "My initial impression was that of a large day camp. All the residents seemed to be having a great time." He soon appreciated "the work involved and the training needed to be able to effectively deal with clients." Bill Robertson could not get the "negative stigma of institutions" out of his mind at first, thinking that the environment had to be bad, but he became a convert. He knew that the program might appear casual, but it was very much goal oriented. The casual air was fostered by the staff's wanting to see boys in a relaxed and "natural setting." "Expressive behavior" was encouraged so its nature and degree could be witnessed and then dealt with, though, added Gordon Boring, you did not want to relax to the point that the boys were denied a "sense of limitations or a sense of security or a sense of guidance." Said Robertson, "We could . . . have a very regimented program in which there wouldn't be an argument in a basketball game or a kid wouldn't be lying around in his room, but then we wouldn't get a look at what that kid is really about." The program tended to "move away from heavily structured things to allow [the boys] a little bit of opportunity for self-expression [so that] staff [can] 'key in' . . . make certain observations and . . . intervene" in meaningful ways. Staff looked for such factors as the degree to which a boy tried to dominate a game or show off, or be self-effacing, or stay in the background; the way the boy handled frustration or disappointment; and whether he was selfish, or wanted to do everything himself. Said Clinic Director Dave Hamel: "There are important factors in evaluating a kid's personality and how he handles other situations. It all ties in together with all the treatment aspects. The more a kid is able to express himself, within reasonable limits, the more helpful it is for us to make an evaluation to see what is going on with this kid and what he needs to work on. It's easier for him to see it too." He added, "These boys are impaired in some way in their ability to develop a healthy relationship with an adult—one in which they feel somewhat safe, and feel some emotional support. This is most clearly seen in boys who come back after their stay." They came to see staff, not other boys.[50]

An interesting dynamic came into play when a physical confrontation threatened to erupt. Generally the boys were more apt to be boisterous or aggressive when a staff member was near, knowing full well that he or she would intervene. Often "let's knock it off" would settle the dispute, according to group worker Gary Beaufait. And sometimes the kid would admit to not being angry with the person, just "restless and edgy." The staff often could anticipate a problem and head it off. Said Dave Hamel:

> The louder and more angry and upset the youngster is, the calmer and softer your voice should be. For a boy who is really angry, really upset, I will repeat the words over and over again—in as benign and mild a manner as possible: 'It'll be all right. We'll work this out. It's O.K. You don't have to go through all this.' Just something repetitive, just to reassure him that he's okay, he's safe now. Generally there's fear under all that, there's anxiety underneath all that the boy's going through. The reassuring presence of someone who is in control and is going to protect [him]—will be the major thing that will calm him down.[51]

He added: "The staff tries helping the kid learn to control [his] raw impulses."[52]

Owen noticed that boys angered to the verge of physical contact would hold off if a female staff member was the only one present, knowing she would not be able to pry them apart. Then, as soon as a male staff member or larger kids came in, they would go to it; it was "safe to fight." She remembered that happening in the gym once: "These kids went around and around in circles for twenty or twenty-five minutes. 'Come on, do something. Come on, let's go. Come on.' Round and around and around. . . . Nobody did anything. They wouldn't listen to me, they wouldn't listen to the other kids. . . . [They were] all heated up and sweaty and ready. When two larger boys walked in . . . POOF. The kids . . . pried them apart."

Hamel concurred that the staff member must take the role of emotional leader: "His emotional tone—the way he is carrying himself, the way he is projecting himself—has an awful lot to do with how the youngsters and their activities are to go. . . . Our approach is one that is very challenging and very taxing and, at the same time, very rewarding. It is somewhat draining." Gary Beaufait observed: "Staff has to be resourceful, very persistent" in showing the boys how to handle their anger in "more socially acceptable ways." Hamel said that almost all the boys knew right from wrong but had to learn to understand what made them lose control and then, when the stressful situation arose, learn to say to themselves: "Don't lose it. You know what happens . . . in this situation, so try something else." Some kids, however, failed to see the "social aspects of right and wrong." They saw right and wrong only as it related to them, "what's right and wrong for me."

Larry Rashad noted that sometimes they could talk until they were "blue in the face about what's right or what's wrong" without getting through to a kid, but then a group situation would drive a point home. A kid might brag about stealing and another might say, "Well, that's fine . . . but if you steal from me, I'll knock your block off." Added Rashad, "The message can get across in various ways. I guess what it takes is what works. You try to use every kind of approach you can." Gary Beaufait said, "There are some instances where you feel what you have to do is prepare the boy as best you can to go back into a less than healthy situation. Try to give as many strengths and help him develop as many insights as he can so that he can manage himself despite what goes on at home." Sometimes parents were not willing to cooperate. Some wanted to forget their kids altogether.[53]

THE RECREATION PLAN

Recreation at the Boys Republic was designed around treatment concepts. Boys learned social skills and could gain a sense of fair play. For the most part the program steered clear of highly competitive activities, and with good reason. New boys seldom knew how to harness anger and were volatile and unpredictable. They needed to learn how to interact and compete without conflict. They needed to build up to competitive activities slowly. The boys did not compete in sports outside the republic because external controls became a problem. If a skirmish arose on the grounds, staff could intervene; in public, the potential for trouble was too great. In addition, when competition was high, recreation directors were more apt to select the best and strongest athletes and overlook others. The republic preferred recreation programs that encouraged active involvement by everyone. Noted board member William Billups: "A program centering around a team reduces the participation of other boys to pure spectators." It was important for every kid to get a chance to play—even the smallest, the weakest. The republic also had to guard against the kind of fever that would erupt if a few of the boys showed real talent. They had to suppress any urges to build a strong team, a team that could compete outside.[54]

Former school principal Rudolph Yanke felt there were too many emotional scars when an institution allowed itself to have star athletes: "I don't want to become melodramatic in this thing, but who is going to be the [one assigned to] 'picking up' the kid" who was crying somewhere "waiting for bedtime to come" because he hadn't been picked for the team and thought of himself as having "flunked out?"[55]

Dave Hamel noted that divergent activities sometimes enabled counselors to pinpoint particular problems. A boy who seemed withdrawn, preferring to watch television or listen to the radio, would be encouraged to engage in less passive activities. A competitive youngster given to outbursts during sports would be guided toward other ways of dealing with frustration. Hamel recalled a "generally fine, kind, cooperative, polite" youngster who changed radically when involved in any kind of competition, even a card game, and was apt to "pop somebody in the face" when things did not go his way. He explained that treatment needs often became crystal clear during recreation times through observations of what a "kid is involved in or not involved in . . . or how he chooses to spend him time." Bill Robertson noted that most often staff would get the activity started and then would pull out.[56]

Bill Burgess liked recreation that taught skills or helped expend energy such as swimming, frisbee, and the ever-popular Capture the Flag. He conferred with the boys to see what they wanted to do; he encouraged all to take part. While involvement was mandatory for home visitation points, he tried gentle urgings at first. He'd speak to a boy about how he was isolating himself and how his goal should be to "get out and interact, grow emotionally." After a week or two, more structured approaches might seem appropriate. Staff might try to devise an activity that would complement a boy's interests or talents. Once the boy was there for a while, he usually became involved.[57]

Gary Beaufait thought that open, honest discussion usually worked best. He'd ask a boy who set himself apart if he was "trying to stay away from kids" or if he was "nervous" or "afraid." It was important, he said, to convey the fact that your interest in getting him involved was part of the treatment process, that it fit in directly with the program that had been established for him. The more he knew about what you were trying to do, the more he would cooperate. He said that they took "mental notes" while watching the boys at play, which later were logged and then used in the treatment plan.[58]

Bill Burgess felt that the people at the republic might not have been able to change a boy's environment, but they could help him "forget it" and learn how to deal with it. They had given up forays into gardening some years earlier because small wild animals—and jealousy—had abounded, but there was not much they had not tried. He thought that the VCR was a real blessing because the kids could see good movies without having to be exposed to the controls necessary in public places and they could get away from regular television, which became boring at times.

They had plenty on the grounds to keep them busy: arts and crafts, ceramics, woodworking, drawing—almost anything, depending on "who can teach what." There were radio, model building, and auto repair clubs. Sperling's office was graced with model cars the boys had built, including one given in gratitude by a youngster at having been accepted at the republic. The boys could also fish in the ravine.

Burgess recalled camping days, which in his estimation were invaluable. It was easier to build more intense relationships faster in the outdoor environment. The closeness, the sense of overcoming hurdles together, helped bond the staff and the boys. And boys got to see the human side of the staff. The boys thought that staff members were not supposed to "get angry or upset. Staff were not human." He added: "They think we're magical people because of our patience. They can't believe we have family problems or get upset or cry sometimes." Once, when he hurt himself in a basketball game, a kid said, "Hey—you're not supposed to bleed."[59]

Former residents liked to recall games they used to play and things they used to make, he said. One talked to him about the hammocks they fashioned. Another recalled a little guy they used to toss in a blanket. Frank Harris remembered the fun they used to have with some military surplus parachutes, big ones used for dropping trucks. On a windy day the kids would catch the air currents until the chute became a huge tent. They'd run around inside and then try to get out before the thing collapsed. Burgess added: "You'd try to get out [before] the guys on the outside . . . pounded you flat." The boys often tried to get the staff in. Eventually the game became a little too rough and had to be discontinued.[60]

Capture the Flag was particularly popular. Harris remembered how much he loved joining in: "It would be funny—a lot of times [as a supervisor] I'd be down in the glen, running around playing [it] with the kids and somebody would say 'Frank, we got a problem up here.' So I'd come up the hill, sweating and wet from the mud and stuff, while having to meet some parent . . . and say, 'My name is Frank Harris. I'm the Group Work Director.' It was fun." Burgess explained that the game involved "running, tagging, hiding and creeping up" and that's what the boys liked the most— "the hiding and creeping up and the sneak attacks." They also liked the game best, said Harris, when the creek was "almost full of water." Although they were not supposed to go in the creek, most managed to get wet from "head to toe." Burgess said: "The one good thing about it [was] whether you were small, large, [or] medium . . . everybody could play. Everybody had a role . . . and if you were small and fast, that's even better."[61]

SCHOOL DAYS

Gordon Boring said that probably one of the most significant things that happened during his tenure was the transfer of education responsibility from the republic to the Farmington School District. At first the boys were taught on the republic campus; then the Farmington School Administration decided it might be easier to handle them at the public school; finally they were housed in an empty facility near the grounds.

One immediate problem was that the boys who were sent off on the school bus each morning were generally the kind that gave teachers the biggest headaches. And when former republic teachers were employed by and hence came under the jurisdiction of the Farmington Board of Education, they were expected to hold to the tenets of that governing body, emphasizing education rather than treatment.[62] Although, as Rudolph Yanke observed, "public school acceptance was unusually good," a rift developed between educators and therapists.[63]

Said Phyllis Griffin, "The major difference between the two [systems] is that we both look at behavior entirely differently," one as good and bad and the other as healthy and unhealthy. "We feel that many times their responses to the kids' expressive behavior is essentially a reward for the kid—and that is to put him out of the school building." He was "excluded from the building for behavior [he was] placed there for."[64]

Sperling saw the problem in much the same way: "Their ideas, educationally, are different from our ideas, clinically. . . . The schools came in with the idea that they could magically make our kids learn. It doesn't work that way. We don't magically make anything happen." At first the faculty "expected [the kids] to function under normal rules, under normal circumstances, under regular school codes." Not having had exposure to "these kinds of kids," they did not understand that "our kids just aren't that obedient."[65] And Bernice Izner, while sympathetic to the plight of regular teachers, understanding why it would be "difficult for them to tolerate the negative behavior of our kids," felt that the punitive action of suspension undercut the program of therapy.[66]

At first republic boys, in Sperling's view, were "treated as step-children—[with an] attitude of 'we are forced to take care of you.'" Griffin recalled a time when neither republic staff nor boys were so much as permitted to enter the school building. Republic people, though technically a part of the educational system, were to stay apart and isolated. This is no longer the case, although Griffin didn't mind a general segregation from the rest of the school population because there were both fewer controls and fewer temptations. She felt that while suspensions used to be handed out too readily, they might have been in order for kids who, experiencing failure in that building, were not being done any good anyway. "It takes a lot to like these kids," she said. "You have to work at that." And the boys knew this. They shared an antipathy toward formal education and a belief, or understanding, that teachers did not like them, said Sperling. He noted also that republic teachers were often more successful than public school teachers in restoring order in the classroom.[67]

Sperling regretted the loss of continuity in having teachers employed by the school board. "They used to come over and have lunch with the kids—they'd share with them—and food is so important to the kids." Instead teachers would go out to lunch and leave at 3:00 instead of mingling. Everyone understood, though, that the school was under limitations in regard to what it could allow or do and all agreed that things were improving. The transitional period was tough, however.[68]

During this time, some of the boys were in the regular high school, some at Shiawassee Center, some at the Oakland County Vocational School, and a few on the grounds under the tutelage of a Farmington teacher. The latter were the ones who were difficult to handle, who might get physical, who might, said Griffin, "present themselves as a threat to the kids or teachers." On-grounds schooling ran from 9:00 to 12:00, followed in the afternoon by an educational film or videotape.[69]

Harris was pleased with the progress in ironing out the problems. He observed: "We will always have differing philosophies, that won't change, but we're doing the best for the kids under the circumstances." He said that most of the boys were functioning at low levels in reading, math, and science. A small percentage were school phobics. He took a practical approach when discussing schooling with the boys. He explained that an education often meant the difference between having a choice of jobs and taking ones that people gave them. He noted that most boys did return to school and he told them that he wanted to get them "in the best shape" he could so that when they returned to the public school system they would "not have the same problems."[70]

Bill Burgess also thought it better for kids to attend school off grounds, since "eventually they have to be able to deal with the normal school teacher." Kids would come back and say, "He's mean, not like you guys," and Burgess would have to explain that the teacher just did not have the time or energy to deal with special problems. He told the kids that they could not "sneak smoke and will have to get used to that." He urged them not to "contag the rest of the class." He explained that on grounds, staff could accommodate them, could be more flexible, but in a regular school, students were expected to adjust, to fit in. Most often the boys understood. Burgess thought that in addition to providing a real-life situation, this setup gave the boys a chance to get off the grounds. Some boys also had part-time jobs after school in the community, which often led to later employment when they left the republic, which took away street time and provided them with money.[71]

Gordon Boring had mixed feelings about the school merger. He believed that the republic was "extremely successful in operating an educational program under Mr. Yanke's direction." Yanke, he said, did "an excellent job, worked very hard, had some tremendous teachers," and added, "We were upgrading our teachers all the time. We had to [sometimes] hire nonqualified people but they were going to school and so forth, until finally all of our people had special education degrees." He doubted, however, that children's homes would one day regain control over the schooling of their charges, even though he believed doing so would be much easier and "more profitable."[72]

DETERMINATION OF SUCCESS RATES

Statistics seldom provide absolute proof of anything. According to the state, a youngster who is sent to a group home within 90 to 180 days after release from an institution is considered a failure, even though the group home option might be the best one for him and is not an indication of failure at all. On the other hand, a boy who truants but stays out of trouble for the same period of time is considered a success. But is one successful if one merely does not fail? What about the youngster who does the very best that he can for himself? Even with the problems of definition, 75 percent of republic graduates have achieved some measure of success. Their own words may serve as a testament.

One boy said, "When I saw no bars or fences, and the people were nice and tried to help me, I couldn't resist being good. I tried to be the other way at first, but it didn't work." Another thought the clinic was a "good deal when a guy had things on his chest, like when I went home on a visit and found my Dad didn't like me. . . . When I was given some responsibility, even after running away, this was encouragement from the staff. I knew I was wanted and could go through the program."[73]

A resident from the 1930s remembered when counselor Sam Rabinovitz damaged the fender on his 1935 or 1936 Chevy and asked him to bang it out: "I was sure I didn't do that great a job, but he praised me for what I done. I was just a young kid. I don't know what he paid me. He was very fair. Chances are that after I got it done, he went out and got it fixed. That's the kind of man that he was—he was a very good man." He added: "I used my democratic experience at the Ford Republic in raising my own sons." Another resident from the 1930s noted: "My initial impressions and reactions of and to the home were mixed with dismay, skepticism, and suspicion. However, my fears were rather quickly dispelled [and] as time went by I gained confidence in the staff and home mostly due to the skillful attention administered to me and the rest of the resident body." He concluded: "I shudder to think of what I might have become if I had not acquired a sense of responsibility, which I'm sure I did during my residency at the home."[74]

A resident from the 1960s was impressed with the patience of the staff. He felt that he was helped most by the freedom, by not feeling cooped up, and by having personal relationships with so many adults: "It did make me more ready for the outside world. Not right away but as I matured and even today. I feel it helped me a great deal." Another resident from the same period felt "it directly contributed to the quality of person I am today. The sports and recreational programs helped to develop my self-confidence." He added: "As a resident I seldom had contact with my family—this was at their prompting, not the Boys Republic." He said: "Boys

Republic has helped develop what I feel are quality members of society today. Men whose feelings and skills were shaped by the staff at the Boys Republic are now community and governmental leaders."[75] Another former resident remembered the summers of baseball, calisthenics, pole vaulting, broad jumping, decathlon, volleyball, and swimming (the glen was the pool), and winters of ice skating, tobogganing, sledding, and war games outside, with Scrabble, reading, and card games indoors.[76]

On April 12, 1982, three one-time residents, along with Bill Burgess, Frank Norah, Frank Harris, and Alice Nigoghosian, director of the 1981 Historical Survey, met at the Boys Republic as part of the Oral History Project. The boys, now grown, successful men, recalled their first reactions to the republic. One remembered feeling perplexed at having a "Big Brother" assigned to "take care of" him and at not seeing "any bars" anywhere. He "kept waiting, figuring, well, when are they going to take me down there and lock me up?" He was astonished upon discovering that he was free to go if he so chose. He recalled his tour of the grounds: "He [the Big Brother] took me around and introduced me to everyone, told me who to stay away from, which guys to watch out for, not to rile these guys up."

Another former resident remembered being impressed with the education program that took him when he was about a half-year below grade and enabled him to graduate a half-year ahead. He remembered, after twenty years, American history teacher Shell Jacobs telling the class that the British had lost the war because "they would march up with this big target 'X' across their chests— saying 'shoot me here.'" He could still "see British uniforms in [his] mind." He also recalled the dress code in the 1960s. Much to his dismay, the boys could not wear jeans, lest they acquire the "image of . . . being a bunch of rowdy boys." He added, in answer to any suggestion that the boys might be rowdy, "They put a fence up around the Boys Republic [not] to keep the boys in [but] to keep the neighbor kids out."

The third former resident remembered being nonplussed by his Big Brother: "He was sort of a strange fellow because [he] used to shave his legs. It sort of made me nervous. I was trying to think how can this guy be my Big Brother? To take care of me and he's shaving his legs?"

One recalled resisting placement, but when the release date was set and there was going to be a campout the following week, he thought, "Damn, I'm going to miss it." This same man "got into drugs pretty heavy" when he got out. It is interesting to note that he turned his life around, but statistically he would be considered one of the republic's "failures" because of initial release problems.

Another had only been back to his neighborhood twice in fourteen years. He had started drinking there at fourteen or fifteen. He said: "I can go into . . . a bar . . . I used to hang around in . . . and find the same guys, in the same damn seat—where they were sitting almost fifteen years ago. And they say: 'Well, how come you don't come back around? This is great!!' I just say 'Sorry.'" This man recalled the time in 1965 when he and his friend were so drunk that they "side-swiped three telephone poles . . . put the engine in the front seat." He fell out of the door, was hit by the spinning car, and knocked clear across the street. He knew then that he had to get out, had to "break the old pattern." He says that he never felt better physically than when he was weight lifting at the republic, but he still got into drugs when he was in college. Eventually he broke that pattern too. Success or failure?

Drugs were definitely a problem in the 1960s. Burgess recalled a kid who thought he was dying. "He kept saying that this big eagle was getting him. He kept seeing this big bird coming down—and he'd be screaming at night." He was given a sedative at the hospital, but the staff did have to sit up with him all night, watching, talking him down. One of the former residents remembered guys having bad trips in the cottages and tearing up the place.

The group remembered the little jokes, too, the ones they played on the counselors, like the time a youngster was able to sneak out a back door with a reefer while others stalled Harris in his search for something that didn't "smell like regular cigarettes."

Another bit of mischievousness led to the destruction of a prize-winning go-cart. The vehicle, winner in the *Detroit News*' Soap

Box Derby, was put on display at the republic. A couple of boys eased a third one through a vent in the garage where it was locked up. He opened the door and for the next few hours the boys ran the thing down the hill, each getting two or three rides. The last rider managed to crash it right off the bridge and into the creek. The boys salvaged what they could and returned the pieces to the garage. The fact that they never heard anything about it left one former resident wondering if the staff had been aware of what was going on. He conjectured that possibly they knew that boys of this sort would never have a chance to construct a go-cart, much less ride a winner. He thinks maybe they just saw the boys having a one-time experience and staying out of trouble at the same time. Harris would neither deny nor affirm, but admitted that sometimes staff overlooked rules.[77]

ONE BOY'S STORY

One resident's story epitomizes those told by people the republic has helped, but it takes an ironic twist. Cef Suarez was, according to his own account, a streetwise kid, an inner city boy "brought up in a hostile environment" that gave him ample opportunity for honing his survival skills. As an adult he earned a master's degree in clinical psychology with a specialty degree in substance abuse and was working toward a Ph.D., had twelve clients in private practice, had a good position with Michigan Bell—and was president of the board of directors of the Boys Republic.

Though he ran the streets, he never joined a gang, thinking them "silly." He was not cut out for following a leader, preferring instead to make his own terms. He was one of very few among his peer group who could relate to both gang members and independent beings. He was an "A" student in elementary school, but was hit hard by the teen years. His parents had trouble gaining control of him, something that Cef did not fault them for, realizing that they were "busy working, trying to make a living." He bore them no resentment and sometimes laughter filled the family gatherings when they went over old times.

He remembered well his first impression of the republic. He was scared because he knew he was going to an institution and expected to be locked up, serving an indeterminate sentence. He realized later that if his length of stay had been spelled out specifically, he would have run away. Imagine his surprise when, after "plotting and figuring out where everything was" so he would "know how to get out," he discovered no one was keeping him there. He was further shocked when introduced to his Big Brother, a large older kid he thought he would have to defend himself against, and found him to be friendly and understanding of his initial nervousness.

He also remembered his first few sessions with his counselor when he sat in stony silence. The man made a few attempts at setting therapy in motion, but nothing worked, so they sat and stared. Finally Cef confronted him: "You're a perfect stranger. I don't know who you are, where you come from. You want me to open up but I don't know what is bothering you." The counselor told him his story at the next session.

Cef remembered being most impressed with the "newness" of the republic. He had "never been in anything new," having lived in an old house in an old neighborhood and having gone to an old school. He also remembered feeling safe, something he had not felt in a long time, now that he was away from the pressures of the street. He made friends and played a lot of handball and basketball, even becoming proficient at competition weight lifting. He learned how to get along with people he did not like. Cef was also impressed with the dedicated staff. The teachers were on the grounds in those days and he remembered them staying late at night for individual tutoring.

In looking back, he realized that the Boys Republic gave him "the opportunity to see [that there was] more to life than running the streets and just protecting" himself. He said he later had an advantage over a lot of people because he had experienced trouble and often could spot "trouble areas" in others. He gained an understanding of how people operated and why they acted out. The biggest lesson he learned was that "there is always hope and people do have the ability to change." The process might be difficult, but it was possible—and the desire to effect change "must come from within."

Cef thought that the streets were much more violent in the 1980s and kids approached the republic program with an attitude of "If you soften me up and put me back out there, it's like throwing a lamb to the wolves." Kids could not let down all their defenses if they were to "make it" back home. The problem of tougher kids from tougher neighborhoods was compounded by the difficulty of finding dedicated individuals who would work with them for little financial gain and with few immediate rewards. Workers seldom had proof of headway until long after it had been gained.

Cef Suarez's election to the board of directors in 1975 was a strange experience for him, since he had "never been involved in anything on that level." He spent the first two years "sitting and watching . . . gaining insight into corporate and sociological functions." As a member of the "lower echelons, the lower middle class," he had always assumed that "monied people were uncaring," but found instead that the board members, even the very wealthy ones, were "talented, sincere, and dedicated." And, he added, the board could boast of having some of the community's most socially concerned people as well as some of the city's and nation's most noted individuals.[78]

Although few former residents have such dramatic evidence of success—from resident to president of the board—the records are filled with their stories of having survived their troubled youths, of having gone on to lead productive lives pursuing various lines of work, to further their education, or to pursue careers in music and sports. College presidents? No. Stable, hard-working citizens? Yes.

Epilogue

By the end of the millennium, the republic of Farmington Hills, Michigan, was a radically different facility in both physical structure and guiding principles. No longer strictly for boys, it had changed its treatment policy as well as its name, becoming the Boys and Girls Republic in 1994. From the boggy seventy-five-acre farmland that Homer Lane brought the boys to in 1907, with a farmhouse, barn, henhouse, icehouse, and blacksmith shop, it has evolved into a modern facility while not totally foregoing the bucolic setting. The corn rows, bean fields, haystacks, and farm animals have yielded to athletic fields, a running track, a tennis court, a softball diamond, and a football/soccer field, but the area is sylvan and peaceful.

THE STRUCTURAL FACILITY

In addition to the outdoors sports areas, there is a new recreation center named in honor of Jack McElroy, recreation worker and cottage counselor from 1970 to 1979. There is also a vastly expanded gymnasium. The old building, constructed in 1956, could no longer serve adequately in an integrated facility, so a girls locker room and restroom were added, as well as a weight/exercise room, a multipurpose room with a cooking lab, and a game room. A media center equipped with computers provides opportunities for research and study.

THERAPEUTIC APPROACHES

The emphasis on exercise and sports reflects the republic's therapeutic philosophy: that learning to use leisure time constructively is essential in stemming delinquent behavior. Director Maryjane Peck notes that young people can "learn how to play by rules; how to respect boundaries; how to cooperate."[1] Needs-based recreation, a form of involvement and physical activity geared toward each youth, is a way to build individual self-esteem that may manifest itself in the classroom.

A new clinical director was appointed in 1998. Dr. Karen Olson Manners, a licensed psychologist, assumed responsibility for all clinical and therapeutic aspects of the residential treatment program, including family treatment and aftercare. Dr. Manners noted that she and Greg Chapman, formerly overseer of the Residential Treatment, Independent Living, and Adventure Course Programs and now assistant executive director, would be "working together closely so [the] staffs [would be] working toward the same goals." She added: "The residents and families will participate with the therapists in establishing goals. All staff working with the youth will be aware of the goals and the youth will receive regular written feedback from the staff regarding their progress."[2]

The emphasis at today's republic is on reality-centered treatment, on helping youngsters understand what they are today rather than why they are what they are. With the goal of returning the boys and girls to the mainstream as swiftly as possible, each counselor asks: How can I help this youngster deal with his or her environment in a healthy, non-acting-out way, without reliance on chemicals, without acts of physical aggression, without property violation?

EDUCATION AND PRACTICAL EXPERIENCE

The on-campus William E. Miller School, named in honor of the principal of the Farmington Public Schools Alternative Education Center for twenty-two years, provides continuity and communication among counselor, teacher, and child that was oftentimes lacking previously. Careers programs that teach such life skills as budgeting money, filling out a job application, handling a job interview, what to consider when looking for an apartment, and buying a car all help in returning the child to the mainstream. Hands-on practical work experience also prepares republic clients for a productive life.

COMMUNITY INVOLVEMENT

The youngsters no longer do farm chores and can beans, but they are much more engaged in the community. A Project Adventure grant from the Chrysler Corporation allowed for the construction of the Boys and Girls Republic High Ropes Challenge Course, which is open to community groups, corporations, and area schools. Bob Kunkel's Pro Golf Caddy Shack sponsored and organized the republic's first three golf outings, which have become an annual fund-raising event.

Yearly newsletters tell of projects, plans, successes, and concerns. The one for 1998 reported on a thriving summer program, with residents working on campus, in the Farmington Hills Community Library, and in the Mercy Center in the city. Six interns from Wayne State University worked with residents. Five groups of employees from Ford Motor Company's Business Leaders Initiatives program, in which employees are required to spend one day in community service, tackled the Challenge Ropes Course and then embarked on painting the auditorium, cottage interiors, and exteriors, staining, refurbishing, hanging blinds, putting up drywall, and sorting books. Through partial funding by the United Way and the Detroit-Wayne County Community Mental Health Agency, residents spent a week at Camp Wathana where they played volleyball and baseball, swam, boated, fished, rode horseback, took nature walks, engaged in archery, worked on arts and crafts, had cookouts, and presented a talent show.[3]

An Eye to the Future

In 1998 Executive Director Peck, citing legislation that placed younger children under the jurisdiction of the adult courts, recommitted the organization to "helping at-risk youth so they do not become adult system statistics."[4] She noted that in the 1997 calendar year, the republic "served 150 youth and their families with a comprehensive program of residential care, group treatment, family therapy, academic education, recreational therapy, prevocational training and on- and off-site employment."[5] She said that "within this program, young people learn to trust themselves and others, to respect boundaries, to set goals and to become productive community members," adding that then "parents learn to work with their children, to set appropriate limits and to foster and expect appropriate behaviors."[6]

The fall 1999 newsletter announced the official accreditation of the Boys and Girls Republic by the Council on Accreditation of Services for Families and Children. Peck noted that when she "first came to Boys Republic in 1991 . . . COA standards were those I wanted the agency to attain . . . to be recognized for reaching for and meeting the highest standards in the industry."[7]

The accreditation process was a lengthy one, beginning with an extensive self-evaluation, vast surveys, peer review evaluations, interviews, and comprehensive reports—eighteen months of work. Resource Director Noreen Haggerty was instrumental in seeing the organization through to its goal of being officially recognized as a leading children's facility. In addition to her responsibility for agency grant writing, volunteer and intern coordination, and the development of auxiliary resources, Haggerty coordinated the self-study, prepared supporting documentation, and organized the peer review and submission of reports to the Accreditation Commission.

FINAL WORDS

Today's republic youngsters are not necessarily more difficult than yesterday's, but their problems are certainly different. A society in flux, with few standard models of the old order to emulate, can prove deadly to youths in need of guidance.

What has not changed at the institution is the underlying principle that a child in need of help deserves a chance. Population changes reflect the disharmony in what Reed's kids called the "outside." The ragamuffins of Lane's day have been replaced by the more seriously troubled, still by circumstances of fortune, but also by abuse or neglect or inner conflicts. The harsh realities of life, with drug availability being just a small part, have had an impact on young people.

The foundation of today's republic, set so long ago by a compassionate woman with a social conscience, remains solid. Through the years the republic has embraced sociological and clinical approaches to the problem of youthful aberrant behavior—always with the child in mind, always with the goal of helping the youngster become a productive member of an ever-changing society. It has been, is now, and will continue to be a friend to children, a major community resource dedicated to the idea that with assistance a troubled child can evolve into a functioning adult.

The republic has proven to be a catalyst that can turn lives bound for destruction into lives with potential for productivity. Again and again it has extended the "mother's arm of love" to help those who have "stumbled on the rough road" until "they were able to step out firmly once more." Mother Agnes D'Arcambal's vision is becoming today's reality.[8]

Notes

INTRODUCTION

1. Dewey quoted in Anthony M. Platt, *The Child Savers: The Invention of Delinquency* (Chicago: University of Chicago Press, 1969), 56.
2. Brace's activities are discussed in LeRoy Ashby, *Endangered Children: Dependency, Neglect, and Abuse in American History* (New York: Twayne, 1997), 38–54.
3. Walter I. Trattner, *From Poor Law to Welfare State: A History of Social Welfare in America* (New York: Free Press, 1974), 107.
4. On late nineteenth-century Detroit, see Melvin G. Holli, *Reform in Detroit: Hazen S. Pingree and Urban Politics* (New York: Oxford University Press, 1969), 56–73; and Steve Babson (with Ron Alpern, Dave Elsila, and John Revitte), *Working Detroit: The Making of a Union Town* (New York: Adama Books, 1984), 2–16.
5. Holli, *Reform in Detroit*, 64.
6. For a list of baby medications prescribed by doctors and used unwittingly by some early twentieth-century mothers, see material from "Habit Forming Nostrums," *Journal of the American Medical Association* (May 1909), as cited under Dangerous Drug Bottles at *http://www.bottlebooks.com*. See also "Cleaning up the Patent-Medicine and Other Evils" at *http://www.bartleby.com* and Otto L. Bettmann, *The Good Old Days—They Were Terrible!* (New York: Random House, 1974), 152–53.
7. Quoted in Platt, *The Child Savers*, 66.
8. For an outstanding survey of turn-of-the-century child welfare initiatives, see LeRoy Ashby, *Saving the Waifs: Reformers and Dependent Children, 1890–1917* (Philadelphia: Temple University Press, 1984). Other important studies include Jack M. Holl, *Juvenile Reform in the Progressive Era: William R. George and the Junior Republic Movement* (Ithaca: Cornell University Press, 1971); E. Wayne Carp, *Family Matters: Secrecy and Disclosure in the History of Adoption* (Cambridge, MA: Harvard University Press, 1998); and the essays in *Growing Up in America: Children in Historical Perspective*, ed. N. Ray Hiner and Joseph M. Hawes (Urbana: University of Illinois Press, 1985).

CHAPTER 1

1. Articles of Association of the Home of Industry, filed May 7, 1890, Boys Republic Collection, Archives of Labor and Urban Affairs, Wayne State University, Detroit (hereafter cited as BRC); LeRoy Ashby, *Saving the Waifs: Reformers and Dependent Children, 1890–1917* (Philadelphia: Temple University Press, 1984), 133–36.
2. Mother D'Arcambal, *Face to Face* (booklet), c. 1903, Burton Historical Collection, Detroit Public Library.
3. Home of Industry Report, 1895–96, BRC.
4. "Mother D'Arcambal Is 75," *Detroit Journal*, March 4, 1898, BRC.
5. Board minutes, February 18, 1899, March 7, 1900; letter to board included in minutes, April 12, 1899, BRC.
6. Temporary Home for Boys "Bulletin," 1902, BRC.
7. Home of Industry Report, 1905, BRC. In its early days, the home issued untitled, printed, pamphlet-like reports, which also contained other miscellaneous material.
8. Ibid.
9. Reports, 1902–1907, BRC; amended Articles of Association, May 12, 1906, BRC.
10. "Friends Greet Fred Butzel," *Detroit Jewish Herald*, August 24, 1927.
11. W. David Wills, *Home Lane: A Biography* (London: Allen and Unwin, 1964), 66.
12. Ashby, *Saving the Waifs*, 136–37.
13. Ibid., 137–39.

CHAPTER 2

1. A. S. Neill, *Neill! Neill! Orange Peel—An Autobiography* (New York: Hart, 1972), 187. W. David Wills, *Homer Lane: A Biography* (London: Allen and Unwin, 1964) contains much valuable documentary material.
2. Wills, *Homer Lane*, 59.
3. In addition to Wills, *Homer Lane*, see LeRoy Ashby, *Saving the Waifs: Reformers and Dependent Children, 1890–1917* (Philadelphia: Temple University Press, 1984), 137–64; and Gay Zieger, "Lane's Way," *Michigan History* 77 (July/August 1993): 32–38.
4. "Homer Lane's Technique Won Boys—And a Job," *Boys Republic* (periodical), September 1944, p. 4, BRC; Ashby, *Saving the Waifs*, 138–39.
5. *The Ford Republic: A Boy Community* (bulletin), 1909, BRC.
6. Homer Lane to Board, March 16, 1908, BRC; Homer Lane to J. L. Hudson, October 27, 1908, BRC.

7. There are numerous letters in BRC from well-wishers, persons who wanted to send boys to the home, and those offering to take in home residents, often in exchange for a boy's labor. See, e.g., John Little to Lane, April 10, 1910, and June 17, 1910.

8. Mary McNabb Johnston to Homer Lane, September 7, 1909.

9. Wills, *Homer Lane*, 89–90.

10. Leslie R. Perry, comp., *Bertrand Russell, A. S. Neill, Homer Lane, W. H. Kilpatrick: Four Progressive Educators* (New York: Macmillan, 1967), 96–97.

11. Wills, *Homer Lane*, 89–90.

12. Ibid., 89.

13. Ashby, *Saving the Waifs*, 148.

14. On Lane's relationship with George, see F. James Clatworthy, "Homer T. Lane's Legacy of Self-Government: An Inquiry into Organizational Synecology at the Boys Republic, 1909–1982" (paper presented at the American Educational Studies Association Conference, Nashville, Tennessee, November 5, 1982), BRC; and Wills, *Homer Lane*, 82.

15. Wills, *Homer Lane*, 82.

16. Minutes, "State meeting of Commonwealth," March 24, March 27, April 3, April 4, July 1, 1909, BRC.

17. Wills, *Homer Lane*, 99.

18. Ibid.; Ashby, *Saving the Waifs*, 263n. 2; *The Ford Republic*.

19. Quoted in Perry, *Four Progressive Educators*, 97 and passim.

20. Clatworthy, "Homer T. Lane's Legacy," 5–8; Homer Lane, *A Boy Farm* (pamphlet), c. 1907, pp. 2–7, BRC.

21. Wills, *Homer Lane*, 103.

22. N. H. Bowen, "Career of Former Street Arab Proves Worth of Boys' Home," *Detroit Saturday Night*, September 16, 1911 (reprint in pamphlet form, BRC).

23. Clyde Reed, "The Story of Ford Republic," January 1935, BRC.

24. Lane, *A Boy Farm*, 2.

25. Ibid.

26. Charles H. Cooley to Rollin H. Stevens, August 27, 1907, BRC; Wills, *Homer Lane*, 78–79.

27. Ibid.

28. Jack M. Holl, *Juvenile Reform in the Progressive Era: William R. George and the Junior Republic Movement* (Ithaca: Cornell University Press, 1971), 214–15; Clatworthy, "Homer T. Lane's Legacy," 5–8.

29. Homer Lane, report to board, 1911, BRC; *The Ford Republic*.

30. Frank Thiesen to Homer Lane, June 11, 1909, BRC.

31. In Wills, *Homer Lane*, 106.

32. Ibid., 115.

33. Clarence Lightner to board, January 14, 1910, BRC.
34. In Wills, *Homer Lane*, 112.
35. See Ashby, *Saving the Waifs*, 161–62.
36. Elsie Theodora Bazeley, *Homer Lane and the Little Commonwealth* (New York: Schocken Books, 1969), 142.
37. Homer Lane, *Talks to Parents*; Elsie Bazeley, *Homer Lane: A Biography*.

CHAPTER 3

1. Susan Tiffin, *In Whose Best Interest?: Child Welfare Reform in the Progressive Era* (Westport, CT: Greenwood Press, 1982).
2. LeRoy Ashby, *Saving the Waifs: Reformers and Dependent Children, 1890–1917* (Philadelphia: Temple University Press, 1984), 88.
3. John McIndoo to G. Stanley Hall, October 21, 1913, BRC.
4. Ruth Colebank, unpublished manuscript, c. 1950s, BRC. This untitled, undated, and unpaginated manuscript is a rich source of material on the republic during the 1920s and 1930s (hereafter cited as Colebank Manuscript).
5. Ashby, *Saving the Waifs*, 167.
6. From a typescript "report," c. 1922, consisting of boys' descriptions of their duties as republic officers (hereafter cited as Boys' Report).
7. Colebank Manuscript.
8. Ibid.
9. Ibid.
10. Superintendent's Report, February 28, 1917, BRC.
11. Colebank Manuscript.
12. McIndoo to G. Stanley Hall, October 21, 1913, BRC.
13. *The Ford Republic* (booklet), 1914, BRC.
14. "Juvenile Court Is Not a Court at All," *Detroit Saturday Night*, April 8, 1916, BRC.
15. Colebank Manuscript.
16. *The Ford Republic*.
17. List of rules, 1916, BRC.
18. Colebank Manuscript.
19. Untitled typescript report, c. 1922, BRC.
20. McIndoo to G. Stanley Hall, October 21, 1913, BRC.
21. Roy Olson's Report on Ford Boys, 1924, BRC.
22. Colebank Manuscript.
23. Ibid.
24. Remarks of Msgr. Edward Hickey, January 1984, BRC.

25. Colebank Manuscript.
26. Ibid.; Ruth Colebank to Milton Huber, August 14, 1956, BRC.
27. Charles Henry statement, March 6, 1953, BRC.
28. Quoted in W. David Wills, *Homer Lane: A Biography* (London: Allen and Unwin, 1964), 122.
29. Colebank Manuscript.
30. Courtland Van Vechten manuscript, 1930, BRC (hereafter cited as Van Vechten Manuscript). One sad note here concerns a dark-skinned boy born of a light mulatto father and a white mother. He had a good IQ and had achieved some success at the republic, but discrimination limited his opportunities outside it. Fred Butzel later explained that he lived a better life "in an institution without a color line" than as a "free Negro."
31. Remarks of Msgr. Edward Hickey, January 1984, BRC.
32. Van Vechten Manuscript.
33. Ibid.
34. Superintendent's annual report, 1930, BRC.
35. Colebank Manuscript.
36. Ibid.; Van Vechten Manuscript.
37. Van Vechten Manuscript; Colebank Manuscript.
38. *Ford Republic: A Self Governing School for Boys* (booklet), 1925, BRC.
39. "Ford Republic, Builder of Boys," *Redford Record*, February 2, 1927, BRC.
40. Ibid.
41. Ibid.
42. Historical survey material (survey of directors, staff, and former residents), 1981, BRC.
43. Van Vechten Manuscript.
44. Board of trustees bulletin, n.d.
45. Jones report to board, 1931, BRC.

CHAPTER 4

1. Alan Clive, *State of War: Michigan in World War II* (Ann Arbor: University of Michigan Press, 1979), 185–213.
2. Ibid.
3. Clyde Reed made several attempts to compile a history of the republic. These materials are not dated or paginated and are contained in the BRC (hereafter cited as Reed Manuscripts).
4. These paragraphs are also based on Clyde Reed, interview by the author, January 15, 1985, Grosse Pointe, Michigan.
5. Reed Manuscripts.

6. Reed, interview.

7. Clyde L. Reed, "The Story of the Ford Republic," 1935, BRC.

8. William J. Norton, Jr., "Ford Republic: The Story of a Boys' Self-Governing Community," *Children's Institutions* (undated clipping [1940]), BRC.

9. Reed Manuscripts.

10. Esther Meredith, historical survey response, 1981, BRC; transcript of taped interview with Esther Meredith by Alice Nigoghosian, June 10, 1982, BRC.

11. Child Welfare League of America Report, 1941.

12. Reed Manuscripts.

13. *Battle Creek Enquirer and News*, April 20, 1947, BRC.

14. Details of home procedure and the boys' routines, diet, and activities are found in Child Welfare League of America, Inc., *Survey of the Boys' Home and D'Arcambal Association (The Ford Republic)* (New York: Child Welfare League of America, 1941), BRC.

15. Reed Manuscripts.

16. Colebank Manuscript.

17. Ibid.

18. Reed, interview.

19. Reed Manuscripts.

20. Transcript of taped interview with Sam Rabinovitz, June 10, 1982.

21. Colebank Manuscript.

22. Ibid.; Reed, interview.

23. Reed, interview.

24. Child Welfare League of America, *Survey of the Boys' Home*.

25. Reed Manuscripts.

26. Meredith, historical survey response; Meredith, interview.

27. Child Welfare League of America, *Survey of the Boys' Home*.

28. Colebank Manuscript.

29. Meredith, historical survey response; Meredith, interview.

30. Colebank Manuscript.

31. Ibid.

32. Ibid.

33. Reed Manuscripts.

34. Meredith, historical survey response; Meredith, interview.

35. Vera Brown, untitled article, *Detroit Times*, October 23, 1944.

36. Reed Manuscripts.

37. Meredith, historical survey response; Meredith, interview.

38. Rabinovitz, interview.

39. Colebank Manuscript.

40. Reed Manuscripts.

Chapter 5

1. Transcript of interview with Gordon Boring, c. 1982. In the early 1980s, researcher Alice Nigoghosian conducted a series of one-on-one and group interviews with former staff members, active and retired, as part of the Republic History Project (RHP). Some were transcribed verbatim from tapes while others appear to have been stenographically transcribed at the time of the interview. Clyde L. Reed kept a log of the transcripts, both stenographic and from tapes, which he made available to the author. The interview transcripts, which are undated and unpaginated, are housed with the BRC. Material from these transcripts will be cited hereafter by interviewee name (e.g., Boring interview, RHP).

2. Bernice Izner interview, 1982, RHP.

3. Boring interview, 1984, RHP.

4. Izner, interview.

5. "Boys Republic, Description of Agency," typescript, c. 1959, BRC.

6. Alan Ternes, untitled article, *Detroit News*, September 22, 1957, BRC.

7. "Time Sequence to Night Watch Job," typescript, c. 1957, BRC.

8. F. James Clatworthy, "Homer T. Lane's Legacy of Self-Government: An Inquiry into Organizational Synecology at the Boys Republic, 1909–1982" (paper delivered at the American Educational Studies Association Conference, Nashville, Tennessee, November 5, 1982), BRC.

9. Alan Clive, *State of War: Michigan in World War II* (Ann Arbor: University of Michigan Press, 1979), 209.

10. The 1949 pamphlet is found among a collection of miscellaneous pamphlets, flyers, and occasional short publications and typescript material in BRC (hereafter cited as Pamphlet Material, BRC).

11. Pamphlet Material, BRC.

12. Minutes of the board of directors meeting, February 26, 1949.

13. Gunnar Dybwad to Charles E. Henry, May 19, 1950, BRC; minutes of the board of directors meeting, June 30, 1950, BRC.

14. Dybwad to Henry, April 13, 1951, BRC.

15. Unidentified clipping, *Muskegon Chronicle*, c. 1950, BRC.

16. Pamphlet Material, BRC.

17. This material on daily routines and activities is usefully conveyed in Martin Armand Adler, "Studies of Boys Republic I: History and Structure of the Agency" (Master's thesis, Wayne State University, 1951), BRC.

18. Adler, "Studies of Boys Republic I."

19. Ibid.

20. Harold R. Bissett, "Studies of Boys Republic II: A Pilot Study to Determine

Methods to Be Used in a Follow-Up Study" (Master's thesis, Wayne State University, 1951), BRC.

21. Norman Polansky to Henry, April 2, 1951, BRC.
22. Polansky to Henry, May 1, 1952, BRC.
23. Ibid.
24. Edward Simon Moscovitch, "Studies of Boys Republic III: Prediction of Institutional Adjustment as Derived from Pre-Institutional Data" (Master's thesis, Wayne State University, 1952), BRC.
25. Colebank Manuscript.
26. Boring interview, RHP.
27. On Huber's background, see Alfred de Grazia, ed., "Notes about the Contributors," *Grass Roots Private Welfare: Winning Essays of the 1956 National Awards Competition of the Foundation for Voluntary Welfare* (New York: New York University Press, 1957), 300; and Colebank Manuscript.
28. Unidentified clipping, *Detroit Free Press*, May 2, 1954, BRC.
29. Jack Pickering, "Gang Crackdown Won't Cure," *Detroit Times*, August 9, 1954, BRC.
30. Warren Stromberg, "A Story on Youth Anonymous Compiled for Either Reader's Digest or Coronet," typescript, c. 1956, BRC.
31. Milton Huber, "Youth Anonymous," undated typescript summary; "Youth Anonymous: A Self-Help and Mutual-Help Program," typescript guide, November 1955; see also Milton John Huber, "Youth Anonymous," in *Grass Roots Private Welfare*, 45–49, all in BRC.
32. Ibid.
33. Ibid.
34. Albert Eglash, "Youth Anonymous," typescript, c. 1957, BRC.
35. Huber, typescript summary.
36. Alfred I. Palmiere, "A Case Study of Seven Boys, Their Post-Institutional Adjustment, and Conceptions of the Boys Republic" (Master's thesis, Wayne State University, 1955), BRC.
37. Board minutes, September 13, 1956, BRC.
38. Board minutes, September 16, 1955, BRC.
39. Board minutes, February 14, 1957, BRC.
40. Board minutes, May 9, 1957, BRC.
41. Board minutes, May 1957, BRC.
42. Board minutes, June 1957, BRC.
43. Boring interview, RHP.
44. Richard Huegli, telephone interviews by the author, July 28–29, 1986; Gillis interview, RHP.
45. Don Harness interview, RHP.
46. Louis Miriani, UCS document, 1954; Huegli, interviews.

47. Responsibility for major funding was finally put in the hands of the state, though as of 1981 the United Foundation had given a yearly contribution of $1,000 to make certain that if state provisions fell through the republic would not have to go through lengthy admissions procedures. That contribution also ensured that the republic would be eligible for support from the United Foundation Capital Fund Campaign held every five years. That campaign involved corporate solicitation, with corporations making a five-year pledge. Without financial support from the foundation, the republic would not be eligible for emergency grants. Support for the republic from the foundation and its predecessor organ—Community Fund, Community Chest, United Community Services—goes back to 1918, said Huegli.

48. State Welfare Department Report, 1939, BRC; minutes of the Budget Sub-Committee on Protective Services, December 23, 1937, BRC.

49. Harness interview, RHP.

50. Jack Pickering, "Boys Republic Totters; in Grave Need of Repair," *Detroit Sunday Times*, July 24, 1955, BRC; "Boys Republic Cheers Start on Its New $1,000,000 Home," *Detroit News*, May 29, 1956, BRC.

51. Clatworthy, "Homer T. Lane's Legacy."

52. Board minutes, September 12, 1957, BRC.

53. Descriptive material on dedication ceremony, September 28, 1957, BRC.

54. Dedication tableau script, n.d. but c. September 1957, BRC.

55. Walter "Red" Barber, "As a Man Thinketh" (transcript of tape recording), September 1957, BRC.

56. Gillis interview, RHP; Harness interview, RHP.

57. Boring interview, RHP.

58. Clatworthy, "Homer T. Lane's Legacy."

59. Board minutes, October 17, 1957, BRC.

60. Board minutes, November 21, 1957, BRC; Alan P. Ternes, "Teen Dance Breaks Ice for 50 in Boys Republic," *Detroit News* (c. October 1957), BRC.

61. Board minutes, January 2, 1958, BRC.

62. Milton J. Huber, "Report of Boys Republic, 1957," c. early 1958, BRC.

63. Gillis interview, RHP

64. Harness interview, RHP.

65. Transcript of Clyde L. Reed interview, September 26, 1984, RHP.

66. Harness interview, RHP.

67. Huber, "Report," RHP.

68. Harness interview, RHP.

69. Huber, "Report," BRC.

70. Ibid.

71. Milton J. Huber, *Which Way Is Up?* (1958), BRC.

72. Board minutes, May 1958, BRC.

73. Board minutes, December 1958, BRC.
74. Board minutes, February 1959, BRC.
75. Board minutes, September 1959, BRC.

CHAPTER 6

1. Fred Auch interview, RHP; Phyllis Griffin interview, RHP; Phyllis Griffin, interview by Gay Zieger, July 16, 1986, Farmington, Michigan.
2. Boring historical survey, 1981, RHP.
3. Gordon Boring, interview by Alice Nigoghosian, May 9, 1984, RHP.
4. "Brief History of the Boys Republic," typescript, April 1961, BRC.
5. "Intake Policy," c. 1961, BRC; Boring interview, RHP.
6. Boring interview, RHP.
7. "General Treatment Concepts and Discipline," c. 1961; Boring interview, RHP.
8. "Intake Policy."
9. Boring interview, RHP.
10. House of Representatives organizational meetings reports, July 18, 1961–August 14, 1961, BRC.
11. Frank Harris, interview by Gay Zieger, June 18, 1986, Farmington Hills, Michigan.
12. Department head meeting minutes, November 5 and 6, 1962, BRC; Administrative Skull Session reports, 1962, BRC.
13. Boring interview, RHP.
14. "Staff Upgrading," undated typescript, c. 1961, BRC.
15. Gordon Boring to Cleve Mason, November 19, 1962, BRC.
16. Boring interview, RHP.
17. Ibid.
18. Department head minutes, November 5, 1962, BRC.
19. Gordon Boring to Mr. Kerinan, April 19, 1963, BRC.
20. Boring report to the board, April 21, 1964, BRC.
21. Boring interview, RHP.
22. Ibid.
23. Harris interview, RHP.
24. Boring interview, RHP.
25. Report on Classification System, February 15, 1963, BRC.
26. Boring memo, May 22, 1965, BRC.
27. Boring memo, September 8, 1967, BRD.
28. John R. Schaupner interview, 1981, RHP.
29. Mark Sperling, interview by Gay Zieger, July 10 and 17, 1986, Farmington Hills, Michigan.

30. Bernice Izner interview, 1981, tape in RHP.
31. "Boys Republic Aftercare Program," undated typescript, c. 1963, BRC; Gordon Boring to William M. Joy, February 25, 1963, with "Annual Report Aftercare Program," c. 1963, BRC.
32. Boring interview, RHP.
33. Ibid.
34. Executive Director's report, December 15, 1966, BRC.
35. Shaupner interview, RHP.
36. Gordon Sokoll, "Afternoon Program Report," January 17, 1967, BRC.
37. Ibid., February 22, 1967, BRC.
38. T. Gearhart, "Afternoon Program Report," June 6, 1967, BRC.
39. Child Welfare League of America, typescript report, May 31, 1967, BRC.
40. Boring interview, RHP.
41. Director's report, September 18, 1969, BRC.
42. Director's report, January 1972, BRC.
43. Allen Ablitz report to board of directors, March 1972, BRC.
44. Boring report to the board, November 1972, BRC.
45. Allen Ablitz report to board of directors, January and February 1973, BRC.
46. Director's report, May 1973, BRC.
47. Director's report, September 1973, BRC.
48. Director's report, November 15, 1973, BRC.
49. Director's report, December 1973, BRC.
50. Minutes of board of directors meeting, 1974, BRC.
51. Sperling interview, July 10, 1986.
52. Harris interview, June 18, 1986.
53. Director's report, 1975, BRC.
54. Ibid.
55. Director's report, January 15, 1976, late 1976, BRC.
56. Director's report, late 1976, BRC.
57. Department of Social Services report, typescript, February 17, 1977, BRC.
58. Ibid.
59. By 1981 the Licensing Review Board showed satisfaction with "the status of the . . . present program," though there remained a need to engage more staff because of a "rougher core of boys in the program and continual minor destruction to republic property."
60. Regulatory Study Reports, April 7, 1977, April 12, 1977, BRC; Frank Harris to Myron Liner, May 19, 1978, BRC; fire inspection reports, 1977, 1978, BRC; Licensing Review Board report, 1981, BRC.
61. United Community Services Report, November 20, 1970, BRC.
62. Gordon Boring to William Miller, spring 1977, BRC.
63. Director's report, 1977, BRC.

64. Griffin interview, September 23, 1982, RHP.
65. Sperling interview, July 10, 1986.
66. Griffin interview, September 23, 1982, RHP.

CHAPTER 7

1. The Nigoghosian interviews conducted in the early 1980s as part of the Republic Historical Project are housed in the BRC and will be cited hereafter as, for example in this paragraph, Boring interview, 1984, RHP.
2. Frank Harris interviews, April 12, 1982, September 23, 1982, RHP.
3. "Staff Problems in a Boys Institution," undated typescript, in Clyde L. Reed to Gay Zieger, December 1, 1986, BRC.
4. Executive Director's report, 1971, BRC.
5. Gordon Boring interview, May 9, 1984, RHP.
6. Director's report, 1976, BRC; Frank Harris, interview by Gay Zieger, June 18, 1986, Farmington Hills, Michigan; Frank Parcells remarks in historical survey, 1981, BRC; Sam Rabinovitz remarks in historical survey, 1981, BRC; Sam Rabinovitz interview, June 10, 1982, RHP; Bernice Izner interview, RHP.
7. Phyllis Griffin, interview by the author, July 16, 1986; William Burgess, interview by the author, June 30, 1986; William Burgess interviews, April 12, 1982, November 10, 1983, RHP; Mark Sperling, interview by the author, July 10 and 17, 1986; Mark Sperling interview, September 23, 1982, RHP.
8. Griffin, author interview; Sperling, author interview.
9. Griffin, author interview.
10. Burgess interview, RHP.
11. Harris interview, RHP.
12. Griffin, author interview.
13. Ibid.
14. Ibid.
15. Ibid.
16. Griffin interview, September 23, 1982, RHP.
17. Burgess interview, RHP.
18. Sperling interview, RHP.
19. Harris interview, RHP.
20. Sally Owen interview, September 23, 1982, RHP.
21. Griffin, author interview.
22. Griffin interview, RHP.
23. Izner interview, RHP.
24. Griffin interview, RHP; Burgess interview, RHP.

25. Griffin interview, RHP; Burgess interview, RHP; Sperling interview, RHP.
26. Griffin interview, RHP.
27. Ibid.
28. Burgess interview, RHP.
29. Griffin interview, RHP; Sperling interview, RHP.
30. Griffin interview, RHP.
31. Ibid.
32. Griffin interview, RHP; Sperling interview, RHP.
33. Griffin interview, RHP.
34. Gordon Boring interview, RHP.
35. Griffin interview, RHP; Sperling interview, RHP; Burgess interview, RHP.
36. Sperling interview, RHP; Sperling remarks, historical survey, 1981, BRC.
37. Griffin, author interview.
38. Joint interview with Griffin and Owen, September 23, 1982, RHP.
39. Griffin interview, RHP.
40. Griffin, author interview.
41. Izner interview, RHP. See also transcript of interview by sociologist James Clatworthy with Clyde Reed, Bernice Izner, and other republic staff members, c. 1979. This undated transcript is contained in BRC and is briefly described in "Boys Republic Historical Committee—Index," undated typescript, included in Clyde L. Reed to Gay Zieger, January 26, 1986.
42. Griffin, author interview.
43. Burgess interview, RHP.
44. Sperling interview, RHP; Sperling remarks, historical survey, 1981, BRC.
45. Griffin, author interview.
46. Burgess, author interview.
47. Owen interview, RHP.
48. Griffin interview, RHP.
49. Sperling interview, RHP.
50. This reconstruction of typical republic activities in the 1970s and 1980s is based on the interview material in the preceding notes for this chapter and on similar, though undated, interview material in the RHP (hereafter cited as staff interviews, RHP).
51. Staff interviews, RHP.
52. Staff interviews, RHP.
53. Staff interviews, RHP.
54. William Billups interview, November 10, 1983, RHP.
55. Rudolph Yanke interview, November 10, 1983, RHP.
56. Hamel, Robertson remarks in staff interviews, RHP.
57. Burgess interview, RHP.
58. Beaufait remarks in staff interviews, RHP.

59. Burgess interview, RHP.
60. Harris interview, RHP; Burgess interview, RHP.
61. Harris, author interview.
62. Boring interview, RHP.
63. Yanke interview, RHP.
64. Griffin, author interview.
65. Sperling, author interview.
66. Izner interview, RHP.
67. Griffin, author interview; Sperling, author interview.
68. Sperling, author interview; Griffin, author interview; Harris, author interview.
69. Griffin, author interview.
70. Harris, author interview.
71. Burgess interview, RHP.
72. Boring interview, RHP.
73. Alfred I. Palmiere, "A Case Study of Seven Boys, Their Post-Institutional Adjustment, and Conceptions of the Boys Republic" (Master's thesis, Wayne State University, 1955), BRC.
74. Ibid.
75. Ibid.
76. These paragraphs are based on confidential material initially deposited in the BRC.
77. Nigoghosian Interviews, group interview, April 12, 1982.
78. Gay Zieger unrecorded conversations with Cef Suarez, summer 1986; Gay Zieger unrecorded five-party telephone conversation with Gordon Boring, Phyllis Griffin, Alice Nigoghosian, and Cef Suarez, July 7, 1988.

Epilogue

The epilogue is based on newsletters, titled *Around the Republic*, supplied by the Boys and Girls Republic. Those made available are dated fall 1997, 1998, and 1999. The republic staff was unable to supply additional material or to arrange for further interviews. The Boys Republic archival collection, held at the Archives of Labor and Urban Affairs, Walter P. Reuther Library, Wayne State University, is described briefly in Margaret Raucher, "Boys Republic," *Walter P. Reuther Library* (fall 1998), 2.

1. *Around the Republic* 5, no. 2 (1997).
2. *Around the Republic* 7, no. 1 (1999).
3. *Around the Republic* 6, no. 1 (1998).
4. Ibid.

5. Ibid.
6. Ibid.
7. *Around the Republic* 7, no. 1 (1999).
8. Home of Industry Report, 1895, p. 96.

Index

Page numbers in italics indicate an illustration

Titles in the Great Lakes Books Series

The Country Kitchen, by Della T. Lutes, 1992 (reprint)

The Making of a Mining District: Keweenaw Native Copper 1500–1870, by David J. Krause, 1992

Kids Catalog of Michigan Adventures, by Ellyce Field, 1993

Henry's Lieutenants, by Ford R. Bryan, 1993

Historic Highway Bridges of Michigan, by Charles K. Hyde, 1993

Lake Erie and Lake St. Clair Handbook, by Stanley J. Bolsenga and Charles E. Herndendorf, 1993

Queen of the Lakes, by Mark Thompson, 1994

Iron Fleet: The Great Lakes in World War II, by George J. Joachim, 1994

Turkey Stearnes and the Detroit Stars: The Negro Leagues in Detroit, 1919–1933, by Richard Bak, 1994

Pontiac and the Indian Uprising, by Howard H. Peckham, 1994 (reprint)

Charting the Inland Seas: A History of the U.S. Lake Survey, by Arthur M. Woodford, 1994 (reprint)

Ojibwa Narratives of Charles and Charlotte Kawbawgam and Jacques LePique, 1893–1895. Recorded with Notes by Homer H. Kidder, edited by Arthur P. Bourgeois, 1994, co-published with the Marquette County Historical Society

Strangers and Sojourners: A History of Michigan's Keweenaw Peninsula, by Arthur W. Thurner, 1994

Win Some, Lose Some: G. Mennen Williams and the New Democrats, by Helen Washburn Berthelot, 1995

Sarkis, by Gordon and Elizabeth Orear, 1995

The Northern Lights: Lighthouses of the Upper Great Lakes, by Charles K. Hyde, 1995 (reprint)

Kids Catalog of Michigan Adventures, second edition, by Ellyce Field, 1995

Rumrunning and the Roaring Twenties: Prohibition on the Michigan-Ontario Waterway, by Philip P. Mason, 1995

In the Wilderness with the Red Indians, by E. R. Baierlein, translated by Anita Z. Boldt, edited by Harold W. Moll, 1996

Elmwood Endures: History of a Detroit Cemetery, by Michael Franck, 1996

Master of Precision: Henry M. Leland, by Mrs. Wilfred C. Leland with Minnie Dubbs Millbrook, 1996 (reprint)

Haul-Out: New and Selected Poems, by Stephen Tudor, 1996

Kids Catalog of Michigan Adventures, third edition, by Ellyce Field, 1997

Beyond the Model T: The Other Ventures of Henry Ford, revised edition, by Ford R. Bryan, 1997

Young Henry Ford: A Picture History of the First Forty Years, by Sidney Olson, 1997 (reprint)

The Coast of Nowhere: Meditations on Rivers, Lakes and Streams, by Michael Delp, 1997

From Saginaw Valley to Tin Pan Alley: Saginaw's Contribution to American Popular Music, 1890–1955, by R. Grant Smith, 1998

The Long Winter Ends, by Newton G. Thomas, 1998 (reprint)

Bridging the River of Hatred: The Pioneering Efforts of Detroit Police Commissioner George Edwards, by Mary M. Stolberg, 1998

Toast of the Town: The Life and Times of Sunnie Wilson, by Sunnie Wilson with John Cohassey, 1998

These Men Have Seen Hard Service: The First Michigan Sharpshooters in the Civil War, by Raymond J. Herek, 1998

A Place for Summer: One Hundred Years at Michigan and Trumbull, by Richard Bak, 1998

Early Midwestern Travel Narratives: An Annotated Bibliography, 1634–1850, by Robert R. Hubach, 1998 (reprint)

All-American Anarchist: Joseph A. Labadie and the Labor Movement, by Carlotta R. Anderson, 1998

Michigan in the Novel, 1816–1996: An Annotated Bibliography, by Robert Beasecker, 1998

"Time by Moments Steals Away": The 1848 Journal of Ruth Douglass, by Robert L. Root, Jr., 1998

The Detroit Tigers: A Pictorial Celebration of the Greatest Players and Moments in Tigers' History, updated edition, by William M. Anderson, 1999

Father Abraham's Children: Michigan Episodes in the Civil War, by Frank B. Woodford, 1999 (reprint)

Letter from Washington, 1863–1865, by Lois Bryan Adams, edited and with an introduction by Evelyn Leasher, 1999

Wonderful Power: The Story of Ancient Copper Working in the Lake Superior Basin, by Susan R. Martin, 1999

A Sailor's Logbook: A Season aboard Great Lakes Freighters, by Mark L. Thompson, 1999

Huron: The Seasons of a Great Lake, by Napier Shelton, 1999

Tin Stackers: The History of the Pittsburgh Steamship Company, by Al Miller, 1999

Art in Detroit Public Places, revised edition, text by Dennis Nawrocki, photographs by David Clements, 1999

Brewed in Detroit: Breweries and Beers Since 1830, by Peter H. Blum, 1999

Detroit Kids Catalog: A Family Guide for the 21st Century, by Ellyce Field, 2000

"Expanding the Frontiers of Civil Rights": Michigan, 1948–1968, by Sidney Fine, 2000

Graveyard of the Lakes, by Mark L. Thompson, 2000

Enterprising Images: The Goodridge Brothers, African American Photographers, 1847–1922, by John Vincent Jezierski, 2000

New Poems from the Third Coast: Contemporary Michigan Poetry, edited by Michael Delp, Conrad Hilberry, and Josie Kearns, 2000

Arab Detroit: From Margin to Mainstream, edited by Nabeel Abraham and Andrew Shryock, 2000

The Sandstone Architecture of the Lake Superior Region, by Kathryn Bishop Eckert, 2000

Looking Beyond Race: The Life of Otis Milton Smith, by Otis Milton Smith and Mary M. Stolberg, 2000

Mail by the Pail, by Colin Bergel, illustrated by Mark Koenig, 2000

Great Lakes Journey: A New Look at America's Freshwater Coast, by William Ashworth, 2000

A Life in the Balance: The Memoirs of Stanley J. Winkelman, by Stanley J. Winkelman, 2000

Schooner Passage: Sailing Ships and the Lake Michigan Frontier, by Theodore J. Karamanski, 2000

The Outdoor Museum: The Magic of Michigan's Marshall M. Fredericks, by Marcy Heller Fisher, illustrated by Christine Collins Woomer, 2001

Detroit in Its World Setting: A Three Hundred Year Chronology, 1701–2001, edited by David Lee Poremba, 2001

Frontier Metropolis: Picturing Early Detroit, 1701–1838, by Brian Leigh Dunnigan, 2001

Michigan Remembered: Photographs from the Farm Security Administration and the Office of War Information, 1936–1943, edited by Constance B. Schulz, with Introductory Essays by Constance B. Schulz and William H. Mulligan, Jr., 2001

This Is Detroit, 1701–2001, by Arthur M. Woodford, 2001

History of the Finns in Michigan, by Armas K. E. Holmio, translated by Ellen M. Ryynanen, 2001

Angels in the Architecture: A Photographic Elegy to an American Asylum, by Heidi Johnson, 2001

Uppermost Canada: The Western District and the Detroit Frontier, 1800–1850, by R. Alan Douglas, 2001

Windjammers: Songs of the Great Lakes Sailors, by Ivan H. Walton with Joe Grimm, 2002

Detroit Tigers Lists and More: Runs, Hits, and Eras, by Mark Pattison and David Raglin, 2002

The Iron Hunter, by Chase S. Osborn, 2002 (reprint)

Independent Man: The Life of Senator James Couzens, by Harry Barnard, 2002 (reprint)

For the Good of the Children: A History of the Boys and Girls Republic, by Gay Pitman Zieger, 2003

For an updated listing of books in this series, please visit our website at http://wsupress.wayne.edu